ENCYCLOPAEDIA OF
INDIAN GOVERNMENT:
PROGRAMMES AND POLICIES

ENCYCLOPAEDIA
OF
INDIAN GOVERNMENT:
PROGRAMMES AND POLICIES

Vol. 2

Urban Development

Edited by

Satish Tiwari

ANMOL PUBLICATIONS PVT. LTD.

NEW DELHI - 110 002 (INDIA)

ANMOL PUBLICATIONS PVT. LTD.
4374/4B, Ansari Road, Daryaganj
New Delhi - 110 002

Encyclopaedia of Indian Government: Programmes and Policies

First Edition, 2000
ISBN 81-261-0515-1 (Set)

PRINTED IN INDIA

Published by J.L. Kumar for Anmol Publications Pvt. Ltd., New Delhi - 110 002 and Printed at Mehra Offset Press, Delhi.

Contents

Preface

Encyclopaedia of Indian Government: Programmes and Policies contains authoritative information on about fifty departmental policies and their future developmental programmes.

Organised to be completed in 40 volumes, this gigantic work covers Agriculture; Atomic Energy; Chemicals and Fertilizers; Coal; Commerce; Communication; Culture; Defence; Education; Environment and Forests; External Affairs; Finance; Food & Consumer Affairs; Food Processing Industries; Health and Family Welfare; Home Affairs and Internal Security; Human Resources; Industry; Information and Broadcasting; Labour; Law, Justice and Company Affairs; Non-conventional Energy Sources; Ocean Development; Parliamentary Affairs; Personnel, Public Grievances and Pensions; Petroleum and Natural Gas; Planning and Programme Implementation; Planning and Statistics; Posts and Telegraphs; Power; Rural Development; Science and Technology; Social Justice and Empowerment; Space; States Affairs; Steel; Steel and Mines; Sugar and Edible Oils; Surface Transport; Textiles; Tourism; Urban Development; Water Resources; Women and Child development etc.

Based on the information derived from authoritative sources, this work contains authentic facts and figures. I am deeply beholden to all the scholars whose writings are cited or substantially made use of in the present work. I am also thankful to Anmol Publications Pvt. Ltd. for undertaking publication of this encyclopaedia. I am solely responsible for shortcomings in presentation of matter.

Encyclopaedic in nature, this will prove a dependable reference work for scholars and academics besides those appearing for different competitive examinations.

—Satish Tiwari

1

Urban Integrating Strategies

Urban fringe has been existing since the emergence of urban civilisation. However, its importance in the planning process has been realised only in recent times, particularly in the wake of the Industrial Revolution. No doubt, the concept of fringe is prevalent more in metropolitan and big cities than in small cities and towns.

It is now established that industrialisation and urbanisation. are inter-related and irreversible processes. These are two sides of the same coin. A small town grows into a big town, a big town intoa city, and then it acquires the status of a metropolis and a mega city. Rapid urbanisation in the country has been accompanied by the emergence of urban fringe and slums in the cities. The existing areas of these cities are put under much pressure, causing excessive clustering and haphazard urban growth. The study on Management of Urban Fringe Land Development in selected Metropolitan cities undertaken by TCPO indicates that too much pressure on urban land during the last two decades has resulted into a decline in the per capita availability of urban land. As of now, a significant percentage 30% to 50% of population in metropolitan cities live in the slum areas in most deplorable and sub-standard conditions.

The emergence of urban fringe depends on various factors like growth of industrial, commercial and institutional activities in the fringe area, the availability of transportation facilities, proximity to the city, the existing spatial capacity of the city to absorb growing population, increasing economic activities and the basic infrastructural facilities being provided in the fringe areas, as well as in the city, etc. Therefore, it is difficult to assign a spatial boundary to define urban fringe.

According to Lewis Keeble the urban fringe is defined "as the land surrounding the town which is not considered as a part of it but whose use is influenced directly by the town".

Richard Mayers considers the urban fringe "as the zone between the country and the city while to Andrews the rural urban fringe outward from the economic city in which there is an intermininglingof charteristically agriculture and urban land uses." George Wherewein defines the fringe "as the area of transition between well recognised urban land uses and the area devoted to agriculture".

As such there is no exact definition for urban fringe land. It seems it is not possible also. This is because no one can exactly say as to what distance ithe fringe land should extend from the city boundary. One may say that fringe land should include those areas which fall on the fringe of the city, that is the areas falling just out side the boundary of the city. But the question is upto what distance one should go?

Some people define fringe areas as those areas which are not contiguous t the existing built up areas of the city, but those which are likely to become contiguous if provided with the right injection of investment towards the right injection of investmnet towards the development of physical and social infrastructure. The structure plan for the Madras Metropolitan Areas has defined urban fringe as those areas that are experiencing considerable pressure form the process of urbanisation.

During initial staes, the urban fringe land would be mostly under agricultural use. However, once migration of population form nearby areas into the fringe land starts, the available land in taken over for housing, commercial, institutional and industial uses.

Rural and urban population : 1901–1991, India

Census year populatin	Populatin (million)		Percentage of total	
	Rural	Urban	Rura	Urban
1901	213	26	89.2	10.8
1911	226	26	89.7	10.3
1921	223	28	88.8	11.2
1931	246	33	88.0	12.0
1941	275	44	86 1	13.9
1951	299	62	82.7	17.3
1961	360	79	82.0	18.0
1971	439	109	80.1	19.9
1981[1]	524	159	76.7	23.3
1991[2]	629	218	74.3	25.7

Source : Census of India 1991. Final Population Totals.

1. The 1991 Census could not be held in Assam. The figures for 1981 for Assam have been worked out by interpolartion.
2. Includes projected population of Jammu and Kashmir.

Table Growth of urbanisation by class of towns

Class of town	Population in ' 000s					
	1901	1951	9161	1971	1981	1991[1]
I. 1,00,00 and above	]6,661 (26.00)	27,507 (44.63)	39,883 (51.42)	61,226 (57.24)	94,504 (60.42)	1,38,802 (65.20)
II. 50,000–99,999	2,892 (11.29)	6,137 (9.96)	8,713 (11.23)	11,680 (10.92)	18,190 11.63)	23,309 (10.95)
III. 20,000–49,999	4,007 (15.64)	9,688 (15.72)	13,139 (16.94)	17,126 (16.01)	22,409 (14.33)	28,079 (13.19)
IV. 10,000–19,999	5,335 (20.83)	8,399 (13.63)	9,902 (12.77)	11,706 (10.94)	14,930 (9.54)	16,531 (7.77)
V. 5,000–9,999	5,159 (20.14)	7,993 (12.97)	5,329 (6.87)	4,756 (4.45)	5,603 (3.58)	5,532 (2.60)
VI. Less than 5,000	1,562 (6.10)	1,906 3.09)	597 (0.77)	473 (0.44)	784 (0.50)	614 (0.29)
All classes	25,616 (100.00)	61,630 (100.0)	77,562 (100.0)	1,06,967 (100.0)	1,56,420 (100.0)	2,12,867 (100.0)
Urban population as percentage to total Population	10.84	17.29	17.97	19.91	23.34	25.72

Source : Part II-A (i) & (ii) 1981.

Note : Exludes Assam and Jammu and Kashmir.

Figures within brackets are percentage total urban population for the census year.

1. Provisional.

Table Age structure projections (as on 1 March)

(Per cent)

Age Group	1980	1985	1990	2000
0–4	14.18	13.91	12.85	10.66
5–14	25.54	24.34	23.15	20.95
15–59	54.07	55.51	57.51	60.80
60 plus	6.21	6.24	6.49	7.59
Total	100.00	100.00	100.00	100.00

Source: Seeventh Five Year Plan 1985–1990.

Table Distribution of villages ccccording to population : 1981

States/UTs	Less than 1000	1,000 to 1,999	2,000 to 4,999	5,000 to 9,999	10,000 and over	Total
Andhra Pradesh	14,085	6,464	5,609	1,058	163	27,379
Bihar 49,617	10,811	5,842	1,054	192	67,546	
Gujarat	9,814	5,108	2,725	418	49	18,114
Haryana	3,275	1,883	1,346	221	20	6,745
Himachal Pradesh	16,348	364	92	3	–	16,807
Jammu & Kashmir	5,017	1,016	393	20	1	6,477
Karnataka	18,631	5,239	2,722	401	35	27,028
Kerala7	13	72	222	905	1,219	
Madhya Pradesh	61,029	8,118	2,016	155	4	71,352
Maharashtra	26,101	8,951	3,691	579	116	39,354
Manipur	1,758	174	90	12	1	2,035
Meghalaya	4,793	85	24	–	–	4,902
Nagaland	921	143	47	1	–	1,102
Orissa 40,710	4,561	1,234	47	1	46,553	
Punjab	8,146	2,819	1,256	120	1	12,342
Rajasthan	26,823	5,468	2,335	321	21	34,008
Sikkim	372	60	8	–	–	440
Tamil Nadu	5,698	4,570	4,381	1,000	182	15,831
Tripura	265	253	274	56	8	856
Uttar Pradesh	83,235	20,830	8,148	751	52	1,12,566
West Bengal	25,319	7,538	4,383	702	82	38,024
A and N Islands	460	23	8	–	–	491
Arunachal Pradesh	3,176	63	16	2	–	3,257
Chandigarh	12	5	7	–	–	24
Dadra and Nagar Haveli	33	27	7	3	–	70
Delhi	54	74	71	15	–	214
Goa, Daman and Diu	185	102	90	34	1	412
Lakshadweep	1	1	4	1	–	7
Mizoram	629	62	30	–	–	721
Pondicherry	209	48	28	6	–	291
All India[1]	4,06,72	3,94,486	46,892	7,202	1,834	5,57,137

Source : Census of India 1981, Series–India. Part II A (i) General Population Tables.

1. Excludes Assam.

Table Population of million plus cities

City	Population in '000s 1981	1951	Growth ratio 1981/1951	1981 Sex ratio	Literacy ratio
Calcutta	9,194	4,670	1.97	781	65
Greater Bombay	8,243	2,967	2.78	772	68
Delhi	5,729	1,437	3.99	808	63
Madras	4,289	1,542	2.78	930	67
Bangalore	2,922	786	3.72	896	64
Hyderabad	2,546	1,131	2.25	919	58
Ahmedabad	2,548	877	2.91	869	63
Kanpur	1,639	705	2.32	804	55
Pune	1,686	609	2.77	880	67
Nagpur	1,302	485	2.68	910	66
Lucknow	1,008	497	2.03	832	58
Jaipur	1,015	304	3.34	861	54

Source : Part II-A (ii) Series I India General Population Table A-4.

Table Population by religion

	1961		1971		1981		1991	
Relmigious group	Number (million)	% to total	Number (million)	% to total	Number (million)	% to total	Number (million)	% to total
Hindus	366.5	83.5	453.3	82.7	549.7	82.6	672.6	82.41
Muslims	46.9	10.7	61.4	11.2	75.6	11.4	95.2	11.67
Christians	10.7	2.4	14.2	2.6	16.2	2.4	18.9	2.32
Sikhs	7.8	1.8	10.4	1.9	13.1	2.0	16.3	1.99
Buddhists	3.2	0.7	2.6	0.5	3.2	0.5	3.4	0.41
Jains	2.0	0.5	2.6	0.5	3.2	0.5	3.4	0.41
Other[1]	1.6	0.4	2.2	0.4	2.8	0.4	3.5	0.43
Total	439.2	100.0	548.2	100.0	665.3	100.0	816.2[2]	100.00

Source : Census of India 1981, Series I-Paper I of 1995 (Religion), Paper I of 1991 (Religion)

1. Including unclassified persons.
2. Excludes Assam and J & K

Note : 1981 data do not include Assam.

Table Population and percentages for principal languages 1971-1981

	Number in (millions)		Percentage	
Languages	1971	1981	1971	1981
Hindi	208.5	264.5	38.0	42.9
Bengali	44.8	51.3	8.2	8.3
Telugu	44.8	50.6	8.2	8.2
Marathi	41.8	49.5	7.6	8.0
Tamil	37.7	3.8	6.9	0.6
Urdu	28.6	34.9	5.2	5.7
Gujarati	25.9	33.1	4.7	5.4
Malayalam	21.9	25.7	4.0	4.2
Kannada	21.7	25.7	4.0	4.2
Oriya	19.9	23.0	3.6	3.7
Punjabi	14.1	19.6	2.6	3.2
Assamese	9.0	0.1	1.6	0.01
Sindhi	1.7	2.0	0.3	0.3
Kashmiri	2.5	3.2	0.5	0.5

Source : Part IV-B (ii) Series- India-1981.

Note :

1. This statement excludes Assam as no census was taken there due to disturbed conditions prevailing at the time of 1981 census.
2. This statement excludes language figures of Tamil Nadu as the entire record of Tamil Nadu state under 'p' sample project have been lost due to flood at the 1981 census.

The NSS estimates of per capita consumption of different sections of the urban population in 1967-68 suffer from similar underestimation. In column 2 of the Table we have reproduced the NSS estimates of per capita consumption of the urban population in 1960-61 only slightly revised to bring them in accord with the official estimate of per capita national consumption. In column 2 are given the NSS estimates of per capita consumption in 1967-68 at 1960-61 prices. It will be seen that the NSS estimate of per capita urban consumption in

1967-68 (Rs. 325.7) is 8.6 per cent below the NSS estimate of urban consumption in 1960-61. Therefore, the estimate in 1967-68 is clearly an underestimate. The nature of underestimation becomes evident from column 4 where the NSS estimates for 1967-68 are expressed as percentages of corresponding estimates for 1960-61. These percentages increase progressively from 77.2 per cent for the poorest 5 per cent to 99.6 for the population lying between 60-70. Thereafter the percentages decline rapidly, implying that the upper middle and the richer sections of the urban population did not do comparatively as well as the middle sections. This is incredible and the conclusion is inevitable that the underestimation of urban consumption has been more serious in the case of the upper middle and the richer sections than in the case of other sections.

Hence, the NSS estimates of urban consumption in 1967-68 need to be revised. As in the case of the NSS estimates for rural consumption, we shall do the necessary revision conservatively in two steps. In the first stage (columns 5 and 6), we suppose that the percentages in column (4) should not decline as they do after reaching the value 99.6 for the class 60-70; hence we hold them at 99.6 for all classes above 60-70.

The results are given in colum (5). It will be seen that this revision causes the NSS estimate for 1967-68 to rise from Rs. 325.7 to Rs. 346.7. It is nevertheless still below the estimate of per capita consumption in 1967-68 namely Rs. 364.9. In fact, it needs to be raised by 5.25 per cent to bring it to that level. We do this by raising uniformly the revised estimates of consumption of all sections (column 6) by 5.25 per cent. The results of this second and final revision are given in columns 7 and 8.

In column 8, the per capita consumption of different sections in 1967-68 are expressed as percentages of corresponding consumption in 1960-61. The results are eye-opening. The lower middle and poorer sections constituting the bottom 40 per cent of the ruban population have not benefited at all by the economic development of the past decade. Indeed, the evidence is that their per capita consumption has declined and greatly so among the poorest 10 per cent. This is not impossible. It is this class which sufferes from rise in prices as was witnessed in the past decade. There are other important reasons for such serious deterioration in the living standards at the bottom of the urban population. We shall refer to them a little later.

Other sections of the urban population have benefited variously. The per capita consumption of the middle sections lying between 40-60 increased by between 1.0 and 3.0 per cent; of the upper middle and the richer sections constituting the top 40 per cent of the urban population, the per capita consumption increased by 4.8 per cent.

All visible and audible evidence points to the possibility that the consumption of the richer sections, the top 10 per cent or the top 5 per cent certainly, has increased much more. But in the absence of positive evidence, we prefer to be conservative. We should be thankful that statistcis could catch even as much of the reality as we have been able to discover.

Growth of inequality

The statistical evidence on growth of inequality is thus clear. A superficial examination and comparison of the NSS estimates of consumer expenditure in 1960-61 and 1967-68, as is commonly done, gives an impression that the inequalities in the distribution of consumer expenditure have narrowed down during the past decade. Unfortunately this is not true. The NSS estimates of consumption in 1967-68 are gross underestimates and the underestimation is particularly serious in the case of consumption of the upper middle and richer classes. The statistical evidence on both these counts is conclusive.

Hence the NSS estimates of per capita consumer expenditure in 1967-68 must be corrected for underestimation. As we have seen, even a conservative revision makes clear that all sections of the population have not benefited equally from the economic development of the past decade. The gains of development have remained largely confined to the upper middle and the richer sections constituting the top 40 per cent of the population. While the overall per capita consumption increased by about 3.9 per cent in seven years, the consumption of the upper 40 per cent of the rural population increased by at least 4.4 per cent and that of the upper 40 per cent of the urban population increased by at least 4.8 per cent.

These increases are not extra-ordinary and they certainly are not undesirable. Unfortunately they have remained largely confined to the upper middle and richer sections of the population. The middle, lower middle and poorer sections of the rural population showed much smaller increases in their per capita consumption and the per capita consumption of the poorest 5 per cent actually declined a little.

The situation in urban areas appears even more serious. The per capita consumption of the lower middle and poorer sections constituting the bottom 40 per cent of the urban population declined and the consumption of the poorest 10 per cent declined by as much as 15 to 20 per cent.

Such unequal distribution of the gains of development inevitably leads to growing inequality and a widening gulf between the rich and the poor.

We have earlier noted that, during the period from 1960-61 to 1967-68, the rural-urban disparity has narrowed down a little. Thus, while in 1960-61 the per capita urban consumer expenditure was 37.7 per cent higher than the per capita rural consumer expenditure, in 1967-68 the urban per capita expenditure was only 35.9 per cent higher than the rural per capita expenditure.

We shall now examine how this slight reduction in the rural-urban differential came about. In particular, we shall ask whether the reduction in the rural-urban differential came about because of a reduction in the differential between the rural-urban rich or the rural-urban poor. We have put together the relevant data. In columns (4) and (7) of the Table we have expressed the per capita urban consumer expenditure as per cent of the per capita rural consumer expenditure for each of the 12 sections into which we have divided the population.

To begin with, we should not that even in 1960-61, the rural-urban differential was much greater between the rural-urban rich than between the rural-urban poor. For instance, the per capita consumer expenditure of the 30 per cent urban poor was then about 27 per cent higher than the per capita consumer expenditure of their rural counterparts.

On the other hand, the per capita consumer expenditure of the 20 per cent urban rich was then about 47 per cent higher than the per capita consumer expenditure of their rural counterparts.

The corresponding data for 1967-68 are given in column (7) of the Table. It will be noticed that the differential between the rural and urban upper middle and richer classes was practically the same in 1967-68 as it was in 1960-61 It increased only slightly.

The urban upper middle and richer classes seem to have done compartively a little better than their counterparts in rural areas. But the situation is quite the contrary in respect of the middle, the lower middle and the poorer sections. These classes in urban areas have done distinctly worse comparatively to their counterparts in rural areas so that the differential between them has narrowed down. This is more true of the lower middle than the middle classes and even more true of the poorer classes than the lower middle classes. The narrowing down of the rural-urban differential is on account of the lower middle and poorer classes in urban areas having thus moved closer to their rural counterparts.

What has happened to the 10 per cent poorest in rural and urban areas is the most striking. As we have noted, the 10 per cent rural poor have stayed practically where they were at the beginning of the decade. On the other hand, the 10 per cent urban poor have difinitely suffered.

As a result, they have moved close to the rural poor. In 1960-61, the consumption of the urban 5 per cent poorest was 27.2 per cent higher than the consumption of their rural counterparts; in 1967-68, it was only 4.5 per cent higher. The same is true of the 5 per cent poor next above them. In 1960-61, their consumption was 29.2 per cent higher then their counterparts in the rural areas; in 1967-68, it was only 10.2 per cent higher. These small margins are certainly not adequate to compensate the higher cost of urban living at this level. It means that in 1967-68 the living standard of the 10 per cent urban poor was worse than that of their rural counterparts.

It is necessary to understand the meaning of this deterioration in the living standards of the urban poor. It does not necessarily mean that the same people were worse off in 1967-68 in comparison with their condition in 1960-61.

This is not imposible. But more generaliy it means that new migrants have moved from the rural area into the growing urban centres and have been compelled to accept life at a level much below what used to be the case a decade ago and hardly distinguishable from the life they left behind and to escape which they moved into the cities. It is thus that the rural-urban disparities have somewhat narrowed down.

We should conclude. During the past decade, the per capita private consumer expenditure increased by less than half a per cent per annum. Moreover, the small gains have not been equitably distributed among all sections of the population. The condition of the bottom 20 per cent rural poor has remained more or less stagnant. The condition of the bottom 20 per cent urban poor has definitely deteriorated; and for another 20 per cent of the urban population, it has remained more or less stagnant. Thus, while the character of rural poverty has remained the same as before, the character of urban poverty has deepened further. This is the consequence of the continuous migration of the rural poor into the urban areas in search of a livelihood, their failure to find adequate means to support themselves there and the resulting growth of pavement and slum life in the cities. All the latent dissatisfaction about the slow progress of the economy and the silent frustration about its failure to give the poor a fair deal, let alone special attention, appear to be gathering in this form. Its shape today is probably no more than hideous; allowed to grow unheeded and unrelieved, it will inevitably turn ugly.

The Urban land (Ceiling and Regulation) Act, 1976 came into force on 17 February 1976. It applies to all the state governments and union territories except Jammu and Kashmir, Kerala, Nagaland and Sikkim hich have not adopted the Act so far. It also excludes Tamil Nadu which had enacted its own law in 1978.

The Act was enacted in order to prevent concentration of urban land in the hands of a few persons and also to curb speculation and profiteering therein with a view to bring about an equitable distribution of urban land to sub-serve the common good. The Act is mainly implemented by the state governments through the competent authorities appointed by them for performing various functions under the provisions of the Act. As per the information furnished by various state governments/union territories, 2,19,506 hectare of land has been estimated as excess vacant land. Out of this, 40,480 hectare of excess vacant land has been vested in the state governments/union territories. The state governments/union territories have acquired physically 14,816 hectare of excess vacant land. On the front of the social housing, 2,980 schemes were approved involving 5,320 hectare of vacant land for the purpose of construction of 4,02,449 dwelling units for the weaker sections of society. In order to make the Act more workable and to simplify the procedure various amendments to the Act have been fomulated and are under consideration of the Government.

Urban Water Supply and Sanitation is a State subject. Schemes are formulated, implemented, operated and maintained by the state governments/union territory administrations. Funds are provided for the purpose under the state plans.

As per the information available, the coverage of urban water supply and sanitation till December 1991 was 85 per cent and 46 per cent respectively. The working group for the formulation of the Eighth Plan recommended to provide drinking water facilities to cent per cent population and with sewerage and sanitation facilities to 75 per cent of the urban population by the end of the Eighth Plan (1992-97). In order to achieve the objective, the Working Group envisaged amount of Rs.

23,634.56 crore for the Eighth Plan. However, only an outlay of * Rs. 1,114.54 crore has been provided for the Annual Plan 1993-94 under the state sector.

During 1994-95, an amount of Rs. 16.99 crore was distributed amongst those staes which were considered earlier for the first instalment. Various training programmes have been initiated for human resource development in planning, design, operation and maintenance and management of urban water supply and sanitation schemes. The Government has introduced use of micro-computer for planning and designing of water supply distribution and sewerage systems besides imparting training to pubblic health engineers. Financial assistance was provided to several state agencies dealing in urban water supply and sanitation sector for procuring micro-computers. The agencies have procured the computers and accessories and installed them in their organisations.

The Ministry sponsors research and development projects to various institutions in the country in order to develop appropriate technologies in the field of water supply and sanitation which can be applied not only in implementation of the project but also in their operation and maintenance and to acheive an overall improvement in the sector. The Urban Development Ministry has developed a Managment Information System (Mis) which has been disseminated to state public health engineering departments and water supply and sewerage boards for implementation. The Ministry provides technical advice and accords technical approval for urban water supply and sanitation schemes in order to get loan assistance from LIC, World Bank and other bilateral agencies.

The Scheme of Urban basic Services for the Poor (UBSP) was launched in 1990-91. The scheme is based on the covergent provision of social and physical inputs in low income, urban neighbourhoods through the programmes of various specialist departments with the active participation of community groups.

The cardinal objective of scheme is to improve the overall quality of life of slum dewllers. The Cabinet has approved the scheme for the Eighth Plan period. From the inception of the Eighth Five Year Plan, the programme is being implemented on a 60:40 sharing basis between the Central and state governments. Further, the per capita expenditure will be Rs. 75 in the first year and Rs. 50/- from the second year onwards after the basic infrastructure hs been established. A total outlay of Rs. 100 crore has been provided for the scheme for the Eighth Plan period.

The scheme is to be implemented in collaboration with the state sector scheme of Environmental Improvement of Urban Slums and the Centrally-sponsored scheme of Nehru Rozgar Yojana. By the end of the Eighth Plan period, it is expected that the benefit of the scheme will extend to urban areas having a total slum population of about 70 lakh and, on a national basis, targets 500 cities and towns. The National Plan of Action (NPA) on Children which is a follow-up of the promises made by the global fraternity at the World Summit for Children in 1990, reiterates and re-affirms India's commitment to the cause of women and child development. NPA goals became opertional from early 1992. One of the major objectives of the UBSP scheme is to achieve the goals of the NPA on Children in the urban poor localities by planning and organising various programmes being implemented by different ministries/ departments.

Upto March 1995, over 3,622 neighbourhood development committees comprising primarily of urban poor women have been set up in around 283 towns taken up for provision of basic services all over the country. This represnets community based structures covering around 48.26 akh low income women and children. It is expected that approximately 70 lakh beneficiaries will be covered under UBSP programme by; the end of Eighth Five Year Plan.

On a national basis, the Eighth Five Year Plan targets 500cities and towns. Around 2,997 mini plans have already been prepared and 460 community organisers are in the field working as catalysts for enriching community participation. In order to monitor the scheme a National Level Monitoring Committee has been set up under the Chairmanship of Secretary, Ministry of Urban Affairs and Employment.

Scheme of Urban Micro-Enterprises

The Scheme of Urban Micro-Enterprises (SUME) is being implemented from June 1990 under the Nehru Rozgar Yojana (NRY). The scheme covers unemployed urban poor whose family income is less than Rs. 11,850 per annum in metropolitan areas, cities and towns, not covered by Integrated Rural Development Programme (IRDP).

Under the scheme, subsidy at the rate of 25 per cent of the project cost is given to each beneficiary subject to the ceiling of Rs. 5,000 for SCs/STc and women beneficiaries and Rs. 4,000 for others. Repayment is made in three to five years with the suitable monthly/quarterly instalments depending upon the surplus cash generation. The applications are sponsored by the Urban Local Bodies (ULBs) viz., Nagar Panchayats and Municipalities which act as nodal agency. Applicants should have lived in the locality at least for three years.

The security for the loan will be the asset created out of the loan and no security or third party guarantee is necessary. While 30 per cent of the funds would be utilised for women beneficiaries, SCs/STs are to be given weightage in proportion to their population share in total urban poor of the ULB concerned. During 1993-94, an amount of Rs. 12,647.69 lakh was sanctioned against 1,78,956 applications.

Prime Minister's Rozgar Yojana (PMRY) for educated unemployed youth was launched on 2 October 1993. the objective of the scheme is to provide sustained employment to about 10 lakh educated unemployed urban youth in micro-enterprises during the Eight Five Year Plan. These enterprises cover manufacturing, service and business ventures. The scheme was implemented in urban areas during 1993-94 and from 1 April 1994, throughout the country. Self-Employment Scheme for Educated Unemployed Youth (SEPUY) has been subsumed with PMRY from 1 April 1994.

The salient features of the scheme are:

- Youth between the age of 18 and 35 belonging to families having incomes of less than RS. 24,000 per annum would be eligijble for assistance under the scheme;
- These educated unemployed entrepreneurs would be given a subsidy of 15 per cent subject to a ceiling of Rs. 7,500 each for starting the micro-enterprises;
- They would be required to bring in five per cent of the project cost as margin money;
- Each entrepreneur will be eligible for a loan upto a ceiling of Rs. one lakh and this loan would not require a collateral gurantee;
- The entrepreneurs selected under the scheme would be provided training before the loan is granted;
- Not more than 30 per cent of the micro-enterprises would be from the business sector;

- Besides matric passed or failed students and ITI passed youth, all the persons who have undergone Government sponsored technical courses for a minimum duration of six months will be eligible for assistance under the scheme;
- Reputed NGOs would also be associated in the implementation of the scheme especially in the selection training of entrepreneurs and preparation of the project under the scheme;
- A reservation of 22.5 per cent for SCs/STs and 27 per cent for other backward castes (OBCs) has been provided;
- Women shuld be given preference and the beneficiary should have been a permanent resident of the urban area for three years. Upto December 1994, 60,513 applicants have been sanctioned loans amounting to Rs. 32,226.65 lakh (by all Indian scheduled commercial banks).

With approximately 27 per cent of its population living in urban areas, India is one of the least urban countries, but with an urban population of 217 million (1991) it is also a country with one of the largest urban populations. India's towns and cities could, by themselves, make up the third largest nation of the world.

Urban India consists of close to 3500 towns varying in size from the smallest district towns with a population of 5,000 to the large urban agglomerations exceeding 10 million people. Nearly two-thirds of the urban population is concentrated in 317 'Class I' towns, or cities with a population of over 100,000 of which half lives in 23 metropolitan areas with populations exceeding 1 million.

The four largest cities—Bombay, Calcutta, Delhi and Madras—between them account for one sixth of the urban total. the Class I towns are the fastest growing urban areas in India. Greater Bombay, with apopulation of 12.57 million, and Calcutta with 10.86 million, are among the largest metropolitan areas in the world.

While over the past four decades the popultion of India has more than doubled, during the same period the urban population has more than quadrupled. The growth has come as much from net migration as from natural increase (about 40 per cent each), with the balance due to reclassification and inclusion of new towns.

The National Commission on Urbanization (1988) states that "these urban centres have also generated tha most brutal and inhuman living conditions, with large sections of the citizens living in squatter settlements.

The overcrowding in the slums and the desperate lack of water and sanitation leads not only to severe health problems but to abject degradation of human life." It further remarks that "in the decades to come, who knows how much political tension and physical viloence will be triggered off by the flrgrant display of wealth which coexists with the rising expectations of the poor and with the appalling conditions of congestion and pollution which form their environment?"

The estimate of proportion of urban people living in slums varies from about 20 per cent to 30 per cent. Looked at by class of town, the highest percentage of people living in slum areas is in the cities with a million plus population and the least in towns with less than 100,000 population.

The growth rate of the slum population, largely through continuing in migration, is significantly faster than that of other segments of the urban population. While this phenomenon is in no way unique to India, it is the sheer size of the problem in India that is staggering.

About 27 per cent of the urban population lives below the poverty line, 30-40 per cent of the population of the larger metropolitan areas live in slums, 27 per cent does not have access to water-borne sanitation. Indian cities also have very high levels of air and water pollution. As a result, the environment that the rural migrant has to live in, is as harsh a choice between environment and development as one can pose.

And yet the choice is made. It is made by over 13,500 people each day who move from rural to urban environments and the several million who continue to live in the highly degraded areas of urban India.

The urban slum is their 'gateway'. It is the 'solution' rather than the 'problem' of urban living. It is both a low cost housing solution and a low cost transportation solution, as the slum is usually close to the place of work. But it makes nevertheless for squalid surroundings. It is a price that is paid, and paid consciously—because the option, where it even exists, is worse. Urban poverty is preferred to rural poverty.

Air pollution is a problem in some urban areas. Heavy vehicles cause 47 per cent of the pollution while accounting for 8 per cent of the total number of vehicles on Indian roads. The production of automobiles in India has increase from 1,891 in 1955 to 116,564 in 1988. Two and three wheelers constituting 63 per cent of the number of vehicles cause 13 per cent of the total pollution. While this pollution does cause localized problems, the number of vehicles is so small that it has negligible impact at the global level. Efficient public transport options, which will cut down on both fossil fuel consumption and pollution need to be explored.

The noise levels in many of the Indian cities is much above the safe limit. This is due to diverse factors which include industrial manufacturing activities, excessive use of vehicle horns, and unregulated use of loudspeakers at social, political and religious events. Awareness must be created in this regard.

The question that is difficult to understand is not so much why the poor decide to stay in slums, but rather how much remains to be done about improving conditions in these areas.

The Report of the National Commission on Urbanization feels that "For whatever reason, resource allocation in the urban field seems to follow a problem rather than anticipate it." Furthermore, "the inefficiency of our cities and towns is being perpetuated by obsolete, rigid and irrational laws, regulatory provisions and norms. The urban centres, with their concentration of diverse activities, should be generators of wealth; instead, they have degenerated into parasites looking elsewhere for support."

- The family Welfare Programme has helped in containing the growth rate of population. Total Fertility Rate has declined from 4.5 in 1981 to 3.5 in 1993 as per the estimates of Sample Registration System (SRS).

The Crude Birth Rate has decreased from 33.9 per provisional estimates of the SRS. The Crude Death Rate has also declined from 12.5 to 9 per thousand population over the same period. The Infant MOrtality Rate dropped from 110 per thousand live births in 1981 to 74 in 1995. The annual average exponential population growth rate has come down marginally from 2.22 per cent during 1971-81 to 2.14 per cent during 1981-91. The population, however, continues to grow as the decline in birth rate has not been as rapid as the decline in the death rate.

- There are, however, inter-State differences in the achievements of the Family Welfare Programme. At one end of the spectrum are the States like Kerala, Tamil Nadu and Goa which have already achieved replacement level of fertility.

At the other end, are the large States like Uttar Pradesh, Madhya Pradesh, Rajasthan and Bihar where fertility levels and bjirth rates continue to be higher than the national average. Therefore, decline in the rate of growth of population for the country as a whole depends upon how the large northern States perform in the family welfare programmes in the future. Unless effective steps are taken to bring about significant improvements in the programme, the performance in containing the growth of population at the All India level may not change significantly.

- Recognising the close relationship between high birth rates and high rnfant mortality, high priority has been accorded to the Maternal and Child Health (MCH) programme since 1985. In order to achieves the main objective of MCH, (i.e. to improve the health status of women and children and to reduce maternal, infant and child morbidity and mortality rates), the Universal Immunisation Programme (UIP) was launched in 1985. From the year 1992-93 the UIP has been strengthened and expanded into the Child Survival and Safe Motherhood (CSSM) programme.

Under this programme, apart from strengthening the existing MCH, initiative has been taken to expand the pilot projects on Acute Respiratory Infection Control and Traditional Birth Attendants training. For this, a provision of Rs.350 crore has been made in the 1996-97 budget as against Rs.220 crore in 1995-96 (BE).

- From 1.4.1996, the Family Welfare Programme is being implemented on the basis of the "Target Free Approach" (TFA). This approach envisages replacement of the system of setting contraceptive targets from the top by a system of decentralised participatory planning at the Primary Health Centre level.

- Pursuant to the World Health Organisation (WHO) goal to eradicate poliomyelitis (polio, a major crippling childhood disease) by the year 2000 A.D., the Pulse Polio Immunization (PPI) was launched in 1995-96.

About 87 million children aged 0-3 years were administered as supplemented dose of oral polio vaccine on 9.12.1995 and 93 million on 20.1.1996, irrespective of their routine immunisation status. Since PPI received an overwhelming response from the public, the exercise was repeated on 7.12.1996 and 18,1.1997 covering about 120 million children in the age group of 0-5 years.

- A Special School Health Check-up Scheme for Primary School Children was carried out in 27 States/UTs in July 1996, and in the remaining 5 States between August and October 1996.

The objectives of this Scheme were to detect common health related problems among primary school children; to conduct screening of children for appropriate referral and check up; to generate health awareness in the community; and to ensure arrangements for follow up and treatment at higher level medical facilities. Reports from 441 districts show 75.9 per cent coverage of schools and 84.9 per cent coverage of enrolled children.

- In order to foster community involvement in the Family Welfare Programme, two new schemes have been started on a pilot basis. Under one of these, one revenue village in every district, among villages with a population of 500 or more, will be given an award of Rs. 2 lakh for achieving a reduction in the

Crude Birth rate, Infant Mortality Rate and Child Mortality Rate.

The second schemes aims to integrate family welfare and health care into the ongoing National Wastershed Development Project for Rainfed Areas (NWDPRA) of the Ministry of Agriculture. Under this scheme, the watershed level community based management structures, known as the 'Mitra Krishak Mandal' (MKM) will conduct surveys and prepare watershed level family welfare and health care plans. An amount of Rs. 5000 will be given to each village in the watershed areas, for specified activities like emergency obstetric care and purchase of essential medicines.

- The Prenatal Diagnostic Techniques (Regulation and Preventation of Misuse) Act, 1994, has been brought into force from 1st January, 1996. This Act makes it illegal to use prenatal diagnostic techniques like amniocentesis for determining the sex of the foetus, a practice that often leads to abortion of female foetuses. Statutory machinery for implementation of the Act has been established.

Uttar Pradesh continued to be the largest state, population wise with 16.44 per cent people of the country living there (13,91,12,287) followed by Bihar with 10.21 per cent (8,63,74,465) and Maharashtra with 9.33 per cent (7,89,37,187). West Bengal occupied fourth place accounting for 8.04 per cent (6,80,77,965) of the country's population followed by Andhra Pradesh with 7.86 per cent (6,65,08,008). Ranking of the states and union territories according to population size is in table 2.

Bombay metropolis continued to be the most populated city of the country with urban population of 12.60 million, Calcutta taking the second place having 11.02 million. Delhi ranks third with a population (urban) of 8.42 million followed by Madras 5.42 million.

One of the important indices of population concentration is the density of population. It is defined as the number of persons per square kilometre. The population density has gone up from 216 in 1981 to 267 persons in 1991 (excluding Assam and J&K). In 1901 it was 77 persons per sq km followed by Chandigarh (5,632). Lakshadweep which has the smallest population size is the fourth most densely populated area with a density of 1,616 persons per sq km. Arunachal Pradesh is the most sparsely populated area of the country with 10 persons per sq km.

The 10 heavily populated districts of the country are Calcutta, Madras, Greater Bombay, Hyderabad, Delhi, Chandigarh, Mahe, Howrah, Kanpur City and Bangalore. All of them have density of above 2,000 persons per square kilometre and 5.01 per cent of the country's population lives in these districts. The average density of these districts is 6,888.

In any study of the population, analysis of the sex composition plays a vital role. The sex composition of the population is affected by the differentials in the mortality conditions of males and females, sex selective migration and the sex ration at birth.

Sex ratio is defined as the number of females per 1000 males. In India, it has generally been adverse to women. The ratio has also declined over the years except in 1981 when it slightly improved to 934 from 927. In 1991, there has been a fall by seven points to 927 per thousand males. But Kerala represented a different spectrum. The state has a higher number of females than males, 1,036 females for thousand males.

In the Indian context, a sex ratio of 950 and above can be considered as favourable to females. The states and union terrtories coming under this category besides Kerala are Himachal Pradesh (976), Andhra Pradesh

(972), Goa (967), Karnataka (960), Manipur (958), Orissa, (971), Tamil Nadu (974),

Dadra and Nagar Haveli (952), Daman and Diu (969) and Pondicherry (979). Chandigarh accounted for the lowest number of females per thousand males with 790.

Table states and union territories by population size

Rank in 1991	State/ Union Territory	Pupulation 1991	Per cent to total population of India 1991	1981	Rank in 1981
1.	Uttar Pradesh	139,112,287	16.44	16.18	1
2.	Bihar	86,374,465	10.21	10.20	2
3.	Maharashtra	78,937,187	9.33	9.16	3
4.	West Bengal	68,077,965	8.04	7.97	4
5.	Andhra Pradesh	66,508,008	7.86	7.82	5
6.	Madhya Pradesh	66,181,170	7.82	7.52	6
7.	Tamil Nadu	55,858,946	6.60	7.06	7
8.	Karnataka	44,977,201	5.31	5.42	8
9.	Rajasthan	44,005,990	5.20	5.00	9
10.	Gujarat	41,309,582	4.88	4.97	10
11.	Orissa	31,659,736	3.74	3.85	11
12.	Kerala	29,098,518	3.44	3.71	12
13.	Assam	22,414,322	2.65	2.90	13
14.	Punjab	20,281,969	2.40	2.45	14
15.	Haryana	16,463,648	1.94	1.89	15
16.	Delhi	9,420,644	1.11	0.91	16
17.	Jammu & Kashmir[1]	7,718,700	0.91	0.87	17
18.	Himachal Pradesh	5,170,877	0.61	0.62	18
19.	Tripura	2,757,205	0.33	0.30	19
20.	Manipur	1,837,149	0.22	0.21	20
21.	Meghalaya	1,774,778	0.21	0.19	21
22.	Nagaland	1,209,546	0.14	0.11	22
23.	Goa	1,169,793	0.14	0.15	23
24.	Arunachal Pradesh	864,558	0.10	0.09	24
25.	Pondicherry	807,785	0.09	0.09	25

(Contd...)

26. Mizoram	689,756	0.08	0.07	26
27. Chandigarh	642,015	0.08	0.07	27
28. Sikkim	406,457	0.05	0.05	28
29. Andaman & Nicobar Islands	280,661	0.03	0.03	29
30. Dadra & Nagar Haveli	138,477	0.02	0.02	30
31. Daman & Diu	101,586	0.01	0.01	31
32. Lakshadweep	51,707	0.01	0.01	32

Source : Census of India 1991 final population total (1) PCA Part-II-B(i), 1991 (2) PCA-Part-IIB(i), 1981 (PPXX).

1. The 1991 Census was not held in J & K. The population projections of J&K as on 1 March 1991 made by the Standing Committee of Experts on Population Projections (October 1989) is given.

Table Sex ratio : 1901-1991

Gensus Year	Sex ratio
1901	972
1911	964
1921	955
1931	950
1941	945
1951	946
1961	941
1971	930
1981[1]	934
1991[2+3]	927

Source: Census of India. 1991 Series I, PCA General Population Part-II B(i) Vol. I.

1. Includes interpolated population of Assam.
2. The sex ratio in India has been generally adverse to women, *i.e.*, the number o women per 1,000 men has generally been less than 1,000. Apart from being adverse to women, the sex ratio has also declined over teh decades. The slight improvement notices in the 1981 census has not been maintained in 1991 and in fact there has been a fall by seven points from 934 in 1981 to 927 in 1991. The reason for the general disparity in the sex ratio and the declining trend over the years need further examination.
3. The 1991 Census was not held in J & K. For working out sex ratio for India the population for J & K as projected by the Standing Committee of Experts on Population Projections (October 1989) has been taken.

Table Population: Scheduled castes: Scheduled tribes: 1981

India	Scheduled castes		Scheduled tribes	
State/UT	Population ('000)	percentage total population	Population of ('000)	percentage of total population
India	1,04,755	15.8	51,629	7.8
Andhra Pradesh	7,962	14.9	3,176	5.9
Arunachal Pradesh	3	0.5	441	69.8
Assam	N.A.	N.A.	N.A.	N.A.
Bihar	10,142	14.5	5,811	8.3
Goa	21	2.1	0.7	0.1
Gujarat	2,438	7.2	4,849	14.2
Haryana	2,464	19.1	–	–
Himachal Pradesh	1,054	24.6	197	4.6
Jammu & Kashmir[1]	497	8.3	–	–
Karnataka	5,595	15.1	1,825	4.9
Kerala	2,549	10.0	261	1.0
Madhya Pradesh	7,359	14.1	11,987	23.0
Maharashtra	4,480	7.1	5,772	9.2
Manipur	18	1.3	388	27.3
Meghalaya	5	0.4	1,076	80.6
Mizoram	Negligible	Negligible	462	93.6
Nagaland	–	–	651	84.0
Orissa	3,866	14.7	5,195	22.4
Punjab	4,512	26.9	–	–
Rajasthan	5,839	17.0	4,183	12.2
Sikkim	18	5.8	74	23.3
Tamil Nadu	8,881	18.4	520	1.1
Tripura	310	15.1	584	28.4
Uttar Pradesh	23,453	21.2	233	0.2
West Bengal	12,001	22.0	3,071	5.6
Andaman and Nicobar Islands	–	–	22	11.9
Chandigarh	64	14.1	–	–
Dadra and Nagar Haveli	2	2.0	82	78.8
Delhi	1,122	18.0	–	–
Daman and Diu	3	3.6	10.0	12.70
Lakshadweep	–	–	38	93.8
Pondicherry	97	16.0	–	–

Source: Census of India 1981. Series 1 India, Part II B(ii) & (iii) Primary Census Abstract.

1. Excludes the population of areas under unlawful occupation of Pakistan and China where Census could not be held.

India's population, as on 1 March 1991 stood at 846.30 million (439.23 million males and 407.07 million females). This includes the projected population of 7.72 million of Jammu and Kashmir. The second largest populous country, India is the home of 16 per cent of world's population. The country, however, accounts for 2.42 per cent of the total world area.

The population of India as recorded at each decenial census from 1901 has grown steadily except for a decrease during 1911-21. In absolute terms the country's population has increased by 162.97 million during the decade 1981-91. Decadal growth of population from 1901, is shown in table 1. An encouraging feature revealed by the provisional results is the decline in growth rate of the population in the last decade compared to 1971-81. It marginally decreased from 24.66 per cent recorded in 1971-81 to 23.85 per cent during 1981-91.

In most states the growth rate declined during the decade. However, Andhra Pradesh, Arunachal Pradesh, Madhya Pradesh, Maharashtra, Nagaland, Tripura, West Bengal, Daman and Diu, Lakshadweep and Pondicherry which account for one third of the country's population, recorded increase in growth rate. Nagaland registered the highest growth rate of 56.08 per cent while Keral the lowest 14.32 per cent.

During recent years, the trend towards rural-to-urban migration as well as urban-to-urban migraton is on the increase and the mobility characteristics are particularly strong towards metropolitan cities. Statistics show populaltion increase annually at national level—2%, at Urban level—3% and in metropolitan cities level—9%. As such, the existing areas of these cities are put under much pressure, causing excessive clustering and haphazard urban growth. According to 1991 census (provisional figures), about 65% of the total urban population live in Class-I cities and 50.6 per cent of urban population live in 23 metropolitan cities alone. Even though the rate of growth to over 40% in 12 metropolitan cities during 1971-81 has been less than the growth of urban population of 46%, the absolute addition of about 12 million people representing 24% of the total addition to urban population is distinctly very high. By the year 2000, India's urban population is excepted to be 325 million, twice the 1981 level, and more than half of India's population growth will occur in urban areas only.

Table Population 1990-91

Year	Population	Decade growth rate (per cent)	Average Annual exponential growth rate (per cent)	Progressive growth rate over 1901
1901	23,83,96,327	–	–	–
1911	25,20,93,390	+5.75	0.56	+5.75
1921	25,13,21,213	–0.31	–0.03	+5.42
1931	27,89,77,238	+11.00	1.04	17.02
1941	31,86,60,580	+14.22	1.33	33.67
1951	36,10,88,090	+13.31	1.25	+51.47
1961	43,92,34,771	+21.51	1.96	+84.25
1971	54,81,59,652	24.80	2.20	+129.94
1981	68,33,29,097	+24.66	2.22	+186.64
1991	84,63,02,688	+23.85	2.14	+255.00

Source: Census of India 1991 Final Population totals and Part-II-A (I).

It could be seen from this data that the pressure on land in urban areas had increased manifold during the last two decades resulting in further decline in the availability of per capita urban land. Further, nearly 30 to 50 per cent of the urban population in these cities has been living in slum areas with poor and sub-standard living conditions, with civic amenities far from satisfactory. The density of population in slums is also very high. Hence, the imbalance between the rapid growth or urban population in the metropolitan cities and relatively slow process of development of additional land for housing, commercial and other purposes has given rise to the following major problems in the metropolitan cities:

- Acute shortage of serviced land for residential, commercial and industrial purposes, resulting in urban sprawl and invasion on urban fringe.
- Continuous increase in density and loss of open spaces, more demand for land for housing and transportation have resulted in large conversion of land in the fringe.
- High land values due to ever-increasing gap between demand and supply of land for various uses.
- Increasing pressure on physical and social infrastructure due to massive spill-over, population pressure/economic activities etc.
- Acute shortage of housing, resulting in unauthorised construction, squatter settlements, up-coming of slums and even invasion of villages by the spill over population/economic activities etc.
- Inadequate finances/investment in urban infrastructure led to the concomitant problems of unplanned urban development on the green-belt leading to serious environmental/ecological problems.
- Fast urbanisation, coupled with sky rocketing land prices has deprived the poor/low income families to have access to shelter or even serviced land. Hence, not only the weaker section of the society but lower, middle income group of society but lower, middle income group of society have also started on public/private land, generally on the urban fringe. The Land Acquisition of land have further acted as a major constraint in smooth and

expeditious a acquisition of land and making it available for urban development.

The TCPO's study on Management of Urban Fringe Land Development in selected Metropolitan Cities of India namely Madras, Hyderabad, Pune, Indore, Lucknow, and Jaipur was taken up to analyse the efficacy of existing policies and programmes in making serviced land available at affordable prices to the poor for utilisation of land, availability of vacant land, unutilised land for meeting future demand etc.

The study has gone into the spatial problems of inner city, density pattern, migration, of various infrastructural facilities like water supply, transport, sewerage, drainage, electricity, roads and other physical amenities in the cities. An attempt has been made in the study to analyse the effects on the management of green-belt, environment and land use transformation, provision of water and transportation for land development. The findings of study are briefly given below:

- The fringe areas of Madras and Jaipur are inhabitated by mostly middle and higher income groups, whereas fringe areas of Hyderabad, Pune, Lucknow and Indore are dominated by poor or low-income people.
- The people living in urban fringe of these six cities are employed in private sector/informal sector. A significant proportion of the total population of these areas are also found to be self employed.
- In case of Madres and Hyderabad, a significant proportion of persons (50-70%) are employed locally. Hosever, in respect of other smaller cities, the majority of the earning members commute to the main city for work or for other purposes.
- Public transport service seems to be the most important mode of transport for work journeys

performed by the households of the urban fringe areas. Public transport facilities appear to be good in the fringe areas of Hyderabad, Madras and Pune, wherwas private transport is playing important role in Jaipur, Lucknow and Indore.

- A good proportion of the households who settled in the fringe areas of Madras, Hyderabad and Jaipur have come from the main cities, whereas the households settled in the fringe areas of Pune, Lucknow and Indore have migrated from nearby rural areas.
- Growth of these urban fringe areas has taken place only around mid-1980s.
- Majority of the households in urban fringe areas of these metropolitan cities have their own houses. It shows that the priority of these households has been to have houses of their own .
- Construction in all these urban fringe areas is unauthorised. This may be due to the impression among the people that these construction or pucca houses would be regularised on the intervention of some social or political pressures later on.
- The majority of the households lack municipal or protected water supply and depend on open wells located within their premises. These households are also deprived of sewerage and drainage facilities. Majority of them have water-borne latrines connected to septic tanks.
- Fringe areas of these metropolitan cities lack adequate basic facilities like education/medicines etc. They have to depend for them on the main cities.
- The reasons for living in the fringe areas are the high cost of urban land within city, the city life being unaffordable for the poor.

- Majority of the households of the fringe areas wanted to have domestic water connections and drainage facilities in their localities.
- Land price in the fringe areas started rising around mid-1980s. The price level between 1980-85 was steady. A sharp rise in the price of land, however, occured after 1985. The Urban Land Ceiling and Regulation Act, 1976, instead of being helpful in preventing speculative transactions relating to scarce and precious land, has added to the misery of land-speculation.

Thousands of hectares of surplus land that the government proposed to aquire nder the Act was caught in the never ending rigmarole of court litigations. In two decades of its existence, the government has been able to acquire barely 15,321 hectares of the total 2.21 lakh hectares declared surplus across the country.

We shall now proceed to examine the crucial question whether as a result of the economic development of the past decade, the poorer sections have profited proportionately more or less than have the richer sections. We have earlier given the distribution of the population in 1960-61 according to per capita consumer expenditure. It would be possible to obtain a similar distribution of the population in 1967-68 namely according to per capita consumer expenditure.

A comparison of the two distributions then may indicate whether, during the period, inequality in the distribution of consumer expenditure has diminished or increased. If the inequality has diminished, it is evident that the poorer sections have profited proportionately than have the richer sections.

There is, however, a more direct method of comparing the improvement in the living standards of the poorer and the richer sections over a given period such as from 1960-61 to 1967-68. For this purpose, we first classify the population according to the per capita consumer expenditure in 1960-61, as we have done in and concentrate attention on the poorest 5 per cent or the poorest 10 per cent and ask what their per capita consumer expenditure was in 1960-61. Similarly, we concentrate attention on the richest 5 per cent or the richest 10 per cent and ask what their per capita consumer expenditure was in 1960-61.

In fact we may ask this question for different sections of the population arranged from the poorest to the richest.

It will be noticed that in this we have divided the population into 12 sections: the poorest 5 per cent, the next poorest 5 per cent (lying between 5-10 per cent), the next 10 per cent (lying between 10-20 per cent), etc., the second 5 per cent richest (lying between 90-95 per cent) and finally the richest 5 per cent (lying between 95-100 per cent). For each of these 12 sections of the, population we have shown their per capita consumer expenditure in 1960-61.

Thus the per capita per annum consumer expenditure of the poorest 5 per cent was Rs. 75.6 and of the richest 5 per cent it was 870.6. These estimates of per capita consumer expenditure of the different sections are as given by the National Sample Survey only slightly adjusted downwards in order to bring them in conformity with the official estimates of per capita national consumer expenditure in that year.

We may now adopt the same procedure for 1967-68 and divide the population into similar 12 sections ranging from the poorest 5 per cent to the richest 5 per cent on the basis of per capita expenditure in 1967-68 and ask what the per capita expenditure of the several sections was in 1967-68. In order to be able to compare the standard of living of the several sections in the two periods, namely 1960-61 and 1967-68, we should express the consumer expenditure in 1967-68 at 1960-61 prices.

The estimates of per capita consumer expenditure given in this column are as obtained by the NSS but expressed in 1960-61 prices.

We may now compare the per capita consumer expenditure of the several sections in the two years 1960-61 and 1967-68 and see how the several sections have benefited by development during the period. It will be seen that for all sections of the population, the per capita consumption in 1967-68 (valued at 1960-61 prices) was below the same in 1960-61. The per capita consumption in 1967-68 for all sections combined was 92.7 per cent of its level in 1960-61.

This is of course a consequence of the fact, earlier noted, that the NSS estimate of private consumer expenditure in 1967-68 is an underestimate. As we have noted, consistent with the official estimate of per capita national consumption, the rural per capita consumption in 1967-68 should be Rs. 268.6 (at 1960-61 prices). The NSS estimate is Rs. 239.8 which is 10.7 per cent below the official estimate. It is therefore necessary to revise the NSS estimates of per capita consumption in different sections of the rural population and bring them in conformity with the official estimate of average rural consumption.

If we examine column 4, which gives the estimates of per capita consumer expenditure in 1967-68 as percentages of per capita consumption in 1960-61, it will be seen that the middle and upper middle classes have done comparatively better than the lower middle and the poorer classes. For instance, the per capita consumption of the poorest 5 per cent is only 93.9 per cent of its level in 1960-61.

This percentage gradully rises until, for the class of population lying between 60-70 per cent counted from the poorest, the per capita consumption in 1967-68 is 99.1 per cent of its level in 1960-61. This appears plausible namely that the middle and upper middle classes should have done comparatively better than the lower middle and the poorer classes. However, judging by the NSS estimates, it seems that the richer classes have done worse than the upper middle classes and indeed very much worse than even the poorest classes. Thus, it seems that in 1967-68, the per capita consumption of the population lying between 80-90 per cent was only 95.0 per cent of its level in 1960-61; of the population lying between 90-95 per cent, the per capita consumption in 1967-68 was only 91.1 per cent of its level; and finally, of the richest 5 per cent population, the per capita consumption in 1967-68 was just 72.9 per cent of its level in 1960-61. This is incredible. There is little reason to believe that the upper middle and the richer sections of the rural population did not do comparatively at least as well as the middle sections.

This evidence coupled with the fact, earlier mentioned, that the NSS estimate of per capita consumption in 1967-68 is more than 10 per cent below the official estimate is conclusive and the conclusion is inescapable that the NSS estimate of per capita consumption in 1967-68 is an underestimate and that it underestimates the consumption of the upper middle and the richer sections much more than that of the middle, lower middle and the poorer sections.

There are prima facie reasons for such underestimation. The NSS secures its estimates of consumer expenditure by interviewing a random sample of rural and urban households and inquiring from them about their cosumer expenditure during the previous month. The limitations of this procedure are well known. For instance, a number of items of consumer expenditure, such as clothing and other consumer durables, which a household would purchase less frequently than once every month, are likely to be missed by this procedure and hence the expenditure on them is likely to be underestimated.

These are the items which are more important in the consumer expenditure of the rich than the poor and they become more important as the rich become richer. It is also known that the upper middle and the richer households, both in rural and urban areas, have become increasingly inaccessible to the NSS investigators who are after all class III government servants. It thus seems perfectly possible that the consumer expenditure of the upper middle and the richer sections has been progressively underestimated.

What part of the underestimation might be on account of underestimation of the consumption of the upper middle and richer sections and what part due to an overall underestimation of consumption of all sections is a matter of judgment and a certain subjective element is unavoidable. But on this judgment will depend our estimate of the growth of inequality in consumption between 1960-61 and 1967-68. We wish to be conservative and avoid all possibility of exaggerating the growing inequality.

Therefore, in revising upwards the NSS estimate of the rural per capita consumption in 1967-68, in order to bring it in accord with the official estimate, we shall attribute only the statistically inescapable minimum part of the underestimation to underestimation of the consumption of the upper middle and richer sections and attribute all the rest to an overall underestimation of consumption of all sections of the rural population, poor and rich alike. This will be clear from the two steps in which we have done the revision of the NSS estimates.

As earlier mentioned, in column (4) of we have expressed the NSS estimates for 1967-68 as percentages of the NSS estimates for 1960-61. The percentages in this column progressively increase from 93.9 for the poorest 5 per cent to 99.1 for the population lying between 60-70. Thereafter the percentages rapidly decline. The first step of the revision consists in supposing that these percentages should not so decline. This is what we mean when we say that the upper middle and the richer sections could not possibly have done worse than the middle sections. on this basis, the statistically minimum adjustment is to hold the percentage in column (4) at 99.1 for all sections above the one lying between 60-70. This is what we do in column (6). Incidentally, we also correct a little the percentage for the section lying between 50-60 as it is obviously out of line with the percentages for the sections 40-50 and 60-70. This is the first revision and its results appear in column (5).

As consequence of this revision, the NSS estimate of per capita rural consumption in 1967-68 is raised from Rs. 239.8 to Rs. 255.1. It is nevertheless still below the estimate of per capita consumption in 1960-61, namely Rs. 258.8. It is of course much below the estimate of per capita consumption in 1967-68 namely Rs. 268.8. In fact it will have to be raised by 5.29 per cent to bring it to that level. We propose to do this by raising the revised estimates of consumption of all sections (column 6) uniformly by 5.29 per cent. This is our second and final revision. The results are given in columns 7 and 8.

The estimates of per capita consumption of different sections of the rural population, thus revised, appear quite plausible. Judging by column 8 where the per capita consumption in 1967-68 is expressed as percentage of its level in 1960-61, it seems that the consumption of the 20 per cent poorest rural population increased by less than 2.0 per cent in seven years from 1960-61 to 1967-68 and that the consumption of the poorest 5 per cent actually declined by about one per cent.

The consumption of the lower middle sections lying between 20-40 per cent increased by between 2.2 and 2.6 per cent; that of the middle sections lying between 40-60 per cent increased by between 3.7 and 4.1 per cent; and the consumption of the upper middle and the richer sections constituting the upper 40 per cent of the population increased by 4.4 per cent. It is possible that the consumption of the richer sections such as the top 10 or 5 per cent actually increased by even more. But in the absence of direct statistical evidence, we prefer to be conservative in this matter.

Thus the process of development during the past decade has affected different sections of the rural population differently. It has benefited the upper middle and the richer sections much more than the middle, the lower middle and the poorer sections. Under the circumstances, a certain amount of growth of inequality is invevitable.

Rural development implies both the economic betterment of the people as well as greater social transformation. Increased participation of people in the rural development process, decentralization of planning, better enforcement of land reforms and greater access to credit and inputs go a long way in providing the rural people with better prospects for economic development. Improvements in health, education, drinking water, energy supply, sanitation and housing coupled with attitudinal changes also facilitate their social development.

Rural development is, in fact, the pivot of administration at the Central, State and district levels in India. Various steps for the betterment of villages have been taken from time to time. Rural development has remained one of the constant and increasingly conscious goals of our Five Year Plans from their inception. As such, in the Ninth Five Year Plan also, high priority has been given to rural development and employment.

Rural poverty is inextricably linked with low rural productivity and unemployment including under-employment. Hence, it becomes necessary to improve productivity and increase employment in rural areas. Moreover, more employment needs to be generated at higher output. It is true that over the last two decades there has been a considerable decline in the incidence of rural poverty.

However, a large number of persons continue to live below the poverty line. Hence, there is a need for continued direct State intervention for poverty alleviation. While the programmes for self-employment and supplementary wage employment would continue in the Ninth Five Year Plan, these would be redesigned in order to make them more effective as instruments of poverty alleviation.

Apart from this, they would be integrated with the various doctoral programmes as well as the area development programmes within the umbrella of the Panchayati Raj institutions.

The decline in rural poverty is attributable both to the growth factor and to the special employment programmes launched by the government in order to generate more incomes in the rural areas. Hence, in its more limited interpretation, rural development has been confined to a direct attack on poverty through special employment programmes, area development programmes and land reforms. Some of these programmes are discussed below.

The Integrated Rural Development Programme (IRDP) is a self-employment programme aimed at enabling poor families to cross the poverty line, via access to income-generating assets and training. During the Eighth Plan, a system of concurrent evaluation of the IRDP was introduced.

Various rounds of the concurrent evaluation revealed that while it had been successful in providing incremental income to the poor, in most cases this was not enough to enable them to cross the poverty line. Thus to make self-employment programmes more effective in the Ninth Five Year Plan, there will be a shift in strategy under IRDP.

Several modifications have been made in order to improve the efficacy of the programme via higher levels of investment, better infrastructural support and strengthening of linkages, as also by a shift towards a group/cluster approach.

Training of Rural Youth for Self-Employment (TRYSEM) aims to enable the rural youth to take up self-employment ventures in different spheres across sectors by giving them assistance under IRDP. During the Ninth Plan, TRYSEM will be revamped in its design, curriculum and method of training in order to improve the employment opportunities of the poor. It will focus on activities in which the rural youth are already engaged and where there exists a potential for skill up gradation or else on activities which would enhance production under the group-cluster approach.

The success of several women's groups under Development of Women and Children in Rural Areas

(DWCRA), which is based on a group approach, suggests that group dynamics work if people are organized into homogenous self-help groups for taking up income generating activities. A mechanism for replicating the successful DWCRA groups would be evolved. Besides, a greater integration of DWCRA with IRDP and TRYSEM will be attempted to provide women's groups with greater access to financial resources and training.

In the Ninth Plan, a new initiative for social mobilization will be taken up, for creation self-managed institutions of the poor. A mechanism for training of social animators to assist the poor to from their own organizations and articulate their felt needs and aspirations would be taken up.

The Jawahar Rozgar Yojana (JRY) was the only wage employment programme at the beginning of the Eighth Plan. The primary objective of the programme is generation of supplementary employment and creation of rural infrastructure required for more sustained employment. However, funds under this scheme went into every single village, though the amounts varied as States were allocated resources on the basis of the incidence of poverty. Apart from JRY, there is another wage employment programme known as the Employment Assurance Scheme (EAS). Both these schemes provide employment for a short duration in the form of casual manual work, during the lean agricultural season. So far, the EAS is being implemented in 3,206 blocks but will be universalized by 1997-98. In the Ninth Plan, this scheme would also be implemented through the PRIs.

In order to provide a greater thrust to shelter and irrigation facilities for the weaker sections, the Indira Awaas Yojana (IAY) for rural housing and the Million Wells Scheme (mws) for provision of open wells/family water harvesting structure were made separate independent schemes since January 1996. In the Ninth Plan, IAY will receive a greater thrust as it is one of the identified basic services for complete coverage in a time-bound manner. The scope of MWS will now be expanded to include borewells/tubewells and lifting devices.

The area development programes confined to drought-prone and desert areas were reviewed and redesigned in an attempt to restore the ecological balance through soil and moisture conservation. Preparation of watershed plans for a unit of 500 hectares with involvement of all members residing in the watershed was made mandatory. Training of functionaries in area planning and watershed management will be expanded.

Access to land remains a key element of the anti-poverty strategy in rural areas because rural poverty is largely among the landless and marginal farmers. In the Ninth Plan, emphasis has also been given to land reforms. The programme of action for land reforms would include the following: (i) detection as well as redistribution of ceiling surplus land; (ii) updating of land records on a regular basis; (iii) tenancy reforms providing for recording the rights of tenants and share-croppers; (iv) consolidation of holdings; (v) preventing alienation of tribal lands; (vi) providing access on a group basis to the poor on wastelands and common property resources; (vii) leasing-in and leasing-out of land will be permitted within the ceiling limits; (viii) preference to women in the distribution of ceiling surplus land and legal provisions for protecting their rights on land.

The Union Finance Ministry has asked the Reserve Bank of India (RBI) to speed up the process of awarding licences to set up local area banks (LABs). There are, currently, about 45 applications pending with the apex bank for the purpose. The apex bank is in the process of finalising the licences for nine local area banks, out of which one will be in West Bengal. Already two such licences have been given, one each for Maharashtra and Karnataka.

The concept of LAB, which was mooted in the first budget of the United Front government for 1996—97, is to gear up the banking operations in the rural and backward areas. The government will thus be relieved from the pains of infusing capital subsidies to the regional banks (RRBs) in order to get rid of their heavy financial liabilities. It is hoped that the LAB will be able to replace the regional rural banks ultimately as the latter are, by and large, plagued with multifarious problems.

As per the guidelines, a local area bank can be set up after its incorporation under the Companies Act 1956, while the licence is granted by the Reserve Bank of India. Like commercial Banks, they are also governed by the Reserve Bank of India Act of 1934. A LAB caters to a maximum of three contiguous districts. The RBI is quite discriminating in giving licence to LABs which are to provide efficient and competitive financial intermediation services in their areas of operation.

As these banks have been set up in district towns, their activities are focussed on the local customers. Their schemes are meant for agriculture and alliled activities, small—scale industrial units, Agro—industrial activities, trading activities and non–farm sector within the area of thier operation. The banks have to observe priority sector lending targets at 40 per cent of net bank credit as applicable to other commercial banks. Of this, at least 25 per cent has to be deployed for the weaker sections.

The promoter's contribution has to be atleast Rs.2 crore. The promoter/s may comprise individuals, corporate entities, trusts or societies. The head/registered office of the bank will be located at a centre within the area of operation of the bank.

Voting rights of an individual share—holder are governed by the ceiling of 10 per cent of the total voting rights as stipulated in section 12(2) of the Banking Reguation Act, 1949. It may be noted that as regards liquidity requirements and interest rates, such banks have to follow the provisions applicable to the regional banks set up under the RRB Act of 1976.

Likewise, a local area bank is subject to prudential norms, accounting policies and other policies laid down by the RBI. It is required to achieve capital adequacy of 8 per cent of the risk weighted assets from the very beginning. Similarly, norms for income recognition, assets classification and provisioning will also be applicable to it reform its very inception.

As for opening branches, LABs can be set up only in the area of operation of LAB by complying with the branch licensing policy as it exists today. It can be said that with a good number of commercial bank branches and RRBs already operating in the rural sector, a local area bank faces great challenges. Rural and semi–urban areas form an important deposit base of commercial banks contribution around 33 per cent of their total deposits. Presently, these banks have a large network in the rural sector with hardly any competition in the mobilisation of deposits.

In case LABs perform well and create in image for themselves, they can surely give a tough time to commercial banks where inefficiency has become the order of the day. As for the RRBs, they are already unviable and perhaps the government may revive the idea of merging them with their sponsored banks. Moreover, the deregulated rates of interest on deposits may create a difficult situation with the local banks by offering better interest rates.

It is also true that around 23 per cent of the nationalised banks' advances go to rural and demi—urban areas. Nationalised banks are now setting up specialised branches for agricultural and small–scale sector. Besides, their large branch network in rural and semi—urban areas, as also their decades of experience in rural lending impart to them an added advantage. Hence, LABs have to employ effective marketing strategies for extending credit in rural areas even if they have to offer competitive interest rates. The field functionaries in rural and semi–urban branches have to be more vigilant and aware about the credit potential in agriculture and allied activities. Besides, they need to ensure adequate suppluy of credit under various government sponsored schemes.

A more comprehensive rural credit strategy can be worked out if strategy can be worked out if NABARD can be granted powers to become the lead form bank with cooperatives, RRBs and local area banks. In that case, the burden of priority sector lending can be taken off the public sector, foreign and private sector banks, along with the concept of concessional credit. Therefore, in that eventuality, banks should be given the option to lend to agriculture based industries without any mandate.

As we all know, agricultural and rural development are a continuous process and banks have to commit themselves to rural financing on a short–term and long–term basis. The focus has to shift to financing of small farmers, landless labourers, village artisans and services. LABs have to ensure that they are adequately organised to handle the task.

Mass social banking has to be the aim along with observing sound tenets of banking. The creating of local area banks must not become one more futile exercise if the attitudes and approaches of banks and their staff continue to remain the same as those of commercial banks, cooperative banks and regional rural banks.

It has been estimated that the demand for agricultural credit in the country would be of the order of Rs. 1,10,900 crore by 1999—2000 A.D., while the supply of institutional credit (including bank credit from all types of banks) would be hardly around Rs. 90,000 crore. This shortfall has to be taken care of by the local area banks with full zeal and commitment for rural development. Since the service area approach is not applied to LABs, they can work with more flexibility. The percentage of agricultural credit to net bank credit has been declining over the last crouple of years. As such, LABs have to take new initiatives.

Finally, it is necessary that the local area banks do not suffer fromthe problem of lack of viability as has been the case with the regional rural banks. In April 1993 there was a demand for setting up a National Rural Bank by amalgamating all the existing regional rural banks but ultimately, the idea floated in Parliament could not fructify.

Perhaps, time has now come when this experiment could be undertaken in such a way that the new national rural bank is made responsible for monitoring the RRBs and LABs so that should any problem arise in their functioning, it should be solved without any delay. There is no doubt that the new set–up of LABs does require some kind of institutional back—up for monitoring and advisory functions on a regular and continuous basis.

Rural development planning in India was introdrced in the light of experiments for rural uplift prior to Independence by the Father of the Nation, Mahatma Gandhi in Sevagram, Rabindranath Tagore in villages around Santiniketan, Spencer Hatch in Travancore (erstwhile), V.T. Krishnamachari in Kasamba near Baroda, and F.L. Brayne in Gurgaon in the 1920s and after Independence by Prakasham, Albert Mayer and Horace Holmes, S.K. Dey et al.

The first massive rural development endeavour called the Community Development Programme was launched with the beginning of the First Five Year Plan itself. This was a co-operative partnership between the government and the people for the all-round development of the people in a particular area. With the commencement of Panchayati Raj, it had to become the programme for the people, of the people, and by the Third Five Year Plan, the entire country was covered with community development blocks numbering over 5,000.

The community development blocks became the units of administration, planning, co-ordination, and development for rural people with the focus on integrated rural development, comprising agriculture and allied activities, rural industries, education, health socail welfare, communications, supplementary employment with special focus on self-help and public partcipation. A schematic budget of Rs. 17 lakh per block—Rs. 12 lakh for stage one (5 years) and Rs. 5 lakh for stage two (another 5 years)—was provided. The staffing patern comprised the Block Development Officer (BDO) 8 Extension Officers (in agriculture, animal husbandry, co-operative, Panchayats, rural industries, engineering, social education, and programmes for women and children), 10 Gram Sevaks, 2 Gram Sevikas, a Programme Assistant, a Storekeeper-cum-Accountant, with some support staff on the ministerial side prescribed for a standard block.

Special Measures for the Poor

The integrated approach to rural development, however, got gradually diluted with the work relating to village industries being handed over to the Khadi and Village Industries Commission (KVIC) and the growing need for self-reliance in food. The greater emphasis on food production resulted in the launching of the Intensive Agriculture Development Programme (IADP) in selected districts followed by the Intensive Agriculture Areas Programme (IAAP), and the High Yield in Varieties Programme (HYVP).

By the late sixties, and the early seventies, it was perceived that even though the intensive effort in agriculture had led to the Green Revolution, the benefits of this remained largely confined to the big farmers and areas which were better placed to receive the benefits of high yielding varieties techonlogy. Therefore, the need to take special measures for benefiting the poorer sections of the population and for development of backward and disadvantaged areas was felt.

As a result, programmes like Small Farmers and Agricultural Labourers (MFAL), Crash Scheme for Rural Employment, Pilot Intensive Rural Employment Programme, Food for Work Programme, Drought-Prone Areas and Desert Development Programmes, and the Minimum Needs Programme were launched.

VI Plan—sharper focus: with the launching of the Sixth Plan the attempts at tackling the problems of the deprived sections of the population and geographical areas were further consolidated, rationalized, and expanded. The SFDA and MFAL were replaced by the Integrated Rural Development Programme (IRDP) which was extended to cover the entire country and its scope expanded to all activities in the primary, secondary, and tertiary sectors.

Under this programme, income-base criteria for identification of the target group was prescribed and household approach was adopted. The programme also aimed to provide skills through Training of Rural Youth for Self-Employment (TRYSEM) and assets (through a mix of subsidy and credit with the ultimate objective of raising people above the poverty line. A special programme for economic betterment of rural women, popularly known as Development of Women and Children in Rural Areas (DWCRA), was also developed and linked to the self-employment programme (IRDP).

The Food for Work Programme was restructured in the form of wage employment programme known as National Rural Employment Programme, the Rural Landless Employment Guarantee Programme (RLEGP) was launched in 1983-84 with the specific objective of providing up to 100 dats of employment per annum to at least one member of each rural landless household.

The programmes of the Sixth Plan were continued with a sharper focus and higher outlays during the Seventh and the Eighth Plan periods. The aforesaid wage employment programmes (NREP & ROEGP) were merged into Jawahar Rozgar Yojana (JRY) and Indira Awaas Yojana (IAY)—a component of JRY—was strengthened both qualitatively and quantitatively. Subsequently, Employment Assurance Scheme (EAS) was introduced for assured employment up to 100 days in the lean agricultural season.

Rural development mey be construed as total all-round socio-economic development of the rural people and not merely the ongoing programmes such as self-emplyment, wage employment, area development, land reforms, etc. A significant step has already been taken to revitalize the Panchhayati Raj institutions with the enactment of the Constitution (Seventy—third

Amendment) Act, 1992 so that 'operation by the people and co-operation by the government' becomes a reality.

Accordingly, the State goverment mey, by law, endow the Panchayats with such powers and authority as may be necessary to enastitutions of self-government and such law may contain provisions for devolution of powers and responsibilities upon Panchayats at the appropriate level, subject to such conditions as may be specified therein, with respect to the preparation of plans and implmentation of schemes for economic development and social justice as may be entrusted to them including those in relation to matters listed, as follows, in the XI schedule to the Constitution (Article 243G):

- Agriculture including agricultural extension.
- Land improvement, implementation of land reforms, land consolidation, and soil conservation.
- Minor irrigation, water management, and watershed development.
- Animal husbandry, dairying, and poultry.
- Fisheries.
- Social forest produce.
- Minor forest produce.
- Small-scale industries, including food processing industries.
- Khadi, village, and cottage industries.
- Rural housing.
- Drinking water.
- Fuel and fodder.
- Roads, culverts, bridges, ferries, waterways, and other means of communication.
- Rural electrification, including distribution of electricity.

- Non-conventional energy sources.
- Poverty alleviation programmes.
- Education including primary and secondary school.
- Technical training and vocational education.
- Adult and non-formal education.
- Libraries.
- Cultural activities.
- Markets and fairs.
- Health and sanitation, including hospitals, primary health centres, and dispensaries.
- Family welfare.
- Women and child development.
- Social welfare including welfare of the handicapped and mentally retarded.
- Welfare of the weaker sections, and in particular, of the Scheduled Castes and Scheduled Tribes.
- Public distribution system.
- Maintenance of community assets.

Indian Development planning has always aimed at removing inequities in the process of development to ensure that the fruits of development are an equal privilege of all. In recent years it has become increasingly evident that women are lagging behind a great deal both in availing of the benefits of development and as participants in the process of development due to several socio—economic—cultural—political impediments. This has become a cause for concern since women number several millions and constitute nearly half of our populaltion.

In the early years of planning the concern for gender took a welfarist perspective which manifested itself in the form of grants, waivers, subsidies and freeships for girls and women in a few relevant programmes. But these concessions did not elicit the required level of participation. In the later half of the 1970's the focus shifted from merely welfare to development and greater emphasis on integration of women into the mainsteam of social and economic development.

In due course many social and economic programmes like NOn Formal Education for Grils, Integrated Rural Development Programme... were evolved exclusively for women or with a percentage set aside solely for them. The benefits derived from these programme had to be sustained and this was posing a challenge. Studies have shown that 'practical gender gains' in improved livelihood, education, nutrition and sanitation are not sustained and easily reversed if the 'strategic need' to give 'women a voice' in the decisions that so directly affect their lives, is not adequately taken care of.

The strategy in the 1990's has shifted to empowerment of women and 'giving them a voice'.

It is in this context of empowerment and given the vulnerability and powerl;essness of the individual women in the existing socio—economic set up that 'Grokup' strategies acquire great relevance. The formation of small informal functional groups of women would give them 'visibility' and create micro level power pockets.

Further, grouping would initiate a learning process through sharing of ideas, skills and interactive capacity and in course of time women would learn to articulate their needs resulting in more appropriate participatory and grassroots level plans for them. Some social barriers would also be broken in the process'. Many groups in recent years have started cutting across barriers of religion and caste and working together harmoniously for economic betterment.

Poverty hits women the hardest, as they balance means and ends at the household level and many a time skip a meal to let the rest of he household avail of the little that is available. These women are subject to economic and social discrimination, and credit is not easily available to them.

Millions of our women live in poverty and their social empowerment would have littlerelevance without first empowering them on the economic front. The World Bank studies have shown that enhancement of women's earnings would hav a more profound effect on the welfare of the family as a whole since 'increases in wmen's income result more directly into better health and nutrition for children. Thus grouping women for economic empowerment is of great importance.

The programme for Development of Women and Children in Rural Areas (DWCRA), launched in 1982—83, inaugurated an era for systematically organising women in groups for enhancing their earnings on a self–sustaining basic and increasing their access to and utilisation of services like health, child care and adult education, among others. The programme called for formation of groups of 10—15 women who would collectively engage in an activity.

A revolving fund of Rs. 15000 (presently enhanced to Rs. 25000) was made available to each group for credit and administrative needs. Supplementing of staff by inclusion of an additional gram sevika and appointment of a lady officer to the post of Assistant Project Officer to oversee implementation to the programme were called for. Subsequently with a view to fortifying the programme further and increasing awareness a

Community Based Convergent Services (CBCS) component and Information, Education and Communication (IEC) component were included.

Upto early 1996, over 1.3 lakh groups covering 2.2 million women were formed. Almost all the districts in the country (except a handful of exclusively urban ones) are presently covered under this programme.

Formation of Thrift and Credit groups of women for self help and economic self reliance has also been encouraged by the government. A Rashtriya Mahila Kosh (RMK) was set in 1993 for extending credit with low transaction costs to poor and needy women and women's groups through Non Governmental Organisations. At present (as in July, 1996), the scheme is being implemented in the fifteen states of Andhra Pradesh, Bihar, Haryana, Himachal Pradesh, Gujarat, Karnataka, Kerala, Maharashtra, Madhya Pradesh, Manipur, Orissa, Rajasthan, Tamil Nadu, Uttar Pradesh, and West Bengal through an network of one hundred and four Non—Governmental Organisations.

The Indira Mahila Yojana (IMY) launched in 1995 aims at coordinating and integrating sectoral programmes relevant to women like health, education, water, sanitation, housing and others at local, block and district levels and increasing their awareness and income through group activities and participation with the aim of empowering women. Indira Mahila Kendras would be established at village level and Indira Mahila Block Kendras at Block level for this purpose.

The programme would be a Centrally sponsored scheme. Non—Governmental Organisations would also be involved in this process. The Programme has been sanctioned for a period of seven years commencing from 1995—96. During the inception year it was to cover two hundred blocks on a pilot basis and a thousand blocks each year in the subsequent years.

The Central Government would provide a one time grant of Rs. 5000 to each Indira Mahila Kendra. Further funds provided at block level would be used for payments of honoraira to individuals who involve themselves in awareness camps, mobilisation of groups, training group members and functionaries and helping survival of groups through creation of outlets for marketing.

Not enough is known about these people who were so poor as not to be able to afford a diet adequate even in terms of calories. In the following, we shall present what little fragmentary data are available regarding the characteristics of the poor which may also indicate the causes underlying their poverty.

One of the reasons of poverty is unduly large number of dependants to be supported per earner in a household. There are no direct data available to support this proposition. But it may be indirectly inferred by examining the size of households (number of persons per household) in different sections of the population. In we give the relevant data.

It will be noticed that the average size of household in the poorest 10 per cent of the rural population is 5.87 (average of 5.77 and 5.97). As we move through the successive ten percent sections of the population with increasing per capita consumer expenditure the average size of the household steadily declines until, for the richest 5 per cent population, it is as low as 3.78.

The phenomenon is even more marked in the urban area. Here, in the poorest 10 per cent of the population, the size of the household is as large as 6.09 (average of 6.00 and 6.18). It declines steadily and rapidly as we move to the better sections until, for the richest 5 per cent of the population, the size of household is as small as 2.25. There is therefore little doubt that the size of a household is an important factor pushing it down the ladder.

It should be noted that a larger household does not necessarily mean a larger number of dependants per earner. A larger household may also have more earners as in a joint family; hence in that case, it would also have a larger income and the fact of a mere large size would not reduce its per capita consumption. When a large household has low per capita consumption, it is evident that it has more dependants per earner.

This would be particularly true of rural households. These households may not necessarily be marked by destitution, with normal earners, but burdened with too large a number of dependants. Nonetheless, for that reason, they will need to be given special assistance in one form or another.

The urban situation is likely to be somewhat different. Here a large household may have more than one earner in the formal sense of the term. However, they earn little. These are cases of the rural poor who have drifted into the cities in search of a living but have not yet been able to secure an adequate one. The mere fact of poverty may bring them together * to constitute a 'household' for the purpose of the census or the National Sample Survey. Their problem is one of employment opportunity for their working members and not so much of special assistance.

Little more information is available on the urban poor. In rural areas, an important cause of poverty is lack of land resources. A number of rural households have no land at all. They live entirely by the personal labour of their members. They constitute some of the poorest sections of rural population. It will be useful to examine what proportion of rural poverty is accounted for by the landless.

The relevant data are available from the Eighteenth Round of the National Sample Survey which refers to the period from February 1963 to January 1964. However, only a few summry tabulations of data from this round are presently available in published form. Therefore we shall supplement these data with the more detailed data earlier collected and published in the Eleventh and Twelfth Rounds of the National Sample Survey which covered the period from August 1956 to August 1957.

In the Eleventh and Twelfth rounds covering 1956-57, besides the general inquiry into the consumer expenditure of a sample of all rural households, a special inquiry was conducted into the employment, earnings and consumer earnings and consumer expenditure of a sample of agricultural labour households. For this purpose, an agricultural labour household was defined as one for which agricultural wage employment constituted the major source of income.

In the Eighteenth Round covering 1963-64, the special inquiry was extended to cover all rural labour households and a distinction was made between agricultural labour households and non-agricultural labour households depending upon the major source of their wage income. It seems that in 1956-57, about 25 per cent of the rural households were agricultural labour households. In 1963-64, only about 20 per cent of the rural households were agricultural labour households but, in addition, about 5 per cent of the rural households were classified as non-agricultural labour households. It is possible therefore that there was a decline in the propertion of agricultural labour households. However, it seems more likely that, though the inquiry in 1956-57 was confined to agricultural labour households, it in fact covered all rural labour houseolds as was explicitly done in the inquiry during 1963-64. In that case, the proportion of labour households seems to have remained more or less constant over the seven years from 1956-57 to 1963-64. In both the periods, about 60 per cent of the labour households had no land and hence they depended almost entirely on the personal labour of their members.

They had no other means of livelihood. The remaining 40 per cent cultivated small pieces of land; nevertheless their main dependence was on wage employment in agriculture or outside agriculture. Nearly three-fourths of the labour households worked as casual labourers, that is, they worked if and when work was available. Otherwise they were unemployed. The remaining one-fourth were attached labourers, that is, they worked for a single employer under some kind of a contract extending to at least a period of one year. The nature of this contract would vary from a proper agreement of an annual farm servant to the feudal tie of a bonded labourer. But all of them had some kind of regular employment. In a sense, they were never unemployed during the year.

Though, as mentioned above, about one-fourth of all rural households are labour households, the incidence varies greatly in different regions of the country. In are given the proportions that the labour households bear to all rural households in different States.

It will be noticed that the incidence of rural labour is very high in the South, namely in Kerala, Tamil Nadu and Andhra Pradesh where more than one-third of all rural households are labour households. The incidence is also high in West Bengal, Bihar and Orissa where nearly one-third of all rural households are labour households. In Maharashtra, about 30 per cent of all rural households are labour is much lower.

It will be noticed that the States with high incidence of rural labour are also generally the States with large proportions of the rural population living below the minimum.

- Tax concession for promoting industrialisation was introduced for the first time in 1949 in the form of tax holiday for the first 5 years of production of new industrial units. This concession was avaliable as deduction from taxable profit, computed at the rate of 6% of capital employed. This incentive was continued till 1980 when, to remove capital bias inherent in it, was reformulated as 80-I to provide for a deduction as percentage of profit rather than capital employed.

This provision was modified and renumbered as Section 80-I w.e.f. 1.4.1991. Under this provision any new industrial undertaking or hotel came into business between 1.4.1991 and 1.4.1995 was entitled to a deduction of 25% from the profits (30% for companies for 10 years).

- In 1968 Planning Commission set up two Working Groups to evolve a criteria for identification 245 out of 396 districts were identified as backward. Government of India also introduced Investment Subsidy Scheme for identified backward areas.

This scheme was, however, discontinued in 1988. States also introduced the Investment Subsidy schemes and these are still in vogue. In 1974, tax concessions in the form of relief in income tax to new units were introduced in Eighth Schedule of Income-tax Act as section 80HH, which was later replaced by notification in 1986. This listed the backward areas.

- In 1987 National Institute of Public Finance and Policy conducted a study to evaluate the fiscal concessions for backward areas.

This study concluded that while the fiscal incentives for the backward development did successfully promote industrial dispersal, the criteria of identifying backward areas in a state with reference to its development indicators rather than any All India norm favoured developed states.

- The NIPFP study as well as the Economic Administrative Reform Commission recommended deletion of Section 80-HH of Income-tax Act which had indicated the backward areas.
- Accepting the recommendations of the study the Finance Act, 1993 modified the tax incentive scheme.

Full tax holiday was introduced for the initial 5 years of production in case of industrial units starting production between 1.4.1993 and 31.3.1998 and set up a backward state or union territories specified in new 8th Schedule. These states were selected because all their districts were earlier classified as backward in notification issued in 1986.

- Following the introduction of the Bill, various representations were received and it was indicated that these concessions were extended to backward districts which would be identified by a Study Group. This has been reiterated by the Finance Minister recently.
- Current approach to industrialisation is based on providing industrial infrastructure. Both the NIPFP Study and the Study by World Bank indicated that location decision can only be marginally influenced. The factor which would be crucial in the location decisions could be the availability of physical infrastructure. This has been the rationale of growth centre scheme.

- Capital incentive in the form of investment subsidy scheme have not been successful in reducing the skewed industrial growth. Infact it may be a better approach to consider harmonisation of incentives.
- While promoting spread of industrialisation, the policy essentially needs to find means of concentration of industries as the complementarity and competitive requirements make such cluster approach more successful.

This ensures diversified industrial base and optimal utilisation of infrastructure and other resources. This is the reason why the growth of centres has been in a corridor or cluster of districts which are geographically inter-linked.

- In a geographically continuous and ethnic homogenous region, industrial development requires consideration of area specific approach. In these areas besides the problem of markets and non local resources there may be constraint of profit, project identification and ignorance about the resources.

This has been the approach for development of backward areas in North East where a North East Development Bank has been set up to cater to the specific requirements of the region, identify areas of investment, infrastructure constraints, technological needs and adoption of a hand-holding approach for the enterpreneurs.

- In other backward districts where there is no geographical continuity, growth centres approach which provide the infrastructure and thereby reduces the cost of operation have better chances of being successful.

However, regional dispersal is a national issue and rquires discussion at all levels for adoption of a comprehensive policy package.

In the first few months of the current fiscal year, industrial performance—both in production and sales—has not been impressive when compared to the previous year. The Economic Times Investment Bureau has estimated that the average growth in turnover of the sensex 30 companies (excluding IDBI, ICICI and SBI) will be between 9.10% as compared to 24% last year.

The net profit growth is also expected to slow down to around 25% as against 46% last year. This along with the relatively poor performance of the infrastructure industries, the depressed stock markets, and slower growth of imports has cast a warning signal about industrial performance in 1996-97.

The Ninth Plan document has to take care of the needs of the SCs/STs and the OBCs. They are the people who are not only poor but they are the politicized communities. Their votes have brought this coalition government at the Centre. The thirteen party government has rightly recognized their needs in the Common Minimum Programme.

This document has reflected the aspirations of these people in their thrust areas. Let us look into the problems of each community one by one.

The peasant tradition: There are two occupational groups in the OBCs. The majority of them are the cultivating classes who depend on the family labour to sustain the farm production. It is the peasant tradition which is sustaining the farm production rather than the market economy which is generating enough profit. That is why they get involved in the farm production. If one takes into account the wages of each family labour who works in the farm, then the small farm economy is neither profitable nor sustainable. A major section of rural people are engaged in peasant production which is not working on market lines.

The State has already withdrawn subsidies in terms of fertilizers and seeds. If they are going to be taxed as the urban rich, then the farm economy is going to collapse. Moreover, they are the victims of vicissitudes of the weather. A majority of our farmers depend on the weather.

It has been studied that because of the changes in ecology, They are the victims of the natural disasters like cyclone, flood and drought. The coastal region of India where a substantive population live, is prone to flood and cyclone. The State is unable to provide any system of insurance which can take care of their losses.

Yearning for quality: Moreover, the peasant families are conscious of health and education. To avail itself of both health and education facilities, each peasant family is spending money directly or indirectly, as the quality of education and health facilities provided by the public system is so poor. The government can charge educational cess from each peasant family. If the government can ensure them quality school education, they would gladly accept the proposal.

The same thing can happen in the health sector if some form of health insurance can be created where both the peasant family and the government can can manage the contribution to sustain such a system. Only the landless families in the rural areas may not carry this financial burden. In the approach paper, allocation of resources in both primary education and primary health services has increased to some extent.

Upgradation of skills: The lower OBCs, who are working as artisans, have lost their market. No technological upgradation of their traditional technology has taken place. Furthermore, education provided by our school system is not creating any skills.

Education without skills creates a lot of educated unemployed who do not fit either in the traditional economy or in the modern economy. The planning of education has to be done in such a manner that the duality of our economy is destroyed. Traditional economic activities have to undergo the process of modernisation which can sustain the modern economy. In this area of thinking, Gandhi's concept of basic education has to be applied in a changed form.

The Ninth Plan approach paper has agreed to make special efforts in bringing about tehnological upgradation of the traditional sector of our economy.

The people of the SC community are without any productive assets. But they work as agricultural labour or do some economic activities which have an insignificant place in the modern economy. A section of the SCs who work as feshermen or cobblers are aleady threatened by the mechanized fishing and modern shoe factory. Can they be absorbed in the modern economic activities if proper skills are added to their traditional knowledge? Mechanisation of agriculture has affected their women, as they actively participate in agricultural operations.

Feminization of poverty has affected nigatively both their level of nutrition and health. It has to be accepted that mechanization of agriculture cannot stop, but at the same time skill of this community has to be upgraded to be absorbed in a meaningful manner in agriculture. Theoretically, the State is providing them free education.

Education to SCs is liked with the job opportunities

in the State sector. As the State sector is shrinking, the job opportunities for these communities are reduced.The cost of educated unemployed in the SC community is an expensive affairs from the State point of view. Unless the State provides education which is directly liked with the skill formation from the modern economy point of view, it is indirectly creating a social volcano which can burst any time.

Rural and urban integration has been a neglected aspect of decentralized planning. The district planning has been nothing more than assembling the various sectoral programmes implemented by various State departments at district level. For the first time, the 74th Constitutional Amendment (243 ZD) has made provision for integration of the rural plan with the urban plan but only at the district level.

It is one of the lacunae of the 73rd and 74th Amendments that they have not made provision for integration of rural areas with urban areas below the district level. No State government including that of Kerala, has made such provision. Therefore, it is suggested that economic development and social justice plans prepared by Nagar Panchayats and Municipal Councils for establishing spatial linkages and effective participatory planning.

A District Planning Committee (DPC) will be constituted as per Section 53 of the Kerala Municipality Act, 1994. The welcome feature of this Section is that the chairperson of the DP and the District Collector have been made Chairperson and Secretary of this Committee respectively. This provision of the Kerala Act should also be emulated by other States.

Section 266 of the Gujarat Panchayat Act provides for a State Council for Panchayats to co-ordinate and advise the Panchayats. The Panchayat Minister shall be its Chairperson. Among others, Presidents of Zilla Panchayats shall be its members. Kerala may incorporate a modified provision in its Panchayat Act making the Chief Minister as its Chairperson.

The above critique of the Kerala Panchayat Raj Act shows that although the Act contains certain positive features which could be emulated by other States, it does not provide an enabling environment for participatory planning because vital issues affecting local government are still in the domain of either the government or its suggestions for its improvement have been offered. If these suggestions are incorporated in the Act they will ensure autonomy of action by the people through the Panchayats. Such provisions in the Act are very important to provide a sound base for capability building of the Panchayats.

In this way, Kerala's enlightened and politically conscious people could practise participatory planning in a more effective way. The example of the Goa Panchayat Act is worth mentioning her. Because of its Section 68, the Querium Panchayat was able to drive out an American multinational corporation "Du Pont" which wanted to construct a factory in its jurisdiction to produce nylon.

The history of Panchayati Raj in the State reveals that the institutions have not become vibrant for participatory planning and the prime mover in enlisting people's participation in development has been the voluntary sector. The Ernakulam model of literacy, the Kalliasseri model of participatory planning and the Alappuzha model of economic empowerment of women have been success stories, acclaimed across the would and could be emulated elsewhere.

Participation of the poor in local development has been ensured by way of reserving seats for them in the

Panchayats. But a critical examination of various provisions shows that the Kerala Panchayat Raj Act fails to give autonomy to the people in their actions through Panchayats, because the vital issues affecting local government have been in the domain of the State government.

Thus, for making Panchayats strong institutions in order to enlist people's participation, Kerala may be benefited from other States like Gujarat, Rajasthan, Assam, Punjab, Manipurm West Bengal and Karnataka. If functional, administrative and financial autonomy is ensured for the Panchayats by amending certain provisions of the Act as suggested in this paper, it may provide a sound base for a sustainable democracy and participatory planning at the local level.

Integrating Strategies

A each agro-climatic level, educational, health or connectivity stratigies will have to be integrated with agricultural and rural edvelopment strategies.

Take the Eastern Plateau and Hill agro-climatic region extending from destricts like Kalahandi in Orissa to Gadchiroli and Chandrapur in Western Maharashtra and including large tribal districts in Madhya Pradesh, the growth strategy is to conserve the rainfall of around 50 cm through waershed programmes and to follow through with forest conservation and optimal cropping patterns. However, the female literacy rate in this region is less than 15 per gcent and so no techology-oriented strategy is possible without remedying this. A destinguished Vice-Chancellor from an agricultural university told me that "sowing" dates were decided by the local Bhuva (witch doctor) rather than the agricultural scientists of the region.

Community organizations are essential for both

aspects as at best co-operation is an educational process and limited sharing of rights on land and water is a way out of landlessness and rack renting. It becomes difficult, if not imposible, to channel structural and limited subsidies and priority credit, to the kind of activities described above, if the land rights of the tiller of land are not clear enforceable. Collateral needed by financial institutions, for example, becomes very difficult to organize, if tenancy arrangements are not recorded. Co-operative arrangements provide a way out.

Even when farming and other economic decisions are left to the initiative of the peasant, and the signals of the market,, for well-defined purpose, for example, land shaping, acquifer management, lower land water delivery systems or even specific mardeting, quality, grading or input supply requirenents, the peasant can co-operate. Self-help co-operateves with will well-defined objectives can than become the crucial interface between the country's manpower, its limited natural endowments and regional and global markets.

Focus on agriculture : While developing macro-economic parameters for the Ninth Five Year Plan, emphasis will th3e overal GDP growth rate is visualized at seven per cent per annum, then the growth in the agricultural sector wil have to be around 3.5 per cent to 4 per cent per annum in valueadded terms and the growth rate of output will be higher.

The precise contours of growth in agricultural sector will be highlighted in the Agricultural Submodel of the Ninth Plan. However, as a preliminary observation, it could be stated that growth in agricultural sector would emanate from improvements in the per hectare yields of crop sector. It is also visualized that diversification and modernization of the various subsets of the agricultural sector would gain momintum in the Ninth Plan and the dynamics of agricultural growth would emanate from growth in non-food grain secters, eg cotton, oil seeds, sugar-cane, fruits and vegetables, spices, plantation crops, etc. along with the development of fesheries, animal husbandry and dairying.

Non-food grain sector: On the assumption that per capita income during the Ninth Plan period will continue to show an annual growth of around 4 per cent, greater emphasis on diversification of the non-food grain sector involving crops like sugar-cane, oil seeds, cotton, fruits and vegetables seems inescapable. Also the output levels in the non-crop based agriculture would rise faster due to (a) increasing flexibility of resource use; (b) response to changing emand conditions; and (c) the technological changes. In fact, these variables would determine the growth process in the economy during the next decade.

The assumption regarding faster growth of non-crop based agriculture is supported by the annual growth rates of output visualized for the Eighth Plan which have been highlighted in the technical note on the eighth Plan, in which agriculture was visualized to grow at an annual rate of 3.25 per cent in value-added terms, feshing at 5.45 per cent, textiles at 5.87 per cent, wood and paper products at 7.63 per cent and leather and rubber products at 16.03 per cent. This structure of output is in tune with the structure of demand anticipated for the economy during the Eighth Plan period.

Exports: The other major development that has taken place is the fast growthof agricultural exports. It has been estimated that while a growth of 15 per cent plus annually ibn agricultural export may be difficult to sustain in the long run, a growth path of around 12 per cent annualy in dollar terms should be aimed at.

The output implications of even fast growth of exports are marginal in an economy of India's size, given the magnitude discussed earlier, but in selected regions, the impacts on income and imployment can be high and the technological implications anyway can be important both on agricultural production and processing and distribution.

2

Administration and Organisation

Shri Ram Jethmalani and Shri Bandaru Dattatreya continued as Minister for Urban Affairs and Employment and Minister of State for Urban Affairs and Employment respectively. Consequent on her transfer as Secretary, Deptt. of Women and Child Development, Smt. Kiran Aggarwal, IAS (HY: 64) relinquished the charge of Secretary, Ministry of Urban Affairs and Employment w.e.f. 1. 12.98 (FN). Shri Ashok Pahwa, IAS (HY: 65) assumed charge as Secretary, Ministry of Urban Affairs and Employment w.e.f. 1. 12.98 (FN). Shri Sujit Sankar Chattopadhyay, IAS (WB: 66) continued as Special Secretary in the Ministry.

This Ministry has two posts of Additional Secretary (including the post of Joint Secretary temporarily upgraded to the level of Additional Secretary as personal to the Officer concerned) and three posts of Joint Secretary.

The Ministry has under its administrative control four Attached and four Subordinate Offices, three Public Sector Undertakings and eight Statutory/Autonomous bodies.

Excluding the work charged staff, the Ministry and its attached and subordinate Offices have as on 31.12.98 a strength 33,033 employees of whom 1430 are in Group A, 3002 in Group 'B' (Gezetted); 530 in Group B (Non

Gazetted); 19932 in Group C and 8139 in Group D. The strength of the work charged staff is 30946. The detailed staff strength is mentioned in Appendix IV.

Budget

Budget Section is responsible for the Budget Work i.e. preparation of Demands for Grants and Performance Budget, their printing and laying before the Parliament. Apart from this, the Section attends to work relating to PAC and Audit paras and Parliamentary Standing Committee. The Section functions under the overall control of Financial Adviser and Additional Secretary.

Demand No. 83—Urban Development, Demand No. 84—Urban Employment and Poverty Alleviation, Demand No. 85—Public Works and Demand No. 86—Stationery and Printing pertain to this Ministry.

The Demand-wise Revised Estimates 1998—99 and Budget Estimates 1999—2000 provisions separately for Plan and Non-plan are as under:-

The Chief Controller of Accounts (CCA) formulates the estimates of receipts.

CCA also looks after the accounting and monitoring functions for the Ministry as a whole including its Attached and Subordinate Offices. He is assisted by a team of Controller of Accounts, Deputy Controllers of Accounts, Pay and Accounts officers and other supporting staff.

House building advance to central government employees

The scheme of House Building Advance to Central Government Employees is aimed at providing assistance to the Government employees to construct/acquire houses/flats of their own. The scheme was introduced in 1956, as a welfare measure. Ministry of Urban Affairs & Employment acts as the nodal Ministry for the same.

House Building Advance is admissible to all permanent Central Govt. employees as well as to those temporary employees who have rendered 10 years of continuous service. The Ministries/ Departments are delegated powers to sanction House Building Advance to their employees in accordance with the House Building Advance Rules.

In tune with the recommendation of the Vth Central Pay Commission, the amount of House Building Advance admissible has been revised to 50 months pay of the employee concerned or Rs. 7.5 lakhs or the cost of constrsuction/ acquisition of house/flat or repaying capacity whichever is the least as against Rs. 2.5 lakhs earlier. Similarly, the cost ceiling limit has been revised to 200 times the basic pay subject to a minimum of Rs. 7.5 lakhs and maximum of Rs. 18.00 lakhs from the earlier Rs. 3.0 lakhs and Rs. 8.0 lakhs respectively.

The rate of interest on House Building Advance continues to be between 7.5% and 12%.

The allocation of funds for House Building Advance as a whole is included in the Demands for Grants of Ministry of Finance. The allocation of fun to Ministries/ Departments from the Financial Ye 1998-99 is being administered by Ministry of Finance to exercise better financial control.

Work study unit

The IWSU of the Ministry performs all O&M functions of the Secretariat of the Ministry and undertakes studies in respect of the Secretariat and its Attached/ Subordinate Offices on various aspects viz. staff strength, working procedures etc. During the year 1998-99, the work measurement study of the Department of Publication, including its sale counters at Delhi was completed and its reports finalised and issued for implementation.

During the year 1998-99, Special drive on Record Management was conducted in the Ministry and its Attached Offices in the month of August, 1998. During the year, 659 files were recorded and 859 files were reviewed, out of which 650 files were weeded out in the Ministry. The Induction Material in respect of the Ministry has been revised and issucd.

Progressive use of hindi

The Ministry of Urban Affairs and Employment, in the category of large Ministries, has been awarded First Prize of Indira Gandhi Rajbhasha Shield Scheme for 1997-98 for achievement of targets prescribed in the Annual Programme on use of Hindi. The 3rd Sub-Committee of Committee of Parliament on Official Language visited the Ministry on 9.11.98 and held discussion with Secretary and other Senior Officers regarding the measures taken for increasing the use of Hindi in the Ministry as a whole and expressed its satisfaction over the initiatives taken and progress made by the Ministry in implementation of the Official Language Policy of the Govt. In response to the suggestions made by the Committee for further increasing the use of Hindi in noting and drafting in the Ministry, 300 staff members (out of 378) now use Hindi in various percentages in their official work

All the Heads of Offices have been regularly reviewing the progress of use of Hindi in their respective offices and have chalked out a phased programme for bringing about further improvement.

Two officials of this Ministry have been nominated for Hindi Prabodh/Praveen/Pragya classes and 5 LDCs and 3 Stenos have been nominated for training in Hindi typing and shorthand respectively during the year. In NBCC more then 90% typists have already been trained in Hindi typing. HUDCO has made Us own arrangement for training its employees in Hindi, Hindi shorthand & typing. It has, so far trained 17,12 and 11 employees in Hindi Prabodh, Praveen & Pragya respectively. 16 clerks have been trained in Hindi typing. Other organisations under the Ministry have also availed of the training facilities provided by HUDCO.

During the year, 19 officials of the Ministry have been trained in two workshops. Hindi Workshops have also been organised by all major organisations under the Ministry. CPWD had organised workshops in Us office at Ghaziabad, Mumbai, Hyderabad, Nagpur & Siliguri. At the behest of the Ministry, the following activities were organised by various bodies:

- L & DO organised two Hindi workshops,
- TCPO organised a special Hindi workshop of 11 days in Sept., 1998 in which the senior officers delivered lectures.
- HUDCO organised a two days Hindi workshop for their nodal officers in December, 1998 at Kanyakumari under the guidance and supervision of Director (OL) of the Ministry in which noted Hindi scholars of three southern States participated.

Action under Rule 10 (4) & 8 (4) of Official Language Rules, 1976

During the year, 156 unit offices of the Ministry (149 of CPWD, 7 of HUDCO & NBCC) under the Ministry, where 80% of the staff have acquired working knowledge of Hindi, were notified in the Gazette of India under Rule 10 (4). The newly notified offices have been advised to specify under Rule 8 (4) the items of work to be done in Hindi. Alltogether 10 out of 45 Sections of the Secretariat of the Ministry stand specified for doing certain number of items of work in Hindi.

Creation of enabling atmosphere for propagation and encouraging use of Hindi.

— The Cash Award Scheme has been made attractive by doubling the amount under various prizes and now a large number of employees are participating in the competition.

— Both Urban Affairs & Employment Minister and Minister of State have been taking keen interest in promoting the use of Official language. The Honourable Minister distributed the prizes to the winners of various Hindi events of 1997-98. He also issued an Appeal to all officers of the Ministry for doing maximum work in Hindi. Various competitive events on Hindi Day, 1998 were organised which created a condusive atmosphere for further use of Hindi. 144 employees participated in these events and 67 were given cash prizes amounting to about Rs. 30,000/- by the Honourable Minister of State in December, 1998. Taking keen interest in Official Language Implementation the Secretary of the Ministry has advised all the Officers of the Ministry to make greater use of Hindi in their official work. As a result all officers have started doing more and more work in Hindi and have chalked out a phased programme in this regard.

— Making available popular Hindi literature to the employees is another area of focus and about 47% of the Library Budget has been spent on popular Hindi literature. The various offices under the Ministry are also following similar systems.

— The National Institute of Urban Affairs (NIUA) has introduced a new quarterly magazine titled "SHAHRI GARIBI" which has nation wide circulation. The other organisations, including some circle offices of CPWD and Govt. of India presses, have also started bringing out Hindi magazines. The BMPTC has been bringing out publicity material bilingually and /or in Hindi only. All offices have been advised to bring out special issues titled "RAJBHASHA SWARAN JAYANTI VISHESHANK" to commemorate the 50th year of Hindi having been adopted as the Official Language of the country.

— All 92 Codes/Manuals/items of Procedural literature have been translated and printed in Hindi also.

— The Ministry inspected Head Quarters of 13 organisations located in Delhi & 18 unit offices of CPWD, HUDCO & NBCC at Bangalore, Mysore, Mumbai & Hyderabad. The Parliamentary Official language Committee, besides inspecting the Ministry on 9.11.98, had inspected unit offices of CPWD and HUDCO at Mumbai, Hyderabad, Chennai & Maduari and expressed their satisfaction over the pace of progress in these offices.

— There are two Dy. Directors, 31 Asstt. Directors, 15 Sr. Translators, 93 Jr. Translators and adequate number of trained Hindi Stenos/Typists under the overall supervision of Director (OL) of the Ministry. In order to facilitate work in Hindi, 16 posts of AD (OL) have recently been created by the Ministry for CPWD in Region "A".

— Adequate number of blingual/Hindi typewriters are available in all the offices.

— The TCPO has continuously been using Hindi in drafting its various survey reports on Urban/ Tourism Development Projects located in Hindi speaking areas

— The detailed guidelines on the following subjects of the Ministry were prepared and issued both in Hindi & English to all national and international organisations/agencies.

(a) National Housing & Habitat policy, 1998.

(b) Clean City Campaign, 1998.

(c) Urban Land Management.

(d) Space standards for Barrier—Free build environment for disabled & elderly persons- 1998

Welfare

Staff Welfare activities in the Ministry and its Attached/ Subordinate Offices continued to receive active attention and encouragement. Nine Recreation Clubs are functioning for the purpose. Ministry's Staff Recreation Club is responsible for promotion of sports and cultural activities amongst the civil employees working in the Offices located in Delhi. The Club looks for ways and means for mass participation of the employees in various sports and cultural activities.

The participation of this Ministry in the various sports and cultural activities organised by the Central Civil Services Cultural and Sports Board is par excellence. During the year 1998-99, this Ministry's team, selected from amongst the employees of the Ministry and its Attached/ Subordinate offices, took part in the Inter-Ministry Tournaments in Athletics, Badminton, Basketball, Bridge, Carrom, Chess, Cricket, Football, Hockey, Kabaddi, Power-lifting organised by the CCSCSB. A large number of sports persons representing this Ministry won medals in the individual events of Bridge, Power-lifting and Swimming.

A number of sportspersons from this Ministry have also been selected to represent the Central Secretariat to play in the All India Civil Services Tournaments. A few outstanding sportspersons of this Ministry even don the colour of Delhi State in Shooting, Hockey, Bridge and Football.

The Departmental Canteen of the Ministry continued to function efficiently, catering to the requirement of the officers and staff.

Parliament Matters

Parliament Section of the Ministry deals with all Parliamentary matters pertaining to the Ministry of Urban Affairs & Employment. During 1998 this Ministry answered 594 Parliament Questions on various subjects relating to Local Bodies, Housing, Central Public Works Department, Water Supply, Urban Development, Urban Poverty Alleviation Programmes etc. While answering these 594 Questions, Assurances were given in respect of 42 Parliament Questions. During 1998, various Divisions in the Ministry implemented 106 Parliamentary Assurances given to both the Houses of Parliament (this includes Assurances given to Parliament in the years prior to 1998 also). As on 31-12-98, 96 Assurances were pending in this Ministry.

During 1998-99 four meetings of the Consultative Committee attached to the Ministry of Urban Affairs and Employment were held, wherein the following important issues, in addition to general discussion on various matters relating to this Ministry were specifically discussed:—

(a) National Housing and Habitat Policy, 1998.

(b) Maintenance of Govt. Bungalows and Rats allotted to Members of Parliament by CPWD.

(c) Private Sector participation in housing.

Annual Reports and Audited Accounts of the following Organisations were laid on the Table of both Houses of Parliament during 1998.—

— National Building Construction Corporation. (1996-97 & 1997-98).

— NCR Planning Board (1996-97).

— Hindustan Pre-Fab Limited (1996-97 & 1997-98).

— Delhi Development Authority. (1996-97 & 1997-98).

— Housing and Urban Development Corporation (HUDCO) (1996-97 & 1997- 98).

— National Cooperative Housing Federation (NCHF) (1996-97 & 1997-98).

— National Institute of Urban Affairs (NIUA) (1996-97 & 1997-98).

— Delhi Urban Arts Commission (1996-97 & 1997-98).

— Rajghat Samadhi Committee (1995-96 & 1996-97).

— Building Material Technology Promotion Council (1996-97 & 1997-98).

— Delhi Metro Rail Corporation Limited (1995-96 & 1996-97).

— Central Government Employees Welfare Housing Organisation (CGEWHO) (1996- 97 & 1997-98).

Vigilance activities

The Administrative Vigilance Unit of the Ministry functions under the charge of Joint Secretary (DD) who is also the Chief Vigilance Officer. The Chief Vigilance Officer is assisted by one Deputy Chief Vigilance Officer of the rank of Deputy Secretary, one Under Secretary, two Assistant Vigilance Officers and Vigilance Officers of the Attached/ Subordinate Offices of the Ministry and also the Chief Vigilance Officers of the Public Sector Undertakings and the Autonomous Bodies under the administrative control of this Ministry. This Unit is responsible for all the matter pertaining to vigilance in the Ministry of Urban Affairs and Employment including its Attached/ Subordinate Offices, Public Sector Undertakings and Autonomous Bodies/Societies/Other Local Authorities.

Vigilance work consist of preventive vigilance, surveillance and detection, and deterrent punitive action. Under preventive action, rules and procedures are reviewed from time to time and surprise inspections are regularly conducted in surveillance areas under the Ministry. As regards surveillance and detection, lists of officers of Gazetted status whose conduct needs to be watched are prepared in consultation with the Central Bureau of Investigation. Under the punitive action, penalties prescribed under the rules are imposed on those who are found guilty.

Generally, the charges related to execution of substandard work in the construction and maintenance of buildings, overpayments to contractors, irregularities in calling of tenders/ quotations and award of contracts, disproportionate assets, illegal gratification, subletting of Government accommodation/shops and violation of the CCS (Conduct) Rules, 1964.

In addition to the departmental examination of complaints and investigation, the Ministry also receives reports from the Central Bureau of Investigation about the misconduct of officers either with a view to taking departmental action or for issuing sanction for prosecution under the Prevention of Corruption Act, 1988

In respect of Public Sector Undertakings, this Ministry processes the cases against the Board Level Officers only. Autonomous Bodies initiate action against their officers themselves. However, in case an officer is on deputation to these bodies from the Central Government, action is taken by this Ministry.

During the period from April, 1998 to December, 1998,124 surprise & regular inspections were carried out, 176 officers were chargesheeted, 299 officers were placed under suspension, major penalties were imposed upon 17 officers and minor penalties upon 144 officers.

Employment of Ex-servicemen

The Director incharge of Administration in the Ministry is the Liasion Officer for the work relating to the Employment of ex-servicemen. Additional Liasion Officers in the Attached/subordinate offices and Public Sector Undertakings also watch the implementation of Government rules, regulations and orders on the subject.

Reservation for scheduled castes and scheduled tribes

A special Cell in the Ministry watches the implementation of Government orders regarding reservation in services for Scheduled Castes and Scheduled Tribes through the periodical returns prescribed by the Government of India for the purpose. In addition, the Cell also monitors the filling up of the backlog vacancies reserved for Scheduled Castes and Scheduled Tribes under the Special Recruitment Drive in respect of the Attached Subordinate offices and the Public Sector Undertakings of this Ministry. The Ministry has also issued instructions to the offices under its control to strictly observe the instructions circulated by the Department of Personnel &Training in respect of the reservations made for Other Backward Classes. The Cell periodically monitors the filling up of vacancies reserved for OBCs in respect of the Attached/Subordinate offices of the Ministry. The statistics regarding the representation of Scheduled Castes/ Scheduled Tribes in the Ministry and its other offices are contained in Appendix VI-IX

Public grievance cell

The Public Grievance Cell in the Ministry ensures redressal of the grievances of public under the overall supervision of Joint Secretary (Admn.) who acts as the Director of Grievances. Grievances are also received through the Department of Administrative Reforms and Public Grievances, Department of Pension and Pensioners Welfare, Directorate of Public Grievances, Cabinet Secretariat, President's Secretariat, Prime Minister's Office, registered associations and members of public. The grievances received in the Ministry are duly acknowledged and referred to the concerned offices under this Ministry for redressal. As per the instructions received from the Directorate of Public Grievances, Cabinet Secretariat & Ministry of Personnel, Public Grievances and Pensions, the grievances are continuously monitored and the over all position reviewed periodically. A watch is also kept on the grievances appearing in the newspaper columns. The cell has contributed to the speedy disposal of genuine complaints and representations during the year.

Computerisation in the ministry

Main ministry

The Cases Monitoring System (CMS) has been developed for the Delhi division for monitoring the status of disposal of various cases referred to the division by concerned offices, departments etc. This is in regular operation. Five computer terminals have been installed with necessary printers. The terminals are used for running CMS besides document preparation and E-mail.

— Parliament Question Information System (PARLIS) is under regular operation in the Parliament Section.

An independent computer system with four terminals and necessary printers have been provided to the section which are being extensively used for running PARLIS, document preparation and E-mail.

— Computerisation of the two million housing programme has been taken up. Discussions have been held and monitoring proforma is under finalization.

— Development of a Computerised Monitoring System for the Swaran Jayanthi Shahari Rozgar Yojana for Urban Poverty Alleviation Division has been taken up. Discussions are being held and monitoring Proforma has been prepared.

— Five Year Information Technology Plan has been prepared for the Ministry. In the plan, a brief description of the hardware and software provided by NIC and various application areas Computerised have been given. A detailed account of new technologies relevant to the Ministry, new application areas to be Computerised, procedural changes to be affected and hardware and software to be procured is also given.

— Local Area Network: In order to provide E- mail, Internet and file sharing services, existing computers (79 nos.) in the Ministry have been connected over a Local Area Network (LAN) which is connected to Internet through RF Tower erected in Nirman Bhawan. The LAN also connects the user's computers in all the other Ministries / Departments in Nirman Bhawan.

— Regular Maintenance and Development work is being carried out on the following operational Office Automation applications.

— VIP References Monitoring System for the Secretary's office.

— Payroll Computation System

— Annual Maintenance Contract System

— CGHS cards Information System

— Telephone Bills Accounting System

— Public Grievances Monitoring System

— Diary Monitoring System for the offices of Cabinet and State Ministers

Website of the Ministry. The website of the Ministry of Urban Affairs and Employment has been launched on 16.2.1999. The Website can be accessed through the address www. urbanindia. nic. in.

Directorate of Printing

Feasibility Report for connection of Printing Presses of the Directorate of Printing: A feasibility report has been prepared which outlines the hardware and software to be procured and procedural steps to be taken for connectivity and timely compilation of the priority jobs referred to the presses by various important Government offices.

Dissemination of new Govt. Publications over NICNET. Monthly lists of new Government Publications are being transmitted to all the State and District Head Quarters over NICNET.

Machine Utilization Monitoring System is in regular operation.

Directorate of Estate

Connectivity: —In all, 38 terminals have been connected to various important sections in the Directorate.

Housing Information System (HIS):— Maintenance and development work have been carried out on the HIS during the year. In view of changed strategy, the Housing Information System is being redesigned for the allotment year 1999.

Dissemination of Regular and change Waiting lists over Internet— Query Modules for registration numberwise, namewise, typewise and joining datewise retrieval have been developed and the data has been loaded in the Pentium Server installed at NIC HQ, alongwith query modules. The data is being updated periodically. For the past over one year, the system is under regular operation.

Eviction Cases Monitoring System has been developed.

Software for on-line waiting list updation has been developed and implemented.

Licence Fees Accounting System: The software for opening the Licence fees card and making the first licence fee bill have been developed and implemented. This is under regular operation.

3

Housing and Human Settlements

A new Housing and Habitat Policy 1998 has been formulated and laid before Parliament on 29.7.98. The objectives of the policy are to create surpluses in housing stock and facilitate construction of 2 million additional dwelling units each year in pursuance of National Agenda for Governance. It also seeks to ensure that housing alongwith supporting services is treated as priority sector at par with infrastructure. The Central theme of the policy is strong public private partnerships for tackling housing and infrastructure problems. The Government would provide fiscal concessions, carry out legal and regulatory reforms and create an enabling environment.

The problem of housing shortage compounded with the population explosion has also been addressed by this policy. This document clearly identifies the respective roles of the Central Government, the State Government, local authorities, Financial Institutions, research standardization and technical institutions. However, since housing is a state subject State Governments have to play primary role in formulating specific action plans and programmes suited to local needs and conditions in consultation with local bodies and citizen groups.

National Agenda for Governance

The National Agenda for Governance has identified Housing for All as a priority area, with particular emphasis on the needs of the vulnerable groups. As per this programme, it is proposed to facilitate construction of 20 lakh additional units every year, with emphasis on EWS & LIG sections of the population as also the needs of SC/ST and other vulnerable groups. Out of 20 lakh additional houses, 7 lakh houses will be constructed in urban areas and remaining 13 lakh in rural areas. This would require an additional investment of around Rs. 4000 crore. HUDCO is expected to meet more than 55% of target i.e. 4 lakh units and the balance 3 lakh units per year will be met by other HFIs recognised by NHB, Cooperative Sector and Corporate Sector. An action plan for implementation of the new policy for achievement of targets has been drawn up and the progress is being monitored closely. As on 31.12.98, HUDCO has sanctioned schemes for construction of over one lakh houses under the 2 million housing programme.

Building Centres and Technology Extension

The National Network of Nirman or Nirmithi Kendras (Building Centres) has been established with Central assistance through HUDCO under a Central scheme. These centres impart training to artisans in low cost construction skills and produce building materials and components by utilizing agro-industrial wastes. Under the scheme a central grant of Rs. 2 lakh was originally granted to each centre. The funding pattern of the scheme has been revised. The Central grant-in-aid ranging from Rs. 3 lakh to Rs. 5 lakh is now available to the Building Centres depending on the level of their activities. In addition, loan from HUDCO subject to a maximum Rs. 22 lakh is also available to these Centres. As on 31.12.98, 560 centres have been sanctioned out of which 324 centres -have become functional. These centres have received Government of India grant of Rs. 9.57 crore and have imparted training to over 1 lakh construction workers. A thorough review of the programme is being undertaken to identify problem areas and to take steps for more effective implementation.

Night Shelter and Sanitation facility for Urban Footpath Dwellers

This Central scheme seeks to provide night shelter and sanitation facilities to footpath dwellers at a per capital cost of Rs. 5000 with 20% subsidy from Central Government and 80% as contribution from implementing agencies or through HUDCO loan. The scheme is being implemented through HUDCO and has now been extended to cover all urban areas, wherever the problem of footpath dwellers exists.

As on 31.12.98, HUDCO has sanctioned loan amounting to Rs. 1217 lakh and Government subsidy amounting to Rs. 1241 lakh for a total of 60 schemes to provide 18470 beds, 6814 pay and use toilet seats, 584 baths and 597 urinals. The guidelines of the scheme were revised in 1993 with a view to widen the scope of the scheme and to make it more attractive and effective,

International Cooperation

United Nations Centre for Human Settlements (UNCHS) is an Inter-Governmental body established through a resolution of the U. N. General Assembly for guiding habitat activities. India is a member of the organisation since its inception. An annual contribution of one lakh US Dollars payable in Indian currency is made by India.

This Ministry has been closely associated with the activities of the UNCHS. The World Habitat Day is celebrated each year as per themes declared by UNCHS.

During 1998-99, the World Habitat Day celebrations were held on 5-6th Oct. '98. On this occasion a two day National Seminar on Safer Cities was held. The Seminar was inaugurated by Shri Ram Jethmalani Hon'ble Minister for Urban Affairs & Employment.

The principal outcome of the Seminar has been as follows:-

— Identification of major issues in evolution of Safer Cities

— Urban Safety &Vulnerable Groups.

— Making cities safer for women and children.

— Barrier free access to built environment for disabled and elderly persons.

— Hazards affecting human settlement.

International Assistance for Housing

KfW/OECF Loan Assistance for Housing Projects

Government had negotiated for line of credit to HUDCO and HDFC from KfW of Germany and OECF of Japan. So far KfW had provided/ Committed assistance by way of credits totalling DM 170 million to HUDCO for undertaking housing schemes for EWS and low cost sanitation scheme. KfW has also sanctioned grant assistance of DM 1 million to HUDCO for the Building Centre Programme in India. Another grant of DM 10 million to HUDCO for Building Centres scheme is under consideration in Ministry of Finance.

KfW has provided loan of DM 25 million to HDFC also for financing EWS housing programmes and has committed a grant of DM 30 million to HDFC for undertaking low cost housing programmes and supporting urban infrastructure. Agreement in this regard was signed in February 1994. Another agreement for grant of DM 30 million is under consideration.

A line of credit amounting to Yen 6,788 million (Rs. 168 crore approximately) from OECF Japan has been secured for city water supply projects of Sholapur and New Bombay. HUDCO has received around Rs. 104 crore through this line of credit. Sholapur project is almost complete.

Another line of credit amounting to Yen 8,670 million has been committed by OECF to HUDCO for infrastructure development projects in several States. This is being received by HUDCO direct from OECF through Bank of India, Tokyo. HUDCO has received Rs. 52.36 crore under this credit line.

IBRD Technical Assistance (Grant)

The International Bank for Reconstruction and Development (IBRD) have extended a grant of US$ one million to HUDCO for strengthening its infrastructure operations. The grant is being utilized mainly for restructuring of HUDCO's infrastructure wing. The objective of the technical assistance is to assist HUDCO in the preparation and appraisal of urban development project to be financed by World Bank.

Infrastructure Financing Project

ADB has committed loan of US$ 100 million to HUDCO, out of which it has already disbursed US$ 20 million.

NRI Investment and FDI in housing

The housing sector suffers from paucity of funds in the backdrop of the magnitude of housing shortage in the country. The available domestic funds leave a huge "resource gap" resulting in unabated increase in the housing shortage. There are significant gaps in resources, technology and management in the sector.

In the ongoing process of economic reforms and liberalisation of trades and industrial policy of the Government, the housing and real estate sectors have emerged as a key area with immense investment potential. In order to pass on the benefits of the liberalisation process to NRIs/PIO/ OCBs and to promote inflow of foreign exchange and augment resources for the housing sector, the Government announced a scheme for NRI investment in housing and real estate development. The scheme covers investment by non-residents of Indian nationality/ origin and Overseas Corporate Bodies (OCBs) predominantly owned by NRIs/PIO in the following areas:-

(i) development of serviced plots and construction of built-up residential premises;

(ii) real estate covering construction of residential and commercial premises including business centres and offices;

(iii) development of townships;

(iv) city and region level urban infrastructure facilities including roads and bridges;

(v) manufacturing of building materials; and

(vi) financing of housing development.

Fiscal Incentives for the Housing Sector

This Ministry has been pursuing with the Ministry of Finance the matter of provision of various fiscal incentives for the Housing Sector. Many of the suggestions had been accepted and the following concessions under Income Tax and Wealth Tax have been given during the financial year 1998-99.

— Urban vacant land held as stock in trade has been exempted from Wealth Tax for a period of 7 years.

- — Rental properties have been exempted from Wealth Tax provided the houses had been rented out for at least 300 days.
- — 25% of rental income to be deducted for repairs and collection charges (under Section 24 of Income Tax Act).
- — Deductions for interest on borrowed capital in case of self occupied properties increased from Rs. 15,000 to Rs. 30,000.
- — Carry forward of losses from *House Property" against future income under the same head to be allowed for 8 years.
- — Reintroduction of Section 8OGG in respect of deduction for rents paid.
- — Tax holiday for approved housing projects: 100% deduction from profits for first 5 year and 30% deduction for subsequent 5 years.
- — Infrastructure status to housing industry subject to certain conditions.

The Government has also been successful in obtaining various concessions under Excise Duty and Custom Duty which will go a long way in stimulating increased productions of low cost building materials and components based on utilisation of industrial wastes and other cost effective technology.

Housing Ministers' Conference '98

This Ministry organised the Housing Ministers' Conference in June '98 to consider the action plan "Shelter for All" for construction of 2 million houses, the draft National Housing & Habitat Policy '98 and other important issues related to urban housing. The Conference was inaugurated by Shri Ram Jethmalani

Hon'ble Minister for Urban Affairs and Employment. The Conference deliberated upon important issues relating to Urban Housing and gave many recommendations/ suggestions for giving a fillip to house construction activity in the country. These include legal reforms, augmentation of housing finance, technological support etc.

Seminar on Housing-Challenges & Solution

The National Housing & Habitat Policy '98 envisages strong public private partnership in housing related infrastructure. With a view to assess the likelihood of public sector participation in Housing, a Seminar on Housing-Challenges & Solution was hold from 28th to 30th Nov. '98 at New Delhi. The Seminar was inaugurated by the Prime Minister and was jointly organised by this Ministry, HUDCO and Federation of Builders & Promoters of Maharashtra. The Seminar offered a number of valuable suggestions on the increased role of private sector in housing, provided some fiscal concessions are granted and impediments to Housing are removed. This included repel of Urban Land (Ceiling and Regulation) Act, 1976 which has since been repealed through an ordinance.

4

Infrastructure and Social Sector Prospects

The scenario around industry, infrastructure and social sector is not comfortable.

According to a report published by Business Times Bureau of The Times of India on 18 January, 1997, 24 industries which have a weight of 50.37 per cent in the index of industrial production recorded a growth rate of only five per cent during April-November, 1996, down from 11 per cent during the corresponding period in the preceding year. The growth rate in output of the infrastructure industries which have a weight of 28.77 per cent in the index of industrial production has also slumped to 3.3 per cent during the first eight months of 1996-97 as against 9.3 per cent in the previous corresponding period. Most of the State Electricity Boards are utterly mismanaged and are running at heavy losses. The power sector also could not be opened to privatization though it was officially decided long ago. The transport and communication sector also needs a thorough restructuring.

Most of the State transport organisation, run on heavy government subsidy, are incurring huge losses. Infrastructural facilities in the agricultural sector like irrigation and flood control measures are still at a very poor level.

There are some areas where the farmers completely lack the basic knowledge of fertilizer and pesticide uses while extension services of government remain only on paper. Likewise, innovative ideas relating to small-scale industries and openings of self-employment opportunities are lacking among the educated unemployed who need proper consultancy services and basic training of entrepreneurship.

In the area of human resource development, the two pillars of literacy movement , viz Operation Blackboard and the Non-formal Education Scheme are floundering mainly due to casual attention of the implementing agencies. The adult literacy movement, for example, was not reoriented until six years after the mission began in 1988.

The recruitment of teachers for the literacy drive was in a shambles. Some vital aspects that need immediate attention now are the strengthening of post-literacy programmes to keep pace with the main drive, formulating a linkage with the formal school system and remedying the lack of vocational education and income generation schemes.

The unfulfilled promise of achieving 100 per cent literacy, renewed several times in the earlier decades, has once again been undertaken by the United Front government with a time-frame of AD 2000. So far, only 5.3 million have been made literate through adult literacy drive and as many as 44 million still remain to be covered.

One does not know how practicable will be the promise. Mere slogan of literacy mission, as has been done so far, is not going to transform the mission into a mass movement. It must be linked to improvement of quality of life, particularly with respect to improved health, nutrition, employment programme and, of course, social justice.

Under a shady family planning programme, INDIA is sitting on a population time bomb. According to the latest census, the country is going to be world's most populous nation by AD 2040 if determined efforts to reverse the growth trend are not made. It is fearful to think that the demography of India is adding every year to her size an additional population at the rate of 18 million, equivalent to the size of six Singapores.

Though during the last four and a half decades of planning the real national income increased by almost six times, the per capita real income could grow by only 2.4 times. Most of the benefits of India's growth and development are eaten up by population growth. Surprisingly enough, though the political class is well aware of the sensitive nature of the issue, especially after the excesses of emergency, the nation did not receive even a single imaginative suggestion of population control during these 20 years. What is more agonising is that there are many politicians who are not even averse to the unchecked growth of a deprived and dependent section which could be a good vote bank. If the country really wants to make progress with assured betterment of life, suitable programmes have to be so framed as to encourage control of births and small family norm at any cost.

Rapid creation of productive employment opportunities is the best way of reducing poverty.

The Economic Survey, 1995—96 reported Planning Commission estimates indicating a sharp increase in additional employment generated in the economy from 3 million in 1991—92 to over 7 million in 1994—95. The employment estimates for 1995—96 have not yet been finalised. However, there is little doubt that the high growth of the last few years would have led to a rapid expansion of employment opportunities.

The Common Minimum Programme (CMP), underpins strong commitment of the Government to the development of social sectors for achieving distributive justice. This commitment is reflected in the increase in Central Government Plan and non—Plan allocations for social services to a record high of 1.19 per cent of GDP in 1996—97 (BE). This ratio was 0.96 per cent in 1995—96. An additional amount of Rs. 2466 crore of Central assistance to States' and Union Territories' plans has also been allocated in the 1996—97 budget for expenditure on basic minimum services.

The Government has also accorded high priority to poverty alleviation programmes. The Central Plan allocations for social sectors and poverty alleviation programmes show highest growth of 85.6 per cent for education in 1996–97 over 1995–96 (BE). The outlay for elementary education has gone up by 247.8 per cent, mainly because of the programme of nutritional support to primary school students. The allocation for health was raised by 21.6 per cent and for rural development, encompassing the major programmes for poverty alleviation, by 12.1 per cent in 1996–97 over 1995–96 (BE).

The weaker sections especially scheduled castes/ scheduled tribes and women have been given importance in special programmes of poverty alleviation and employment as well as in several other programmes. The PDS has been steamlined recently in order to target the poorer sections of the population.

Population : According to Planning Commission estimates, population figures are expected to go up from 856 million in 1991-92 to 938 million in 1996-97, showing an annual average growth rate of 18 per cent . If the growth rate remains around two per cent, this figure will go up to 955 million, According to current indications, the actual figure will be in between these two figures since the death rate has fallen below even the 2000-2001 and in any case will be below the rate of around two per cent as estimated by the current UN projections, of around 1,042 million in that year.

If India is able to achieve a population growth rate of around 1.6 percent in the decade 2000-2001 to2010-2011, its population will reach 1,171 million, if the Planning Commission projections are used as a base. Even if this target is exceeded, the figure will be less than 1,224 million as estimated by the UN. These projections have not incorporated the detail of the 1991 census. The Registrar—General's Working Group on Population Projections set up conventionally by the Planning Commission, will have to firm up these alternative conjectural projections, in terms of underlying fertility, mortality and expected life span-behaviour, by age—group and rural-urban categories.

Land: The other major category needing examination on this kind of perspective is the land or resource base of the economy. The Planning Commission has correctly projected that the net area sown or arable land of the country will remain constant at 141 million hectares.

Growth in net area sown at around one per cent annually in the early period of planing fell to around 0.6 per cent and then to 0.3 per cent in subsequent decades and is now not growing at all. It is reasonable to assume that the exploitation of the geographical area of the country or the extensive land frontier has reached its limits. This is an important issue, the implications of which are not being realized with the urgency they deserve, since at a basic level resource constraints of a more severe kind faced by certain East Asian economies are now being approached in India. Organizations, communities, households and individuals will have to grasp this fact and live with it.

The intensive frontier for land use, however remains. It has been known for example that cropping intensity depends on irrigatin. Thus gross cropped area or harvested area has been shown in the past to be strongly determined statistically, in an econometric sense, by net irrigated area and irrigation intensity. This fundamental relationship can be used to project the intensive resource base of the economy.

Water management: Recognizing these problems the Finance Minister has been persuaded to introduce an Accelerated Irrigation Benefit Programme in the Annual Plan for this year. An outlay of Rs. 800 crore has ben provided for large irrigation project where substantial achievement can be expected—say in completing a section of the canal systems in the next two or three years and Rs. 100 crore for delivering water to the field in the next two agricultural years.

These programmes will be strictly monitored. More important, a blue ribbon commission has been set up with the following terms of reference:

- To prepare an Integrated Water Plan for development of water resources for drinking, irrigation, industrial, flood control and other uses;
- To suggest modalities for transfer of surplus water to water-deficit basins by interlinking of rivers for achieving the above objectives;
- To identify important ongoing projects as well as new projects which should be completed on a priority basis together with phasing;
- Identify a technological and interdisciplinary research plan for the water sector with a view to maximizing the benefits;
- To suggest physical and financial resource generation strategies for the water sector; and

- Any other related issue.

The projections assume a vastly improved performance on the land and water management frontiers. It needs to be remembered that the balance ground water reserves towards the later half of the nineties will be nore and more limited. A very dramatic effort will be needed to harvest and carefully use the available water. Otherwise, the projected increase in cropping intensity will simply not take place. Cropping intensity increased from around 1.3 in the early nineties. In the nixt two decades, this effort needs to be considerably strengthened, so that cropping intensity can increase from 1.3 to 1.5. Harvesting of rainwater, recycling water from agricultural drainage systems, more judicious use of water for cropping, will all be required, Non-agricultural use of water will have to be far more econmical.

Another way of looking at the severe land constraint is to see that a net area sown per person will go down from around 0.17 ha to around 0.10 ha. The gross area sown per person currently around 0.2 ha will, even if cropping intensity increases very rapidly, go down to around 0.15-0.18 ha.

It has been shown elsewhere that limited co-operation in waer use has been successful in many watershed projects in resolving the land constraint. The same is true of lower level surface irrigation systems. Community involvement is also important for judicous management of aquifer systems and ground water use.

In many cases, land management questions are equally important and are inextricably linked with water management, eg land shaping in hill slopes and on farm investment in irrigation commands.

The technology interface is important, both for land

and water management and for cropping and non-crop farm systems that are optimal, in this class of issues. While a lot of research has been done and is available, the real issues are policy rules for fast replicability of existing knowledge and success stories. Community institutions have to be at the heart of this process. ICAR, its centres and sponsored institutions, have not easily participated in this process.

Work force: This kind of development is simply not possible if the functional literacy skills of the farm population arenot improved and if the peasant who works on the land, does not have rights to make improvements on it. There are a number of significant examples where based on local initiative, educational and training institutions led to knowledge-based growth in rural areas. These include the Charotar Vidya Mandal at Vallabh Vidyanagar (later Sardar Patel University), Dharamasthala Educational Trust (efforts of Veerendra Heggade) and many co-operative sponsored institutions in Maharashtra (for example the Pravara Ecucational Trust at Loni). Recognizing the importance of such efforts, the government of India has set up a National Council for Rural Institutes. The ICAR and its affiliates must be one of the major thrust institutions in this effort and its educational and extension wings must sponsor, acredit and support the effort.

BMSs: The government's Basic Minimum Services (BMSDs) Programme also has the same objective. It consists of the following programmes which need integration with our agricultural strategy:

- 100 per cent coverage of provision of safe drinking water in rural and urban areas.
- 100 per cent coverage of primary health service facilities in rural and urban areas.

- Universalization of primary education.
- Provision of public housing assistance to all shelterless poor families.
- Extension of mid day meal programme in primary school to all rural blocks and urban slums and desadvantaged sections.
- Provision of connectivity to all unconnected villages and habitations.
- Streamlining the public distribution system with the focus on the poor.

The major problems that confront India are poverty and unemployment. And both are interrelated. There is a lot of controversy regarding the estimates of poverty in the country. Estimates of Tendulkar and Jain show that rural poverty has increased from 37.5 per cent in 1990-91 to 39.7 per cent in 1993-94. On the other hand, urban poverty has declined from 35 per cent in 1990-91 to 30.9 per cent in 1993. The upshot of the argument is that even in 1993-94, around 40 per cent of the rural population (around 250 million) and 31 per cent of the urban population (around 65 million) were below the poverty line, or food insecure in terms of not having enough calories.

The continuance of poverty at such a colossal level has created great distortions in the economy. There are several reasons why poverty has persisted in rural areas. One obvious factor which has hurt the poor is the sharp increase in the prices of food grains. During the last five or six years, procurement prices of food grains have increased considerably recultural labourers. Secondly, the rural poor appear to have been left out of the gains of increased productivity in the agricultural sector. Thirdly, the rate of growth in employment in rural areas (both males and females), during the period 1987-88 to 1993-94 was significantly lower as comparesd to the urban areas as shown in .

According to the 50th Round of the NSSO, while 'Open' unemployment at a little over 6.0 per cent, remained more or less unchanged. And casualization increased with a corresponding decline in self-employment, both in rural and urban areas. Casual wage employment increased from 31.2 per cent in 1987-88 to 33.5 per cent in 1993-94, while self-employment declined from 53.6 per cent to 51.9 per cent. Regular salaried employment also declined from 15.2 per cent to 14.7 per cent.

The census figures have given an alarming new for Indian planners again. The data paint a dismal picture both with regard to increase in population and unemployment. By 2040, India is set to become the world's most populous country with a population of 126 crores. And as far as unemployment situation is concerned, one-third of the populztion—300 million were estimated to be without work in 1994.

This implies that unless some effective steps are taken to control population, the rate of employment will increase in future.

The approach paper, however, recognizes that a sustained and long-lasting solution to gthe problem of poverty depends on the creation of adequate employment opportunities through a broad based programme of development and economic growth. Therefore, in the Ninth Plan, a great deal of emphasis has been given to agriculture and rural development. And agriculture has been delinked from rural development in order to emphasize the development of irrigation, watershed development, animal husbandry schemes, social forestry and so on.

Technology is the "in" thing for elite circles in industry as well as in agriculture for operational policies to be determined. This has implications—economic, social and political—which should not be missed in the wider context of the course and content of the entire economic and social development process.

There is, first of all, a high cost financing improvements in production and productivity of viable farmers and the marketing of surpluses from may be generated in the farm sector. The gains in agriculture too are monopolized in their entirety by the rich and party middle farmers who constitute hardly ten per cent of the farming population. The so-called incentive prices, guaranteed for the marketable surpluses, which under the system of public procurement have been scaled up even as production and productivity have risen, have distorted the structure of relative prices within agriculture and as between agriculture and non-agricultural sectors. Surpluses for investment in industry and for relief to the vulnerable sections of society, especially those which have no viable assets in land, have consequently eroded and processes of balanced economic and social growth have been blocked instead of receiving a boost from agricultural growth in the last three decades.

Precedence to Profit: It is interesting to note in this context the new ambitions which the beneficiaries of the new agricultural strategy have been nursing and have now acquired a critical importance after the structural adjustment based on market-oriented liberalization-globalization process was initiated in 1991. Important in this context too is the proposition which began to be advanced in influential quarters in the late half of the seventies that the "export principle" should apply as much to agriculture as to industry; more so to agriculture in which in recent years surpluses to effective demand in the domestic market have begun to appear from time to time and are creating their own set of problems.

This is an extension of the demand for the so-called principle of "parity of prices" between what the surplus farmer sells in the Indian market and what he buys. The idea is that price determination for agricultural produce should be governed relative to the highest price which can be fetched in the global market and not by any reference to a system or structure of relative prices of goods or labour (that is, wages) in the domestic market. There is, of course, at the same time a demand for protection against competitive prices. A logical further extension of this reasoning necessarily is that it is right economically to export agricultural surpluses rather than use them for satisfaction of the needs of those in the country who for want of adequate purchasing power are unable to provide a profitable market for increases in production. The commercial principle, after all, has a logic of its own had if applied to agricultural surpluses it must grant precedence to profit of the surplus producer rather than to the satisfaction of human wants.

Agriculture vs Industry—Distortion of Reality: Of special interest in this context again is the agriculture versus industry debate which began forcefully to be raised as commercial agriculture made headway. It is suggested by the votaries of higher priority for agriculture that India's development programmes and plans have been a failure because more resources have been pumped into industry, specially heavy industry, during the planning era and agriculture has been starved of funds and investment. It is argued that this resource allocation pattern should change and agriculture should have higher share in total financial outlays in development plans. It is, however, a distortion of reality to say, since after the launching of the new agricultural strategy in the mid-sixties, that agricultural development has suffered on account of greater priority for industry in the economic development process. The resource stringency has, on the contrary, been a far bigger constraint on industrial investment. The worst hit, of course, has been the social services sector. So far as the agricultural sector is concerned, the diversion of resources in favour of commercial farming has been considerable and impressive.

Rich Farmers Benefit Most: It is not at all enlightening to examine the allocation of resources in terms only of the budgetary allocations in the plans. There have been crash programmes for agricultural production outside the framework of the plans with their accent on additional non-Plan allocations.

Though the commercial banks have been oriented towards providing working capital needs of industry, agriculture began to claim a sizeable share in bank credit also. But the most important change has been a shift in the terms of trade in favour of agricultural sector through the policy of "incentive" procurement prices, especially of food grains. The huge income derived by surplus farmers on this account have been supplemented during the years of comparative shortages by black market prices extracted by the rich farmers in collusion with traders. The higher incomes originating in the agricultural sector have, moreover, been tax-free. The surplus farmers have been getting, in addition to subsidized supplies of various inputs, like irrigation, power and fertilizers.

The huge public investment in irrigation, power and fertilizers, therefore, does not give returns and has been showing big losses so that resources for additional investment on infrastructural facilities for the development of the agricultural as well as the industrial sector has had to be drawn from other than those who benefit from these subsidies.

Industry—Need for Growth at Faster Pace: It is indiputable, opf course, that strains in the economy cannot be relieved unlwss indian agriculture is able to produce adequate surpluses. The question, however, is whether it is at all possible to achieve this objective merely by budgetary allocation at the cost of further decay in social services and stagnation in industrial investment. The fact is that any scheme for the development of agriculture and uplift of the rural economy qas a whole cannot become viable and will not be possible to sustain unless industry and more specifically heavy industry grows at a rate faster than that of other segments of the economy,l including agriculture. This is borne out by elaborate input—output calculations and exercises in material balances and linkages that are involved in the growth process.

It was in the very initial stages of framing an economic development strategy in India that he question of the relative weight and pace of the development of heavy industry in relation to wage goods production, especially in the agricultural sector, was closely examined.

A galaxy of internationally renowed economists who assisted aIndian planners in drawing up the I and the II Five Year Plans during the fifties was unamious that heavy industry would have to be developed at a rate taster than the overall rate of development of the national economy. By simple calcuations with respect to material balances in a developing Indian economy, it was established that the desired rates of agricultural output and consumer goods production would require import of machinery and equipment on a scale which would be difficult to finance. The development of an indigenous heavy industry to meet this requirements was, therefore forced by the course of development of the Indian economy in the last three decades, particularly in respect of developments in the agricultural sector.

It may be noted that a high growth of even more than seven per cent can be achieved in India if the economy is geared up only in those sectors where production efforts are selectively concentrated to enhance goods and services mainly required by the top expenditure classes.

In such a case, even heavy taxation and substantial rise in price level could be absorbed by the consumers. However, the Indian economy cannot take such a step. A sustained growth of the economy has to give balanced attention to all the sections of society and particularly to the weaker and vulnerable groups of the people. So long the people were told that the poverty figures of India were declining at a fast rate. The way the statistical jugglery was used by the earlier Planning Commission and the earlier government to present a picture of fast declining poverty with the figures of the people below the poverty line coming down from 35 per cent in the 1980s to just 19 per cent in the mid 1990s, there should not have been poverty concentration in the country by now. Surprisingly, however, the present Planning Commission has rediscovered poverty and finds that the people living below the poverty line comprise almost half the population.

The modified version of the methodology for measuring poverty was suggested by the expert group of Lakdawall Committee as far back as in 1992 to unveil the ground reality. Poverty line is fixed at Rs. 264 for rural areas at 1992-93 prices. According to the new estimate, the number of people below the poverty line at the moment would not be less than 45 per cent of the total population.

It is important here to note that while the earlier method put the poverty rate at 29.9 per cent in 1987-88 and 203 per cent in 1992-93, the new method shows the figure at 39 per cent in both these years. What it means is that the liberalization and new economic reforms have not led to any improvement in the life-style of the masses.

If we go by the UNDP's Human Development Report and its "Capability Poverty Measure" which are put together by the National Council of Applied Economic Research, we also get the impression that the proportion of population who may be defined as poor on the basis of capability poverty measure would now be as high as 45 to 50 per cent of the population.

Thus, the fact remains that after half a century of freedom from colonial rule during which the net national product at factor cost of 1980-91 prices increased by 493 per cent from Rs. 40.454 crore in 1950-51 to more than 240,000 crore in 1955-56 and the real per capital income rose by 128 per cent from Rs. 1,127 in 1950-51 to Rs. 2,573 in 1995-96, almost half the population of the country still lives in poverty. What it indicates is that a total of 493 per cent growth during the decades of planning has remained incapable of reducing the gap between poverty and prosperity by any significant measure.

The benefit has mostly been eaten up by the high growth rate of population and the little improvement in real per capital income that could be achieved has made the rich section richer more than they have made the poor well off.

The confusion relating to earlier poverty figures centered round the limited definition under which the government did not take into account the components of poverty like morbidity, health status of people, education and skill-levels, frustration of the unemployed, etc.

The poverty ratio was defined purely in terms of food intake while assuming the much needed education, health services and employment opportunities to be provided by government. Hence, the growth rate envisaged in the Ninth Plan draft must be qualified with an in-built mechanism structured to remove the earlier defects. Needless to say, the mechanism to deal with these shortcomings is to pursue economic policies that could promote a high labour-intensive growth with the combination of redistributive justice under high income generation and public investment in social infrastructure. Agrarian economy needs a thorough shake-up in the direction of redistributive justice since the gap between poverty and prosperity in the sector has gradually assumed a large dimension due to the wrong policy of discriminatory treatment in favour of the rich farmers. This is perhaps the key to a dent in rural poverty.

As the "Human Development Report" of UNDP, 1996 emphasizes, "it requires a combination of government and private sector initiatives to turn economic growth into human development. And investment in health and education along with growth-oriented redistributive economic policies could generate a 'virtuous cycle' of growth and development. "

An area of priority in the Ninth Plan is to improve project implementation and delivery mechanisms and to ensure that the intended benefits actually reach the people. Further, several social sector programmes are formulated without addressing the isssue of sustainability of benefits and most programmes run with ever-increasing government budgets and thus pre—empt resources which could find better alternative uses. The Ninth Plan must introduce necessary correctives to reverse many of the unsustainable trends in the implementation of poverty alleviation programmes. Just allotting higher outlay for rural development will mean nothing unless a major streamlining takes palce in the implementation and delivery systems.

The existion schemes whose delivery costs are disproportionately high or which fail to make the desired impact should be considered for reorientation and discontinuation.

It is necessary to shelve such schemes whose delivery cost exceeds, say 15 to 20 oer cent of the total cost of operating the programme. Monitoring and evaluation of programmes have to be made equally effective and purposeful. Therefore, the Centre, States and the grass roots level organizations/institutions would need to be involved to ensure the effectiveness of the system. It is encouraging that the Planning Commission would bring out compendium of evaluation studies and give wider publicity of the findings of research studies conducted and sponsored by it. This would be helpful for a meaningful public debate on issues involved.

An overall increase in the level of real wages of the unorgainzed workers will also help empowering them to be able to secure maximum advantage from the other developmental programmes of the government. The very concepts of democratic decentralozation and empowerment of the people imply a steady reducation in the paternalistic role of the State and increased emphasis on empowerment of the people themselves. It is hoped that during the Ninth Plan there will be much more attention on bringing about awareness among the unorganized workers as also on providing effective redressal mechanisms to enforce their rights.

The approach document of the Plan rightly observes that one of the most important weaknesses of the Indian social sector programmes has been is inabiligy to inform the target benefiviaries about the schemes that are available and to which they have a rightful clain. The Ninth Plan will, hopefully, stress the creation and deployment of an effective information dissemination system,and the necessary redressal mechanism for making the demands effective.

Finally, of course, there is no unique way to describe an ideal gorwth process. It can be hoped that the Ninth Plan will lay down foundations for a more progressive process of planning than has been the case so far. Growth involves a dynamic interaction of linked changes. The economic endocrine gland has to be clear as to how much other matters mingt have advanced. As such, it can also be argued that little attention is required to any particular rate of economic growth so long as it is positive.

Wouldn't it then make little sense to worry whether a baby will end up five or six feet tall when the real anxiety should be whether the baby can be safely brought through the problems of infancy, childhood and adolescence? The slower rate of growth, once under way, can pick-up speed and, of course, can slow down too. But the higher growth rate has the prospect of slowing down only. It is desirable to have a steady growth as it has more possibility of ending up with the fastest rate of growth of the economy just as the movement on a highway gives to the motorest the highest speed. The crux of planning is to find the turnpike and reach it. Also gorwth is no longer the guarantor of trickle down effects. To what extent these plan promises are taken care of in the Ninth Plan, can be anybody's guess.

The philosphy and practice of the policy of market-friendly liberalization, privatization and globalization has a logic of its own for planners and policy-markers. With profit maximization motive, to which private enterprise, Indian and foreign responds rather than economic and social priorities which are of crucial importance in the process of planned development, there is bound to be a shift in the content and direction of the economic growth process.

Without the step-by-step removal of policy and administrative constraints on the play of market forces and pull of effective demand on the economy, investment flows, production structure and incomedistribution cannot conform to an order of meaningful and equitable socio-economic priorities. Any attempt to obfuscate this truth is a deception. The play of market forces cannot, of course, be denied. But the market mu;st be regulated to ubserve planned economic and social priorities.

The issue at stake in this context is the prime responsibility and obligation of the democratic State not only to direct healthy activity for economic growth and social development in all sectors, public private and co-operative, but also mobilize adequate resources, material, human and financial, for public investment.

There were defaults and lags in the planning process and the implementation of the polans inthe process under way for the last five years, the development role of Indian State is being attempted to be extinguished even as the content and direction of India's socio-economic development is increasingly determined and supervised by private terests, Indian and foreign, and the Indian State is asked and obliged to provide law and order and security to the vested interests entrenched in the socio-economic structure. The approach to the Ninth Plan as delineated by the Planning Commission and endorsed by the National Development Council has only made a laborious excercise to give a gloss of populism to amarket-driven growth path which is not amenable to authentic planning to subserve the needs and aspirations of themass of the people.

Hiding the Facts: The shift to non-planning actually started, though rather gingerly, before the market-oriented policies overwhelmed real and meaningful planning. The charade of planning is still, however, kept up by the ruling elite for political-populist considerations. The planners are being used to give respectability to populist promises and gestures. The approach document on the Ninth Plan is, therefore, full of rhetoric on agricultural growth, productive employment, poverty eradication and self-reliance to hide the fact that economic policies being pursued by the government of the day are promoting growth objectives which far from helping the poor and the vulnerable mass of the people and give added strength to the claims and demands of the rich and powerful in society.

The high growth rate of seven per cent per annum with low domestic savings, drastic reduction in public investment and boost for private enterprise not only in organized industry and services sector but also agriculture is directly linked to a strategy in favour of giving commanding heights of the economy to foreign investors, especially multinational corporations and their collaborators among Indian big business. The ongoing structural adjustment programme for the economy launched in 1991 and the Common Minimum Programme (CMP) of the United Front government cannot really provide a sound basis for development planning. The CMP, after all, is a compromise between disparate political and ideological entities, a hotch—potch of contrary objectives and contradictory policies which do not add up and provide a basis for an integrated view and coherent strategy for meaningful development planning.

It is a bundle of preference of conflicting interests, economic, social and political which have only temporarily combined to run a coalition government. Already, the differences in the interpretation and priorities of CMP have surfaced and look like becoming sharper and sharper.

The vested interests, Indian and foreign, in positions of vantage in the economy, society and polity, on their part, are eager to partake of the joys of "indicative planning" such as it has now become, to further stengthen their position. It is wrong really to make light of planning based supposedly on a division of labour as between public investment and private enterprise in socio-economic development process.

It is a grand deception to talk of reduction in poverty, increase of employment through agricultural growth and labour-intensive industry, vast expansion of the social infrastructure of education, health, and mass welfare when, side by side, private enterprise is relied upon to take care of investment for high profit-yielding production and distribution of goods and services to satisfy "effective" demand in the market. The Ninth Plan targets and projections, have, therefore, tended to be financial assumptions.

The challenges

The life and vitality of human beings depend crucially on certain vitamins and minerals that help in the efficient functioning of the brain, immune system. reproduction and energy metabolism. The body needs only small amounts of these nutrients, but it cannot synthesize them. They must be provided through diet. Deficiencies of even the small amounts required cause learning disabilities, impair work capacity and bring illness and death.

Micronutrient malnutrition (silent hunger) is most devastating for pre—school children and pregnant women but is also debilitating for all ages. And it is debilitating the national economy as well. The most important and well studied micro-nutrient deficiencies are vitamin A, Iodine and Iron. Virtually every developing country has deficiencies in the micro nutrients large enough to constitute a public health problem. Many developing countries have multiple deficiencies. Taken together micronutrient deficiencies affect a far greater number of people in the world than Protein-Energy malnutrition. 1.6 billion people live in areas where soils lack sufficient iodine, 655 million suffer from goitre, 26 million have had brain damage and 5.7 million cretinism.

Two billion pre-school children suffer from iron deficinet anaemia. 254 million pre-school children are affected by subclinical, severe and moderate deficiencies of Vitamin A.

In India, 167 millions are exposed to the risk of Iodine deficiency of which 54 million have goitre. Surveys conducted by DGHS indicate that 186 districts are IDD endemic area with goitre rates over 10 per cent. As regards Iron deficiency anaemia, multicentre study conducted by ICMR reveal that 87.5 per cent were anaemic. Deficiency of Vitamin A has long been known to be the largest preventable cause of blindness.

The main intervention strategies against micronutrient malnutrition are:

- Diet supplementation of vulnerable population.
- Dietary improvements.
- Fortification of common foods.

The richest sources of micronutrients are green leafy vegetable and fruits. India is rich in vegetable crops, some of which have good carotene content. Future programmes with respect to horticultural products must be directed towards identifying and propagating high micro-nutrient concentration varieties. People know when they are hungry but they have no natural hunger for vitamin. A, Iron, Iodine and other micronutrients. They do not know they need them and they often do not know what foods provide them.

Deficiency in soil nutrients reflect in the plants grown in the soil. One—half of all soils in all developing countries are deficient or low in available micronutrients. Soil depletion of S, Fe, Mn, Zn and Cu are due to intensive and indiscriminate irrigation and heavy use of high analysis chemical fertilisers. This gets reflected in the plants grown in these soils. Hence, in the national soil health care programme, we should ensure that both the macro-and micro-nutrient needs of soils are addressed.

The term Green Revolution was coined by Dr. William Gadd of USA in 1968, when our farmers brought about a quantum jump in wheat production by taking to semi-dwarf, non-lodging varieties with great enthusiasm and when similar progress appeared feasible in rice. Punjab took the lead because of the scientific and educational backstopping given by the Punjab Agricultural University on the one hand and on the other, by the presence of the essential pre-requisites for progress such as land consolidation and leveling, rural communication, rural electrification and above all, owner cultivation.

Twenty eight years after the term "Green Revolution" was coined, we are in a position to draw a balance sheet and chalk out a strategy for the future.

Apart from erasing the "begging bowl" image of India, the most important gain has been the saving of forests and land, thanks to the productivity improvement associated with high yielding varieties. This year, Indian farmers harvested over 60 million tonnes of wheat, as compared to 6 million tonnes at the time of our Independence in 1947. Punjab farmers have raised the average yield of wheat to over 40 quintals per hectare. Likewise, Tamil Nadu farmers have raised the average yield of rice to over 50 quintals per hectare.

If the yield improvement associated with the Green Revolution in wheat and rice had not taken place, we will need another 70 million hectares to produce the wheat and rice we now harvest. Thus, the productivity inmprovement associated with the Green Revolution is best described as forest and land saving agriculture. The productivity improvement has taken place not only in wheat and rice but also in relation to milk and eggs. Only in the case of pulses, we are lagging behind.

The population of India is growing at a rate of 1.8 per cent per year. If this trend continues, our population will double itself in less than 40 years. Only Kerala, Tamil Nadu, Goa and Mizoram have so far achieved a demographic transition to low birth and death rates. Besides population increase, improved purchasing power among the poor will enhance the demand for food, since undernutrition and poverty go together. In contrast, per capita availability of arable land is shrinking. Water efficiency is still on the whole low and water disputes are growing.

In addition to the gradual decline in per capita availability of land and water, various forms of biotic and abiotic stresses are spreading. There is still a widespread mismatch between production and post-harvest technologies. In perishable commotities like fruits, vegetables, flowers, meat and other animal products, this mismatch is often severe, affecting the inyterests of both producers and consumers. This is why foreign experts frequently refer to the setting in of a fatigue of the Green Revolution. Lester Brown and Hal Kane in their book "Full House" released last year predict that at the current rate of population growth and environmental degradation coupled with an improvement in the consumption capacity of the poor, India will have to import annually over 40 million tonnes of food grains by the year 2030. This is four times the quantity we imported in 1966 i.e. before the onset of the Green Revolution.

We should examine this issue seriously and should not allow complacency overtake the farm sector, just because we now have over 30 million tonnes of food grains available with Government.

Industrial countries are responsible for much of the global environmental problems such as potential changes in temperature, precipitation, sea level and incidence of ultraviolet-B radiation. While further agricultural intensification in industrialised countries will be ecologically disastrous, the failure to achieve agricultural intensification and diversification in developing countries where farming provides most of the jobs will be socially disastrous.

This is because, agriculture including crop and animal husbandary, forestry and agro-forestry, fisheries and agro-industries provides livelihood to over 70 per cent of our population. The smaller the farm, the greater is the need for higher marketable surplus for increasing income. Eleven million new livelihoods will have to be created every year in India and these have to come largely from the farm and rural industries sectors. Importing food and other agricultural commodities will hence have the same impact as importing unemployment. Thus, what we need now is an environmentally sustainable and socially equitable green revolution or what may be termed as ever-green revolution.

Those who advocate going back to the old methods of farming ignore the fact that just a century ago when the population of undivided India was 281 million, famines claimed 30 million lives between 1870 and 1900.

The famine eradication strategy of India comprising the following steps is perhaps the most important achievement of independent India:

- Enhanced production and productivity.
- Better distribution through the public distribution system.
- Adequate grain reserves.
- Purchasing power enhancement through various employment generation and guarantee schemes.
- Special intervention programmes for children, pregnant and nursing mothers and old and infirm persons.

While famines have been prevented, widespread under-nutrition prevails among the economically underprivileged. Since non-food factors like health care, environmental hygiene and literacy play an important role in promoting sustainable food security of the level of the individual, we should redefine security.

Steps for achieveing sustainable food security are as under:

First sustained physical access to food will involve a transition from chemical and machnery intensive to ecological farming technologies.

Second, the emphasis on economic access underlines the need for promoting sustainable livelihoods through multiple income-earning opportunities.

Third, environmental access involves on the one hand attention to soil health care, water harvesting management and the conservation of forest and biodiversity, and on the other to sanitation, environment hygiene, primary health care and primary education.

If the political vision to implement this mission is forthcoming, population stabilisation can be more readily achieved. The prediction of Margins de Condorcet made in 1975 that population will stabilise itself, if children are born for happiness and not just for existence, will then come true.

The emphasis on the individual is important, since the household is not often a homogenous unit. Women and girl children tend to suffer more from under-nutrition than men and boys. UNDP's 1995 Human Development Report contains distressing data on the growing feminisation of poverty. To give operational content to such a concept of food security, we should initiate a Hunger-Free Area Programme (HFAP) consisting of the following components:

— Ensuring sustainable availability of food production over population growth through the development and dissemination of ecotechnologies, supported by appropriate packages of services and public policies. Ecotechnology involves the blending of the ecological prudence and technologies of the past, with the best in frontier technologies, particularly biotechnology, information technology, space technology, renewablre energy technology and management technology. Without ecotechnological empowerment, farm men and women will not be able to produce more food and other agricultural commodities on an environmentally sustainable basis from less land, water and energy resources.

— Sustain the productivity of the natural resource base, by conserving and improving the ecological foundations essential for continuous advances in crop and animal productivity.

— Ensure adequacy of household incomes through promotional social security, such as accessing assets, employment and organisational and marketing empowerment. Agricultural programmes should concurrently aim at more food, more jobs and more income. Integrated attention to farm and non-farm employment and value-addition to primary agricultural commodities will be necessary to enhance income and rural livelihood security.

— Provide entitlement to food through protective social security measures to the vulnerable groups, such as employment guarantee and food for nutrition programmes.

— Introduce a National Food and Livelihood Security Act for the purpose of paying integrated attention to:

- Conservation of lands, water, forests, biodiversity and the protection of the atmosphere.
- Enchancing productivity through ecotechnologies.
- Improving distribution in order to eliminate endemic hunger.
- Maintenance of adequate food security reserves.
- Strengthneing the techno-infrastructure for better post-harvest technology and expanding the coverage of sanitary and phytosanitary measures, and
- Efficient research, education, extension, marketing systems both to take full advantage of emerging

opportunities in international trade and to ensure that research and extension designed to promote public good receive adequate support.

In 1993-94, the Planning Commission stated that only 18.96 per cent of the Indian people were below the poverty line. Now we are told that it is 40 per cent. A couple of shocking statistics, recently released by the National Council of Applied Economic Research (NCAER) provide a horrifying picture of where we are.

The first figure is that 39 per cent of India's population of nearly one billion remain under the poverty line, a number that has not changed in a decade. In real terms, this means a very large number of Indians have an earning capacity of a couple of chapatis. According to another survey by the NCAER, 37 per cent lof the country's rural population are landless and therefore unable to grow their own crop to put off hunger.

The second figure, less publicised but avilable from international agencies, is that food grains production is 1991 million tonnes in 1994-95 to 185 million tonnes in 1995-96 and in the case of wheat from 65.5 million tonnes to 62.6 million tonnes in same period. Unsurprisingly the worst shortfalls are in the politically volatile States of Uttar Pradesh and Bihar and yet the naked face of hunger continues to be maskedby the hypocrisy that India is a food grain exporter.

Apart from the rising poulation, agro-economists put forward a number of reasons for fall in food grain production, among them soil exhaustion and the larger number of landless that are concentrated in the States of UP, Bihar and eastern India. What they don't spell out is the endemic political instability and coruption these States, and the interminable cycle of fodder scams and caste wars, that are pushing the poor deeper into the poverty trap.

Economic reports do not point out that the agricultural ministry for many years has been managed by ministers, who only represent the narrow interests of wealthy landed farmers like themselves, and have no truck with the poor landless peasants.

The Ninth Plan will be an heir to the same hypocrisy despite agriculture being put on the top by all then nine objectives of the Plan.

Population time bomb: J. Gaur, a retired officer of Rajasthan government has a telling story about his visit to one of the villages of Dungarpur district. He was shocked to know from one of the poor schoolboys that he was served the family had ten members. This speaks volumes about our rural development and family planning programmes. The population clock outside the Capital's (Delhi) All-India Institute of Medical Sciences is galloping ahead but, for India's shoddy family planning programme, time has stood still.

The latest census data is proof, if any were needed, that we are sitting on a population time bomb. By 2040, India will be the world's most populous nation. In a situation where over 18 million—or six Singapores—are being added to the population every year, it can be of little comfort to learn that curde birth rates have declined from 34.7 per cent in 1991 or indeed that fertility levels have shown a negligible decrease of two per cent in that period. If the population has to stabilize at even a staggering 100 crore by 2001-2005, the average birth rate has to be reduced to two children per woman. But so far, only Kerala and Tamil Nadu have achieved this with Madhya Pradesh stated to do so only after 2060, Rajasthan by 2048, Bihar by 2039 and Uttar Pradesh by 2100. The government has confined itself to making tall claims about running a family planning campaign which is so "people oriented" that all targets have been removed.

The truth is that it is Central run and almost totally dependent on female sterilisation ignoring the variety of options which are available.

The desired goal of population as mentioned as one of the objectives of the Ninth Plan could be achieved only through the willing co-operation of the population and specially of the rural people. The magic words are 'literacy' and 'healthcare'.

There is no "political will" as is evident from the fact that no political party has cared to emphasize the need for some concrete steps to restrict population growth in their election manifestoes. There is no mention of family planning even in the Common Minimum Programme of the United Front government.

Education : It should be a matter of deep concern for every thinking Indian that after 45 years of the so-called planning, the country does not have a comprehensive education policy. This is despite the constitutional objective to provite universal primary education and eradication of funding, enormous sums have been wasted on subsidies and populist schemes from which money is easily diverted into the pockets of corrupt politicians and officials. Even in education, priorities have been misplaced. While primary and vocational education, which would improve the skills of the work force, have been neglected, money has been spent on creating an army of inadequately unemployable at various levels. The crying need of the hour is not elaborate plans but the 'political will' to act and innovate.

Development—real criteria : The late S.K. Dey, a Minister of State in Nehru's Cabinet once visited Tamil

Nádu. He met the late Kumarappa at Gandhi Niketan and with some pride of achievenment he claimed that the Community Development Programe was a grand success. Kumarappa was sharp to retort : "What is your scale for measuring the success of your projects? S.K. Dey answered by giving elaborate statistics of the miles of roads constructed, number of wells dug, school-buildings built, dispensaries opened, fertilizers distributed, improved seeds introduced, the manure pits constructed, and all the usual figures. Kumarappa looked doubtfully at S.K. Dey and said in a derisive voice, "this is your scale" and laughed. Pricked by Kumarappa's remarks, Dey asked, "what then is your scale of success?"

Kumarappa in a very emphatic tone said: "Mr Dey, before I cover an area with the Community Development Programme, I would select some six poor persons, count their ribs and if after three years (or five years) of implementing the C.D. Programme, there is some flesh to cover these ribs, thn I will call it a success". Dey was dismayed and implicitly accepted that his approach was defective. Kumarappa continued to say thay S.K. Dey was "trying to throw a silk shirt on a hungry person". The essentials of development are brought out in this one sentence. In other words, villages have developed and not the villagers.

Rich vocabulary : Kalia a poor villager at the time of India's Independence thought, he was poor. He was told he was not poor but needy. Then as to be called needy was self-defeating, he was addressed as deprived which was again changed to underprivileged. This term was also later changed to disadvantaged. Kalia said : "I have no dime or rupee yet but a rich vocabulary". He further said : "I have no idea of Five Year Plan". He was about 20 years of age at the time of India's Independence. Now he is about 70 years of age. In the last two-and -a-half decades, he was not able to eat chapatis with pulses. His earnings are so meagre that he is unable to afford prices to buy pulses for his family consisting of six members.

Against the per capita net availability of 501.9 gms of cereals the estimated consumption of cereals was of the order of 394 gms i.e. 78.6 per cent of the net availability. similarly in the case of pulses, per capita consumption was 28.05 gms. i.e. 75.8 per cent of net availability. Inequality in the consumption of foods among different income groups gets masked in the overall consumption estimates. Among the poor, nearly 80 per cent of consumption expenditure goes for food items. Recent surveys indicate:

- Percapita cereal consumption has declined over the years resulting in the aggregate energy intake of 1859 k.cal per capita as against 2200 k.cal recommended.
- 47.7 per cent of households have calorie inadequacy and 19.8 per cent of households have protein inadequacy. 19.5 per cent of households have both calorie and protein inadequacy.
- The exetent of moderate and severe growth retardation in preschool children varied from 34 per cent in Kerala to 72 per cent in Gujarat.
- 47 per cent of adults have body mass index value below 18.5 indicating large scale prevalance of chronic energy deficiency in the community.
- Haemoglobin levels among pregnant mothers reveal that as many as 87.5 per cent of mothers were anaemic.
- About 30 per cent of infants born had low birth weight.
- 167 million people are considered to be at risk for iodine deficiency disorders and 54 million have goitre.

- Preventable blindness due to Vitamin A deficiency still large.

Looking back the distance travelled and counting on various milestones towards food security, the country can be proud of some of the achievements so far. Yet the final milestone looks to be a long march. Shrinking arable land resources, soil degradation and depletion of nutrients from the soil, poor water management and unsustainable use of ground water, loss of momentum in the growth of food output, inefficient biological utilisation of the nutrients consumed due to poor environment and growing population are some of the problems the country faces in the march towards the final milestone of a hunger-free nation. The over-exploitation of the aquifer is also leading to the leaching of high levels of arsenic from natural underground sources into thousands of village wells in West Bengal. As estimated 200,000 people already have arsenic-induced skin lesions.

It is estimated that there are about 20 million species of poants, out of which 50,000 are edible. However, we are not using more than 200 plants as food, 80 per cent of our food supply however comes only from about eight species.

We are today laying much emphgasis on developing new varieties of these few plants. We should enlarge the food basket by including the excluded. Many nutritious grains fall under the classification "coarse grains". It is time we start referring to them as "nutritious grains". They are rich in micronutrients like Fe and Ca.

Seeing that between 75.0 and 80.0 per cent of the total expenditure at levels a little below the average is spent on food and its preparation, we might briefly examine the nutritional adequacy or otherwise of food at this level. In we show the per capita daily consumption of foodgrains and substitutes at different levels of expenditure.

As is to be expected, the consumption of foodgrains increases as we move from the poorest to the somewhat better. This occurs much more rapidly in rural area than in the urban area. In rural area, the per capita daily cosumption of foodgrains and substitutes reaches 616 grams for households with per capita monthly expenditure of Rs. 13-15 or per capita annual expenditure of Rs. 170.8. Calculating at the rate of 3.3 calories per gram of foodgrains (including substitutes), 616 grams of foodgrains give 2,033 calories per capita per day. As we have seen, this takes up nearly 60.0 per cent of the total consumer expenditure of these households. They spend another about 20.0 per cent on other items of food such as edible oil, ghee and butter, sugar and gur, and a little milk, meat and fish. The quantities of these items are rather small and they yield about 200 calories per capita per day.

Thus the entire food at this level seems to give about 2,250 calories per capita per day. Nutritional experts regard this as adequate under Indian conditions of climate, etc. It means that, in 1960-61, an annual per capita consumer expenditure of Rs. 170 was essential to give a diet adequate at least in respect of calories.

At consumer expenditure below this level, the diet was inadequate even in respect of calories. With reference to the population lying in monthly per capita expenditure classes Rs. 0-8, 8-11, 11-13 and half the population lying in the class Rs. 13-15 had per capita expenditure below this level. These classes add up to 33.123 per cent of the total rural population. Thus, in 1960-61, about one-third of the rural population lived on diets inadequate even in respect of calories.

Global action for sustainable food security

The commitment of the international community to ensure food and nutrition security to every child, woman and man on our planet has been reiterated at several international conferences held during this decade. Some of them are: World Summit for Children, New York (1990); International Conference on Nutrition (ICN, 1992), Rome; UN Conference on Environment & Development (UNCED, 1992), Rio de Janeiro; World Conference on Human Rights (WCHR, 1993), Vienna ; 1994 International Conference on Population & Development, (1994) Cairo ; UN Conference on Social Development (1995), Copenhangen ; World Food Summit (1996), Rome.

Despite such high level political reaffirmation of the need to achieve speedily the goal of "Food for All", over 800 million human beings now suffer from hunger and malnutrition. Hidden hunger, arising from the deficiency of the essential micronutrients is widespread. Endemic hunger is now more due to the lack of adequate income at the household level than due to the lack of food in the market. Both poverty as well as non-food factors such as environmental hygiene, sanitation and lack of safe drinking water are becoming major contributors of food insecurity at the level of communities and individuals. A majority of the food insecure live in Asia.

There is also increasing concern about the earth's capacity to produce adequate food for the growing population. The increase in human population, now mostly confined to the developing countries, coupled with enhanced purchasing power leading to greater capability to buy food and increasing urbanisation will lead to a higher growth rate in demand for food as well as more diversified food products in the coming millennium.

Thus, on the one hand, there will be need for intensification and diversification of agriculture, particularly in the developing countries, on the other, the ecological foundations essential for sustainable advances in crop and animal productivity are getting eroded. This situation has led to the ringing of alarm bells by experts concerning the earth's capacity to produce adequate food to meet growing needs. Lester Brown has concluded; "Constraints imposed by the earth's natural systems, the environmental degradation of land and water resources and the diminshing backlog of yield-raising agricultural technologies are slowing the growth in world food production, raising questions about the earth's population carrying capacity.

The earth's capacity to produce enough food to satisfy expanding demand is now emerging as the overriding environmental issue as the world approaches the 21st Century".

The year 1998 will mark the bicentenary of Malthus's essay on population. The onward march of science and technology, supported by appropriate public policies, has so far helped humankind to keep Malthusian forebodings on the population-food supply equation at bay. It is, however, becoming increasingly clear that without concerted national and global action to arrest environmental degradation, promote economic and gender equity and check population growth, the Malthusian spectre may still come true in the next century.

The Food and Agriculture Organisation of the United Nations (FAO) therefore, organised a World Food Summit in Rome from November 13 to 17, 1996.

At this Summit, a Rome Declaration on World Food Security and a World Food Summit Plan of Action were adopted.

The Declaration makes a commitment to reduce the number of undernourished people to half their present level no later than 2015. It also states:

"We will pusue participatory and sustainable food, agriculture, fisheries, forestry and rural development policies and practices in high and low potential areas which are essential to adequate and reliable food supplies".

"We will strive to ensure that food, agricultural trade and overall trade policies are conducive to fostering food security for all through a fair and market-oriented world trade system".

The Plan of Action includes the following seven commitments:

- Create an enabling political, social and economic environment designed to create the best conditions for the eradication of poverty, and for durable peace.
- Implement policies aimed at eradicating poverty and inequality and improving physical and economic access to sufficient, nutritionally adequate and safe food and its effective utilization.
- Pursue participatory and sustainable food, agriculture, fisheries, forestry and rural development policies and practices in high and low potential areas.
- Ensure that food, agricultural trade and overall trade policies are conducive to fostering food security for all.
- Prevent and be prepared for national disasters and man-made emergencies.
- Promote optimal allocation and use of public and private investments to foster human resources,

sustianable food agriculture, fisheries and forestry systems, and rural development, in high and low potential areas.

- Implement, monitor and follow-up the Rome Plan of Action at all levels in cooperation with the international community.

The above plan of action integrates the principles of (a) conservation of the ecological foundations essential for sustainable advances in agricultural productivity and production, (b) sustainable production through ecotechnologies and (c) equity in acces to food through an appropriate blend of national and international action in the area of entitlements and employment. The Science Academies Summit held in Madras in July, 96, recommneded that all nations may provide an overall public policy support to action at these three levels through the enactment of a National Food and Livelihood Security Act designed to achieve the following objectives:

- That every individual has the physical, economic, social and enviormental access to balanced diet that includes the necessary macro-and micronutrients, safe drinking water, sanitation, environmental hygiene, primary health care and education so as to lead a healthy and productive life.
- That food originates from efficient and environmentally benign production technologies that conserve and enhance the natural resource base of crops, animal husbandry, forestry, inland and marine fisheries.

The Chief Minister of Tamil Nadu, India in his budget speech delivered on July 17, 1996 made the following announcement.

Feed the people who are hungary Educate the people to uplift the World"

To fulfil this dream of Mahakavi Bharatiyar, this Government will launch a new "Hunger Free Area Programme" with an aim to eradicate poverty induced hunger. A number of schemes are already under implementation to alleviate poverty and to cater to the nutrition requirements of different groups of the population.

Gaps in this coverage will be identified which can then be specifically targeted under the Hunger Free Area programme. Preovision has been made in the Budget for preparing a detailed strategy to implement this programme in association with Dr. M.S. Swaminathan.

Studies at MSSRF have shown that by adding a horizontal dimension to numerous vertically structured programmes and by promoting a coalition of all concerned with ending hunger and deprivation, it is now possible to provide opportunities for a healthy and productive life for all.

The problem of food and nutrition security at the level of the individual has to be viewed in 3 dimensions. First,, inadequate purchasing power leads to calorie-protein under-nutrition. Second, the lack of the needed quantity and variety of micronutrients and vitamins in the diet leads to several nutritional disorders including blingness caused by Vitamin A deficiency.

This kind of problem is referred to as "hidden hunger", a problem which affects today more than 2 billion people in the world. Third, lack of environmental hygiene and sanitation leads to a low biological absorption and retention of food, due to intestinal infection and diarrohea. Thus, both food and non-food factors assume importance in determining the nutrition secu;rity of an individual. Concurrent action at all these levels is necessary in a Hunger-Free Area Programme. The various steps involved in this process are described below:

- Step No. 1: Identify the basic underlying reasons for chronic under and malnutrition.
- Step No. 2: Collate information on available programmes and opportunities for the sustainable end of hunger.
- Step No. 3: Articulate the steps needed to provide the 'missing elements' in achieving the end of hunger.
- Step No. 4: Mobilise local level community action and commiotment for achieving the end of endemic hunger by the end of the Ninth Five Year Plan and enlist mass media support for this purpose.
- Step No.5: Assess the extent of (i) Financial resources required (ii) Technical resources for technological empowerment necessary (iii) Managerial and Organisational resources needed.
- Step No. 6: Foster the organization of a Grassroots level Coalition for Ending Hunger in each HFAP area comprising representatives of

— Elected representatives of the people.

— Government agencies.

— Civil society-non-governmental organizations, voluntary agencies, services organizations like Rotary clubs, Lions clubs, etc.

— Academia-Research, Training Instituitons and Universities.

— Corporate Sector.

— Financial Institutions and

— Mass Media.

The Coalition for Ending Hunger will be responsible for designing, implementing and monitoring the Hunger Free Area programme.

Grasroots level action

The challenge lies in converting HFAP from a concept into an operational programme. In such a programme, emphasis will have to be placed during the remaining years of this century on generating additional livelihood opportunities for those living below the poverty line in villages and towns. The increasing feminisation of poverty demands that priority attention be given to women and girl children. Based on these considerations, the following operational framework is suggested for a National Hunger-Free Area Programme.

This phase will relate tot he analysis of gaps and constraints. Under the Gap Analysis Programme, an inventory will be made of all the entitlements currently available to those living below the poverty line both through the Central and State Government programmes. The inventory will be suitably classified so as to differentiate social security and nutrition intervention programmes from those relating to employment generation.

Once the Entitlements Database is compiled detailed study based on random sampling techniques will be conducted in about 100 villages of a district to assess the extent to which the entitlements have actually reached the intended families. Within families, special studies will be conducted to ascertain the extent of male-female differences in access to entitlements. The gap between what the poor are entitled to and what they are actually receiving will be grouped according to gender and economic status (I.E., those having assets like land or livestock or fish pond or tress and those who do not own any productive asset).

Once the GAP Analysis is completed, a careful identification of the reasons for the gap and the contrainsts faced by the pooring getting their entitlements will be made. Such a gap and constraints analysis will be the starting how direct and imdirect opverty elimination programmes can be made to reach the unreached organisationfunctioning in the villages including under the GAP Analysis would be made together with an assessment of their effectiveness in serving as bridges between Government agencies and the poor. Discussions will be held with both voluntary organizations and men and women members of elected Panchayats and Nagarpalikas on how the gap can be ended and how the delivery systems of poverty in thier efficiency and impact.

This phase will be a strategic planning phase giving particular attention to the following:

(a) Steps needed to fill the gap between entitlements and actual delivery.

(b) Opportunities for mobilising human, financial resources in the concerned areas for improving the efficiency of delilvery of on-going programmes and for initiating new programmes to meet the unmet minimum needs of the population.

(c) Identification of methods of achieving synergy and convergence among all the programmes, whether governmental or non-governmental.

(d) Articulation of new livelihood opportunities based on both farm and non-farm occupations.

(e) Introduction of organisational and management methods which will ensure the oversight and effective participation of the primary stake holders in the implementation of programmes designed to strengthen the security of their livelihoods, and

(f) Identification of young women and men in the concerned villages for forming a Corps of Hunger Fighters. The young hunger fighters would undertake responsibilities such as creating awareness of entitlements, improving delivery systems and promoting environmental hygiene and garbage and sewage recycling.

The hunger fighters would be given a small honorarium for meeting their travel and other expenses and for compensating them for thier time. The members of the Corps of Hunger Fighters will be drawn from those who have a social or economic stake in living in their respective villages. There will be equal number of women and men in such a corps.

As a result of the work done during phases 1 and 2, awareness of the possibilities for ending hunger and deprivation, analaysis of methods of achieving the desired goals and an implementable action plan would have emerged. The Action Programme, to be effective, must emerge from discussions with the poor families and on the basis of their suggestions. The phase will therefore be opportune to establish a broad based local level Coalition for Ending Hunger and Deprivation. Such a Coalition for Ending Hunger could consist of representatives of local self-government institutions, government agencies responsible for fighting poverty and hunger, academic community, the civil society, corporate sector, women's and youth organisations, financial institutions and the mass media. Such a coalition will assign specific tasks to each member of the coalition in the areas of awareness generation, resource mobilisation task implementation, monitoring and evaluation. The Coalition will aim to add a horizontal dimension zto vertically structured government programmes. Coalition members will also help to develop methods of achieving gender equality and eliminating social evils like dowery and alcoholism.

During ths period, HFAP will be converted from a desirable concept to anb implementable local level action plan. Intensive efforts will be made to sensitise all sections of the community to the uncommon opportunities now available for achieving a sustainable end to hunger. The poor themselves will play an active role in both the planning and implementation phase. Many of the members of the grassroots level Corps of Hunger Fighters will come from landless labour families. The Corps of Hunger Fighters will include elected members of Panchayats and Nagarpalikas, so that they are able to serve as links between the elected bodies and the people. There should be a minimum of two members of the corps drawn form every village/town, so that they are able to play a role in improving environmental hygiene and sanitation as well as the health and nutrition secutity of the families living in their village/town.

Ours is a land of the young. Nearly 400 million women and men are below the age of 21. The nation's future depends upon the opportunity they get for a productive and healthy life. Youth can be attracted and retained in farming only if farming becomes and economically rewarding. This is where ecological agriculture, which is knowledge intensive, can prove to be a double advantage.

Our society is characterised by cultural, religious, linguistic and political pluralism. Political pluralism at the level of the central government provides an opportunity for elevating issues relating to hunger elimination and poverty alleviation to a level of overriding priority, transcending political frontiers and placing them at the top of the political agenda.

The world Conservation Strategy has recommended greater public participation in planning and decision-making concerning the use of living resources and proposed environmental education programmes and campaigns to build support for conservation. The Panchayati Raj is institutionalization of public participation in planning and decisison-making in rural India. The following issues can be listed for capacity building in Panchayati Raj for environment protection and improvement.

Through Panchayati raj institutions are not directly linked with the Indian federal system, they are closely related with State governments. Most State government departments, particularly departments of agriculture, education, public health, forests and finance have close functional relationship with PRIs.

The activities of State governments may be broadly analysed as general administration, technical assistance in the fields ofpersonnel, financial assistance, correction of errors, excesses and negligences. State governments provide administrative guidance and advice to PRIs n problems and issues. The 73rd Constitutional Amendment Act 1992 has strengthened the organizational aspects of PRIs. The success or failure of the object of environment protection through PRIs would largely depend on administrative ability, leadership and motivation of personnel. It becomes even more significant because of the fact that administrative capability is an important means of converting programme inputs into outputs with economy and efficiency. The administrative and transforming quality of the leadership would significantly determine the administrative capability of the Panchayati Raj. The administrative capability involves the ability to mobilize, allocate and combine the actions that are needed to achieve the objectives of environment protection.

India is one of the few countries of the Third World which has enshrined in its Constitution a commitment to environment protection and improvement. The environment law ia a new division of law. Even though it appears to be of recent origin and yet it not a sudden creation. Many provisions dealing with the environment are scattered in pieces and found in different enactments.

The Environment (Protection) Act 1986 was enacted with the objectives of protection, regulation of the discharge of environment pollutants; handling of hazardous substances; speedy response in the event of accidents threatening environment safety and health. The World Conservation Strategy has suggested reviewing and strengthening of legislation concerning living resources to ensure that it provides sufficiently for conservation, paying particular attention to enforcement as also to remove loop holes. The lack of proper co-ordination and co-operation among the administrative institutions is an important loophole. A greater degree of co-ordination and co-operation between Central, State and local governments is needed for the implementation of environmental programmes.

The other important weakness of the legislative enactments is its lack of recognition of the crucial role that the PRIs can play. The involvement of PRIs as the eyes and ears of the government in terms of grass roots monitoring of environmental quality, needs to be duly recognized. In due course, as experience is gained, particularly with regard to the respective roles of PRIs, enactment of new legislation for environment protection could be considered.

Though PRIs are not sound in their organization for technical tasks and do not have technical and professional experts, decentralization below the State level ensures technical expertise of a high order required for environment protection and improvement in rural India.

The Ashok Mehta Committee on Panchayati Raj has asserted that technical assistance and organization of a high order is necessary to sustain the momentum. The State governments have the requisite competence in this regard and the decentralization process at the district level is now under way. When the process of administrative decentralization is already taking place, analysis of the changes, and the ensuring emphasis on development point to the need for democratic management or rural development below the State level so that the entire programme can be effectively implemented, co-ordinated and supervised.

The inescapable conclusion is that the first point of decentralization should be at the district level. District heads of sufficient competence are already stationed here. Their capabilities ae also being upgraded. The district is also traditionally a unit of administration to which all are acclimatized. Further, it is the key planning unit for evolving the overall strategy, resource allocation including credit and the delineation of the different types of projects.

The establishement of a strong Panchayat tier at the district level appears to respond both to the organizational needs within district and the demands of emerging links with the State.

Despite the emphasis on the active role to be played by PRls, they were not, much effective in the past. A number of efforts were undertaken to bring forward the Constitution Amendment Bill 1992, to provide constitutional status to Panchayati Raj bodies and to strengthen them by making suitable provisions for this durability, continuity, adequate representation to all the sections of society and financial allocations.

The Act has empowered the State legislatures to authorize the Panchayats to levy, collect, and appropriate suitable local taxes and also provide for making grants-in-aid to the Panchayats from the Consolidated Fund of the State. In addition, a Finance Commission has to be constituted once in every five years to review the financial position of the Panchayats and make suitable recommendations to the State on the distribution of the funds between the State and the local bodies.

The Central Finance Commission shall also suggest measures necessary to augment the Consolidated Fund os a State to suppliment the resources of the PRIs in the State. Thus, a large amount of assured funds will flow to the PRIs involvement in environment protection and improvement.

In rural India, all the life support systems are now under serious stress and strain. Both human and animal population pressures have reached a level where the flora, fauna, soil and water and also atmospheric conditions are getting more and more depleted and pollutted. Consequently, in a predominantly agricultural country, the renewable base of land resources has been eroded and environmental degradation has taken place in the name of development. The Panchayati Raj institutions have existed for long in India, but these institutions have not been effective in environment protection and improvement. Against this backdrop, the 73rd Constitution Amendment Act assumes greater importance. Now it will no more be possible for any State government to fiddle with these institutions, as has been the case in the past. The continuation of these institutions will automatically result into strengthening of both horizontal and vertical linkage with the administration at different levels. This, in turn, will provide these institutions an opportunity to play their legitimater role in environment protection and improvement. Besides this, PRIs can play an educative role in environmental matters for younger generation as well as adults, with due consideration to the underpriviledged. This is essential in order to broaden the basis for an enlightened opinion and responsible conduct by individuals, enterprises and communities in protecting and improving the environment in its full human dimension.

Integrating environemntal considerations into development planning is not an easy task. Unless concern is backed by an ability to take ameliorative action, little can be achieved. India has been very conscious of this and has, over the past few decades, taken important steps to increase its capacity to handle environmental issues.

The initiatives have come equally from the Government, NGO's and individuals. Many collaborative and joint programmes exist today between the Government and the NGO's.

Environment and development problems are complex and there cannot be generalized and simplified solutions. Answers have to be found which are ecologically, economically and socio-culturally consistent in the particular milie. Given the size and diversity of a country like India, this task becomes extremely difficult.

Expertise is requied in framing appropriate policies and legislation, in planning, in creating mechanisms for implementation, in education and public awareness. India also needs to be above to bring its perspective to global forums and participate in evolving international treaties, protocols and conventions. Most importantly, with the increasing emphasis on decentralized decision—making and the stress on micro-planning, this capacity-building is taking on a greater urgency. Capability is required to enable decisions to be made in a decentralized manner—decisions which are not imported solutions, but are appropriate to the particular situation.

Addressing the plenary session of the UN Conference on Human Environment in Stockholm in 1972, Prime Minister Indira Gandhi and said, "Even though our industrial development is in its infancy and at its most difficult stage, we are taking various steps to deal with the incipient environmental imbalances, more so because of our concern for the human species, whic is also imperilled." It was at her initiative that a National Council Environmental Planning and Coordination (NECPC) was set up in 1972 to identify and investigate the problems of preserving or improving the human environment in the country, and to propose solution to environmental problems.

Another Empowered Committee, the Tiwari Committee, was set up in 1980 to review and recommend legislative measures and administrative machinery for ensuring environmental protection. On the recommendation of this Committee, the Department of Environment was set up in 1980 as the focal agency in the administrative structure of the Central Government for planning, promotion and coordination of environmental programmes. This department became part of the new Ministry of Environment and Forest in 1985.

The Ministry is the apex body under the Government of India for planning, promotion and coordination of environmental and forestry programmes. Its activities include conservation and survey of flora and fauna, prevention and control of pollution, afforestation and regeneration of degraded areas, impact assessment, forest conservation and research, and education and information. The National Wastelands Development Board and the Ganga Project Directorate are major components of the Ministry.

Most of the states have also set up their own Departments of Environment, Pollution Control Boards and other associated bodies. Various other ministries and departments, including those of Urban Development, Oceanography, Non-Conventional Energy Sources etc., at the state and central levels, are also concerned with different aspects of the environment. Greater coordination among these various agencies—government and non-government-would strengthen environmental efforts. State Governments are in the process of involving themselves seriously in environmental planning.

The Directory of Environmental NGOs, brought out by the World Wide Fund for Nature - India (WWF-I) in 1989, lists about 850 NGOs working in this field, but there are porbably at least four times this number. Their involvement is clearly seen. As the Secretary General of WWF-I says, "India's impressively large body of NGOs is becoming active on the environmental front because fo the increasingly clear nexus between meaningful, equitable, sustainable economic growth and the conservation of the environment.

For instance, the National Environmental Awareness Campaign promoted by the Ministry has successfully encouraged many NGOs whose primary concerns are rural development, appropriate technology, civil rights, women's development, tribal welfare etc. The interaction between NGOs and State Governments is largely confined to functional matters (clearance, information, advice etc.) whereas for financial and technical support various central departments and agencies have to be relied upon. However now there is a concerted effort by the Government to use their expertise for their own programmes."

NGOs range from clubs which encourage and assist in adventure travel, exploration, and dissemination of knowledge about an ecosystem to agencies which deal with various issues like creating gainful employment, wastelands development, afforestation, rehabilitation of tribals, and with preparation of educational materials and aids. They may be as small as groups of two or three persons, or as large as organizations with an eight-thousand-strong membership.

One of the most important signs of environmental awareness in India is the rise of people's movements which are challenging existing socio-political structures and development models, and are showing alternative paths. These have led not only to action at the grassroot level, but are also helping to shape developmental policies.

If Volunteer Service is as old as manking, its use as a tool in international development is relatively new. Within the United Nations, its importance was first officially recognised in 1961 in a resolution passed by the United Nations Economic and Social Council (ECOSOC).

In 1969 the subject came before ECOSOC again: this time the UN Secretary General was requested to explore the possibility of creating an international volunteer programme. The following year, Secretary General U.Thant, formally recommended that such a programme be launched: and on December 7, 1970 the Un General Assembly passed resolution 2659 (XXV) calling for the creation of the United Nations Volunteer (UNV) programme.

UNV is the world's unique multinational volunteer-sending organisation and has become one of the United Nations' foremost suppliers of middle and upper level specialist—professionals who work with national and international personnel in over a hundred developing countries in Africa, Asia, the Pacific, Central and Latin America, the Caribbean and the Arab States.

The most important objective of the programme, which came into operation in 1971 was to mobilise dedicated, skilled volunteers as an alternative source of technical cooperation, personnel capable of assisting developing countries in achieving these development objectives.

The aim of the programme is also to favour the development of domestic development services and to promote grassroots development activity based on a participatory process. Moreover, its objectives is to undertake operational activities promoting the active involvement of youth in development. Besides, it aimed at providing more people throughout the world with the opportunity to use their dedication and talents for the cause of development in countries other than their own and upon, returning home, to share their enhanced knowledge and experience with others.

The overall responsiblity for UNV was given to the United Nations Development Programme (UNDP). An executive coordinator directs UNV's activities and is responsible for promoting, managing and developing the programme.

UNV works closely with UN agencies involved in development and humanitarian cooperation, such as FAO, ILO, UNESCO, UNHCR, UNICEF, UNIDO, WFP and WHO. In their country of assignment, UNVs work in projects executed by the government by one or other UN agencies, or by the UN itself. In the respective country, UNC specialists and flied workers benefit from the general back stopping of the UNDP Resident Representative. The UNDP field office also provides logistic and administrative support for them, in most cases with the assistance of a UNV Programme officer.

There are more than 2000 qualified, experienced and motivated women and men of over 100 nationalities currently serving in developing countries as volunteer specialists and field workers. A further 6,000 who completed their assignments in UNV are themselves citizens of developing countries; one fifth coming from the industrialized world.

They work in technical, economic and social fields, under three main headings—in technical cooperation with skills—short governments, with community based initiatives for self—reliance, humanitarian relief and rehabilitation. They are professionals who work on a peer basis. They listen and talk. They encourage and facilitate. They share and exchange ideas, skills and experience. They teach and train. They care.

The UNV programme involves a number of sectors: it maintains a roster covering 115 professional categories. Agriculture, health and education feature prominently, as do social conditions, community development, vocational training, industry, transport and population. Humanitarian relief and rehabilitation count for some 10% of assignments.

Over the years, they have served in more than 130 countries. Tiday, half are at work in Africa, a third in Asia and the Pacific, the remainder are to be found in the Arab States, the Caribbean, Central and South America, and with new programmes in Central and Eastern Europe. Nearly three quarters serve in the world's poorest nations—the least developed, the land locked and the Small Island economies.

Half work outside capital cities, frequently in remote towns and villages. This is in response to expressed needs, and it reflects the commitment which volunteers bring. Included here are the field workers serving at grassroots level within UNV's Participatory Development (or 'DDS'—Domestic Development Service) Programmes in Asia/Pacific and Africa. These are practitioners with excellent track records in village level community animation; they exchange skills and knowledge among countries of these regions.

The great majority of the finance comes from country and regional funds provided by UNDP. Other significant sources include the regular programme budgets of UN agencies, contributions from host governments, special purpose grants by donor governments, and the UNV Special Voluntary Fund. The average annual outlay on a UNV specialist assignment is some 20–25% that of comparable technical personnel working on market terms. Budgeting for field workers is based on local grass roots comparators.

Critical issues

Faith in & Use of Selection Procedure : The massive publicity and tremendous thrust given by the Government coupled with the increasing unemployment among educated youth caused in influx of seminal enthusiastic individuals to take up entrepreneurial career.

Enthusiasm creates a complex problem for the support agencies in the matter of choice of individuals to given necessary support for enterprise launching and management. There is always a danger by supporting those who are not genuinely interest but have been attracted to the support programme for many other reasons. The resources used for developing such persons by way of investment on training etc. often go waste. Besides being wastage of scarce resources, the wrong selection may also contribute to the volume of entrepreneurs facing closure and sickness.

Therefore, there is a need for choosing right type of people to be given support facilities. A three-tier system commonly used for selection purpose includes "the analysis of application blanks"; psychological tests and group planning exercises"; and "personal interview". Presently each of the above areas are given different weightage by different organisation. Also there is variation in selection of psychological tests, games and exercises for selection purposes. The standardising of such selection procedures requisites longitudinal studies spread overt long period of investigations. The administrators generally do not support such longitudinal studies. Since empirical evidences are lacking many organisations avoid conducting selection tests or apply a non-standard procedure as per their convenience (some time which). This erode the quality of EDP and may endanger even its credibility in the long run.

Inadequate Information : Industry specific information play vital role in selecting, designing and deciding the size of units, and market strategy. The inadequate information prevents entry into an Entrepreneurial venture. The lack of information also contribute considerably to the wrong decision resulting into sickness. Often the healthy units also have been reported stagnating format of appropriate information.

Problems are acute and the national organisation set up for collection, storage and dissemination of such informationm may require heavy reinforcement or even decentralisation at lower level. The existing network of industrial information is proving the major hurdle in accelerating the process of entrepreneurship develoment.

Transfer of Technology : Technology is fast changing. What is new technology today is likely to be obsolete in next five years. It is more true in case of the technology adopted by small entrepreneurs in general. With a change in technology, the unit loses its capabilities of competitiveness.

Subsequently, entrepreneurs are continuously worried about the product development in given period of time but their access to latest technology is very poor. Many of them do not have internal R&D and trade totally dependent on the technology/processes developed elsewhere. The urgency, however, is often not appreciated by research staff of technical institutes/ centres of excellence. This is one of the major hurdles in promoting Hi-Tech small industry. Mere physical proximity between researchers and industrialists may not necessarily eliminate the barriers which inhibit the meaning full interaction resulting into development and flow to technology. This issue requires continues attention an innovations in formulating strategy for the development quick flow and transfer of appropriate technology to the small entrepreneurs.

Effective Training : The human factor refers to the attitude, desire and motivation of individual, his capability to perceive the environment change and opportunities as well as his ability to solve the problem which an entrepreneurs is likely to fact.

The training is effective in developing all these aspects of human factor provided it is planned well with balanced emphasis on all aspects. An analysis of the development process that helps emergence of people opting for entrepreneurial career in the society and succeeding in setting and running self-employment activites, reveals that it follow a sequence of development in individual personality, capability and ability.

The first generation of entrepreneur requires to develop:

- Entrepreneurial quality/motivation;
- Capability for enterprise launching/motivation;
- Ability for enterprise management; and

- Sense of responsibility to the society that promote/ support them.

These aspects related to individual behaviour, abilities and capabilities follow the logical sequence of development which ultimately drive prospective entrepreneurs to actual entrepreneurial career.

The training has been the common component of most of entrepreneurial development programmes conducted by various organisations. Of course training conducted by these organisations vary in terms of their duration, content and methodology. Probably depending on the availability of faculty and orientation of the organising agencies, the emphasis shift towards one or the other. Training varies in methodology as well.

Of late, the efforts have been made to standardise such training by evolving 'Model Syllabi' for entrepreneurship development training at national level. But the issue related to standardisation of training in order to achieve the desired result is still alive to ensure the minimum standard.

Management Consultancy : The growth in number of small business is very rapid all over the world. But the percentage of small business unit facing closure or sickness are growing significantly. One of the every 12 units started in US is facing closure every year.

In India, according to the data available with the RBI, the number or sick units during 1982 was as high as 50,549 out of 10,44,405 units claiming 5.6% SSI units becoming sick. The Reserve Bank of India defines a unit as sick if "it has incurred cash loss for one year and in the judgment of the bank is likely to continue to incur such losses for the current year as well as the following year and which has imbalance in its financial structure such as, current ratio of less than 1:1 and worsening debt equity ratio (total outside liabilities to the net worth)".

According to the diagnostic study of a sample conducted by the Development Commissioner (SSI) India, the major causes of sickness are:

- 30% due to shortage of working capital/inadequacy and untimely assistance from the banks.
- 22% due to scarcity of raw-material.
- 13% due to lack of demand.
- 10% due to management deficiencies.

No account has been given for the remaining 25% except for the first case which explains for 30% sickness, the remaining factors can be broadly attributed to the management functions.

Even if certain percentage is assigned to environmental factors, beyond the control of the owner/ manager of small business, considerable percentage of sickness appears to emerge from management inadequacies. Moreover, against the great potential of further growth and graduating small business to medium & large industry, the majority of small business units beyond large are found stagnating with same level of operation.

The dominant factors may be the lack of management insight & competency. The great growth potential demand greater emphasis to devise content and methodology for management education, training and consultancy.

Most of the modern management techniques have been developed for the use of large business establishments. Theoretically and in principle these hold good also to small business management. But their scale of operation and the need of specialist for their application appear to be the major bottleneck in the use of such management techniques in small business management. This suggests testing and adaptation of such management practices.

Capital-A Critical Resource : The small entrepreneurs is up against considerable odds, when he goes out looking for funds either fixed or variable capital financing. This is not because the finances are not available or schemes have not formulated for meeting varieties of need for capital financing. India is probably one of those countries which have multiple schemes launched by various financial institutions under the leadership of IDBI. Although various schemes have been instituted, they are all functioning at a sub-optimal level.

The kind of venture capital support that is needed to nurture and sustain small technologically innovative and dynamic business is perhaps not present in most of the developing countries.

The another hurdle in raising capital financing by small entrepreneurs more often arise out of the comparison with medium and large industries. In a comparison to medium and large industries small entrepreneurs are often very helpess in providing assets and security which on paper, not required but in practices never ignored. Again for the purpose of industrial growth and rehabilitation of sick units the necessary funds should flow fast.

For sustaining entrepreneurship, the capital financing requires that the officials belonging to both industrial extension system and financial institutionms develop comprehensive understanding of health of industrial untis, posses diagnostic skill to assess the health and acquire counselling skill to influence needy SMI to implement remedial growth measures and above all develop favourably attitudes towards extension approach which is basically opposite to the concept of a donor.

Points of Caution : Entrepreneurship Development has been found a forceful movement to fight the acute problem of growing unemployment. When it has been attempted sincerely and systematically, it has yielded very rewarding results. In the past, many mistakes have been committed as a part of 'hit and miss' trial methods. The success is bound to be there provided we formulate strategy by understading the concept, process and techniques of developing entrepreneurship.

One area of caution is also necessary to understand the similarity and distinction between entrepreneurship and self-employment. All entrepreneurs are self-employed but all self-employed are not necessarily entrepreneurs. The tendency to ignore such differences may make the strategy weaker.

A diluted strategy for developing entrepreneurship may result in failure and consequently the task of piece-rate-workers. Both may be necessary and useful at different stages but should be attempted with clear-cut distinctions and omitting the confusion by titling the programme differently.

Middle-class families (middle-income group) seem to be the direct benefitciaries of EDPs. This group is important in terms of both number and influencing public opinions. In the course of developing entrepreneurship, the supply of inputs (including finance) plays a crucial role. Instead of treating such inputs as development requirements, there may be a tendency to use them as a means to earn favour. There may be temptation to politicize the whole movement.

The entrepreneurship movement which started in India, in mid sixties have proved its potential. Now the dynamics and methodology are clear, strategies are more or less standardised. The scope and coverage, however, is so vast and widespread that the movement requires active involvement and enthusiasm of all the government voluntary organisations and social reformer. Through entrepreneurship, it is possible to build new economic order with progressive socio-psychological make-up.

It is evident from the above discussion that the Panchayats have been denied the possibility of carrying out participatory planning for local development at the grass roots level. This vacuum has been filled by the voluntary efforts of the people with the participation of intellectuals and voluntary network organizations like the Kerala Sastra Sahitya Parishad, Bharat Vigyan Samithi. The results of their efforts have been remarkable. In the field of literacy, the "Erankulam model" is acclaimed across the world and replicated elsewhere in India.

The alphabet literacy has provided a sound base for a mass initiative in the field of environment protection, gender equality and women's empowerment. Thus social development in Kerala has been the contribution of an awakened and vigilant public.

Majumdar (1995) rightly observed that "The enlightened and politically conscious electorate in Kerala closely monitors the functioning of schools, including those in the rural areas. Here, cases of shirking on the part of teachers evoke strong collection protest (e.g. many such cases are immediately publicised through posters in public places), and as a corollary, elicit appropriate policy responses.

The expansion of literacy has given a sound base for participatory planning which has successfully been operationalised in Kalliasseri Panchayat in Kannur district of the State.

The Community Development Society (CDS), with its thrift and credit activities, has improved the lot of poor women in urban Kerala. The Alappuzha CDS is an example, where "poor women have mobilized up to Rs. 37 lakh from their own savings. In two years, the Alappuzha CDS has generated more than 4,000 jobs ensuring 100 per cent loan recovery and repayment to banks as on date". Due to this exemplary work, the Alappuzha model has received "We the People Award" in 1994 from the United Nations.

Although Kerala could not provide a successful model for participatory planning through Panchayats due to political instability, its people, with the help of dedicated voluntary organizations have offered one. The other States could benefit from its success stories in participatory planning.

We have seen that Panchayats in Kerala have not become a viable and pulsating institution for ensuring participatory planning. The prime mover in this sphere has been the voluntary sector, But after the 73rd Constitutional Amendment which, among other things, has ensured regular elections to the Panchayats and reservation of seats as well as of posts of Chairpersons for the weaker sections at all the tiers, they have to assume this role. The elections to these institutions were also held last year.

The People's Campaign for the formulation of the Ninth Plan has also been launched in the State for making decentralized Planning the key input in preparing the State Plan. All these efforts on the part of the State government are in the right direction. But the main question is whether the Panchayats have really emerged as institutions of self-government (as envisaged in Article 243 G of the Constitution) to help materialize participatory planning.

As mentioned earlier, the two important dimensions of the people's participation are: who are the people and how would the participation occur. The answer to the first question is given by M.A. Oommen (1991) while discussing the formulation of a methodology for district planning with people's participation in Kannur district where he says, by people we mean those below the poverty line. The poor people, including other marginalized sections of society, have been statutorily given berth in Panchayats. The second question is also answered by constituting the Panchayats in the State.

But the most important question regarding realization of the objective of participatory planning is whether people enjoy autonomy in their actions.

In other words, whether the various provisions of the State Panchayat Act establish Panchayats as an Institution of Self-government (ISG), i.e. whether they have institutional existence, institutional capacity and financial viability. Therefore, the question discussed in this part of the paper is whether the various provisions of the Kerala Panchayat Act enable Panchayats to usher in participatory planning. And if not, what amendments need to be made.

Planning is not only an instrument of economic growth but it is accepted by all that it is an instrument of social integration. Indian society consists of many social groups both in caste, community and ethnic terms. During the national movement it was realized that political mobilization has to be done in the context of the castes and community terms. That is why Gandhi is known as a political fold. Their participation fold. Their participation in the political movement brought their economic and social needs into sharp focus. Any planning has to recognize their needs.

As such, the Indian Donstitution has recognized these social groups. They are socially and economically backward. They do not have access to modern education and social services. Planning as a concept was developed during the national movement. The democratic experiment of India has to take into account the needs of SCs/STs and the OBCs. It is mandatory.

New dimensions

Planning is an integral part of our political culture. Strengthening democracy is possible with planning,. Planning accepts the role of State in the market economy. The role of the State is to reduce the regional disparity. It is to reduce the income disparity between various sections of our society. Liberalization process has restricted the role of the State in the area of industrialization.

The private capital is today strong enough to stand on its own feet. Withdrawing the State from economic activities is a welcome step. But historical experience of the Third World countries show that the first decade of economic liberalization generated lot of economic distress. The approach paper to the Ninth Five Year Plan document has recognized this new development.

First, the regional disparity between poorer regions and richer areas has increased. Regional disparity has created already a lot of political mobilization on ethnic line.

Secondly, investment in agriculture has slowed down during this phase which sustains a majority of our people to earn their livelihood. Even after 50 years of industrialization, our agriculture is not self-sustaining. It needs State intervention for its growth.

The lack of agricultural growth has reduced the employment opportunities that is reflected in the rise of unemployment and underemployment in rural India and which has pushed them to overcrowd the cities. As a result, it has increased urban poverty. Both rural and urban poverty have a close relationship.

Thirdly, urban areas are facing the crisis, in terms of providing drinking water and sanitation where the urban poor are living.

Fourthly, the decade of economic liberalization has increased the number of poor, people below the poverty line. Who are these poor people in the rural areas and urban slums? They are nobody except the people from the SCs/STs and the lower OBCs. These social classes are today the worst victims of the economic process.

The approach paper to the Ninth Plan has looked into the factors explained in the above paragraphs. It demands the reorientation of the State role and definite thrust on the poverty alleviation and employment generation without which the poor are going to distrust the democratic system. Once alienation of these communities from the system starts growing, then the system itself is going to be vulnerable.

The Kerala Panchayat Act is full of provisions which empower the State government to interfere with impunity in the functioning of the Panchayats. These provisions have not created and enabling environment for participatory planning. They are as follows:

- Section 159 (1) of the Act empowers the State to remove the democratically elected Chairperson, and Vice-Chairpersons of the various Standing Committees on certain grounds.
- As per Section 161 (8) of the Act, the copies of the minutes of every meeting of a Panchayat shall be forwarded within 48 hours by the Secretary either to the government or its authorised officer. This is

against the spirit of decentralization. What is the rationale for sending these minutes to the State authorities? This may be repealed as it will unnecessarily increase the burden of the secretary's work without any gain.

- Section 188 of the Act empowers the government and its officials to call for any record of Panchayats for verification, audit or examination. Section 190 empowers the government to direct the Panchayats to perform their responsibilities properly. The government can by an order fix a period for the performance of such duties. Similarly, Section 191 empowers the State government to cancel or suspend any resolution adopted by the Panchayat. The State government as per Section 193 can dismiss popularly elected Panchayats if they do not perform their duties properly.
- The Act empowers the State government to make rules and by-laws to carry out all or any purpose of this Act (Section 254). The State government, instead of making rules and bye-laws, may prepare model rules with flexibility which the Panchayats can modify keeping in view their requirements.
- The State government can delegate powers enjoyed by the VP, BP and DP to an authorized officer (Section 275). It means powers given to Panchayats by one hand can be taken back by another. Section 278 militates against Section 156 because as per the former, "executive functions of the President be construed as a reference to the Secretary of the village Panchayat," while as per the latter Section, the Chairperson is the executive head of the Panchayat. Thus Section 278 may have to be repealed.
- As per section 282, disputes between Panchayats

> will be referred to government officials. This Section should be amended to provide for referring disputes between Panchayats to the next higher tier of Panchayat.

Thus, a number of provisions in the Act are retrograde and reduce Panchayats to an agency of the State government. In order to ensure proper control with adequate safeguards over them, the following suggestions are made.

To establish an organic relation between and among the three tiers of the Panchayat Raj system for participatory planning, the VP should work under the direction of the BP and the BP should work under whose direction the DP. Now the question arises under whose direction the DP should work. Sometimes, due to political reasons, the upper tier of Panchayat may misuse its authority. The following measure is suggested to prevent such misuse.

A body under the chairpersonship of a person, qualified to be a judge of the High Court and comprising the representatives of the VP, BP and as members to be nominated by the government may be constituted. This body may handle all the cases relating to abuse accounts and other issues relating to decentralized governance.

The idea here is that Panchayats should in real sense emerge as an institution of self-government without any threat of political onslaught.

Participatory planning denotes people's involvement from initiation to the completion of the Plan. It is an indivisible concept as it encompasses people's participation in decision-making, implementation of the decision, sharing of the benefits and evaluation and monitoring of the plan. Thus, people's particulation has to be threaded like warp and woof in every stage of planning.

According to the Working Group on District Planning (1984), participatory planning has three dimensions: nature of the participation, participants and the way of participation.

The answers of the first two, i.e. the nature of the participation and who should participate, are based on the dictum "people plan and the government supports". The Panchayats are the institutions through which participation occurs. Thus, the whole concept of participatory planning depends on the extent of the autonomy of the people.

The objectives of the present paper are: (i) to review the role of the Panchayats in Kerala in a historical perspective with a view to examining the extent to which they have succeeded in ensuring people's participation in planning. (ii) to evaluate the role the community and the voluntary sectors have played in creating an environment for participatory planning in the State, and (iii) after critically reviewing the Kerala Panchayat Act, suggest changes in it so that it facilitates people's actions.

While examining the last question, a comparison of the Kerala Act with other State Acts has also been made.

The State of Kerala was formed in November 1956 by merging the Travancore, Cochin and Malabar regions to create a single State. Since its formation, the State has had a chequered history in the sphere of democratic decentralization. In April 1957, the first leftist government led by E.M.S. Namboodiripad was installed in the State. It introduced the Kerala Panchayat and District Council Bills in the Assembly. But these Bills could not become law as the government was dismissed on 31 July, 1959 by the Centre.

The succeeding government headed by Pattom Thanu Pillai, however, succeeded in enacting three Bills, the Kerala Panchayat Raj Act, 1960, the Kerala Municipalities Act, 1961. These Acts not only unified the laws in operation in the Malabar, Travancore and Cochin regions, but also enhanced the functional and financial autonomy of the local government institutions.

In 1964, the Kerala Panchayat Union Council and Zilla Parishad Bills, modelled on the recommendations of the Balwantray Mehta Committee report, were introduced in the State Assembly by the next government. These too could not be enacted due to the fall of the government.

In March 1967, the CPI-M government headed by E.M.S. Namboodiripad again introduced a Bill called the Kerala Panchayati Raj Bill 1967 in the Assembly which envisaged a two-tier system of Panchayati Raj at the village and the district levels and induction of an organic link between the two tiers by putting the Gram Panchayat under the supervision and control of Zilla Panchayat. This Bill was referred to a Select Committee which recommended substantial amendments in it. It enabled the district level institution to function as the district government. But it could also not become law as the State Assembly was dissolved in August 1970.

In 1971, the government headed by C. Achutha Menon came forward with the Karala District Administration Bill the Select Committee set up in 1968 to consider the 1967 Bill. This Bill also could not become law. In August 1978, the A.K. Antony Ministry introduced the Kerala District Administration Bill in the Assembly. But this Bill was passed by the Legislature during the Chief Ministership of the CPI leader P.K. Vasudevan Nair and got the Presidential assent in May 1980 when the office had passed into the hands of the CPI-M leader, E.K. Nayanar, who incidentally holds the reins at present. But this could also not be implemented as the Ministry fell in 1981. The government however, commissioned a study on the shortcomings in the Act. This study was undertaken by a senior IAS officer, V. Ramachandran.

In May 1982, a new government assumed office but it did not demonstrate the necessary political will to strengthen Panchayati Raj in the State. In 1987, the Left Democratic Front (LDF) government led by E.K. Nayanar again came to power. It implemented, although not fully, the recommendations of the Ramachandran report on the measures to be taken in democratic decentralization at the district and lower levels, which was submitted in July, 1988.

This government also did very little for strengthening Panchayati Raj in the State, because at that time every political party was afraid of decentralization as V. Ramachandran (1995) had observed: "A fear has taken hold in the State that there was voodoo about decentralization in Kerala as every government, overcoming this fear showed political courage and announced elections to the District Councils in December, 1990. For the first time in the history of the State, District, Councils came into being in February 1991.

The provision of reservations for SCs, STs and women made in the Act enabled these marginalized sections of the society participate in the development process. The results of the elections held for the councils revealed that the share of SCs and STs in their total membership was 17 per cent. This was much higher than the ratio of their population in the State. The percentage of the SCs and STs in the total population in the State was 10.02 and 1.02, respectively. The LDF captured 13 out of the total 14 District Councils. The reservation for the marginalized sections of rural society in the District Councils gave them a Panchayat to enable them to participate in the system of decentralized governance and development.

But this welcome process could not be sustained for long as fresh elections to the State Assembly along with the parliamentary election were held in June 1991. In these elections, the LDF government law replaced by the United Democratic Front (UDF) regime led by K. Karunakaran. The first step this government took was to amend the District Administration Act, 1979. The amended Act made provision of appointing a junior officer as Secretary of the Council in place of the Collector who was its ex-officio Secretary under the original Act.

The State government was also empowered to amend, delete or add to the powers and functions devolved to the Councils. In nutshell, the District Council was reduced merely to an agency of the State government.

The village Panchayats (VP) in the State also have a poor track record. It only in 1963 that had their first elections with the second after a long spell of more than one and a half decade in 1979 and the third in 1988. After the expiry of the term of the elected representatives, the government officials have been made their administrators. The latest elections to the Panchayats (i.e. VP, BP, DP) were held last year after an amendment of the State's Panchayat Acts in accordance with the Constitution (73rd Amendment) Act, 1992.

It can be seen that the Panchayats in the State have not yet become vibrant institutions for enabling the people to participate in local development. The factors responsible for this plight of these institutions, among others are the vested interests, i.e. the political leaders and bureaucrats who have not been interested in parting with powers in favour of the Panchayats. The LDF, which wanted to make the Panchayats the fulcrum for participatory planning could not succeed fully as its governments had fallen for one reason or the other. Otherwise, an enlightened and articulate public coupled with land reforms could have made panchayats a sound base for people's involvement in planning.

That is why M.A. Oommen (1991) commented that "Kerala is probably on State where people's participation should be strong and successful given the level of literacy. However, the progress made, has been very poor".

Not giving membership to MPs and MLAs in Panchayats, not tampering with the VP and Block Panchayats (BPs) boundaries for the membership of the BPs and the District Panchayat, (DP) respectively and making the Chairpersons of the lower tier members of the immediate upper tier for establishing an organic link among them are welcome features of the State Act, which should also be emulated by other States.

But there are certain features of the Act which need to be amended as they are against the spirit of the Central Act and participatory planning. These are:

- In Chapter II of the Act, reorganization of the boundaries of the wards of Panchayats has been vested in the State government, which is against the provisions of Articles 243 k and 243 O of the Constitution. All functions pertaining to the delimitation of boundaries, including disputes between or among Panchayats, should be performed by the State Election Commission.
- A provision for reservation of OBCs should also be made in the Act to enable them to participate effectively in decentralized governance.
- The election of the Chairperson of the VP should be

made direct as is the case in most States. In this way, the Chairperson will be able to draw authority from the people. Besides making Chairpersons accountable to the people, this will also strengthen the institution of the GS.

- To provide more space for weaker sections to participate in planning and development, the reservation for SCs, STs, OBCs and women should be extended to include the post of Vice-Chairperson of different tiers. At present, Punjab is the only State where such a provision has been made at the intermediate and apex tiers. Kerala may do well to go one step further and provide reservation for these sections at all tiers of the Panchayats.
- As per Section 151 of the Act, if the government is satisfied that a Panchayat at any level cannot be constituted for certain reasons, like failure to elect the majority of the members, it can appoint an Administrative Committee consisting of at least the elected members and a President and Vice-President, or appoint a special officer for period not exceeding six months. This provision is against the spirit of the Constitution. If such an eventuality arises, only the elected representatives should govern the Panchayats for a specified period and not a special officer. Therefore, the provision of a special officer provided in this section should be deleted.

Devolving of adequate and clear-cut functions and powers to the Panchayats is very important for enabling them to function in a free environment.

Let us examine the scope of Kerala Panchayat Raj Act (KPRA) in this regard.

- Under Section 164 (2), a provision has been made for constituting a Ward Committee for each constituency with the purpose of informing the VP on the needs of the constituency. But the GS will also be held at the ward level only, which among others, will list out its needs as is also envisaged as the role of the Ward Committee. The VP may also constitute a vigilance Committee as suggested earlier in this paper. Keeping these provisions in view, constitution of the Ward Committee is dispensable.

- The District panchayats, Block Panchayats and Village Panchayats shall perform their functions under the financial and technical guidance of the State government [Sections 166 (2), 172 (2) 173 (2)]. This is wrong in principle and operationally difficult as it does not put Panchayats on a firm foundation. Through provisions of this nature, the government can meddle with the functioning of the democratically elected institutions and deprive the people of freedom of action which is essential for participatory planing.
- These provisions in the State Act may have to be suitably amended so that the VP takes help from the BP which, in turn, takes help from the DP and the DP from the State government, if it is required. The State may be benefited from the Panchayati Raj Acts of States like Gujarat, Assam, Manipur and Madhaya Pradesh which have enabling provisions for consultation among the three tires without much intervention from the State.
- Functions to be performed by different tiers of Panchayats have been listed in Schedules 3,4 and 5 of the Act. Looking at their distribution among the three tiers, an hour glass picture emerges, because they have been concentrated either at the lowest level or at the apex. This shows that in deciding the distribution, proper thought has not been given. For

example, functions relating to education do not figure in the list for the BP, which thus emerges as a weak tier of the PR system and, therefore, does not provide sufficient scope for its members to play a role in participatory planning.

While participating in the Conference of Chief Ministers on basic minimum services 4-5, July, 1996 in Delhi, the Chief Minister of Kerala mentioned that less than one per cent of the total habitations in the State were fully covered as regards the availability of safe drinking water against the national coverage of 57 per cent. Shortage of clean drinking water is an important reason for the high morbidity in the State.

This is one of the basic needs and could be handled effectively at Panchayat level. But very little responsibility to this basic necessity has been devolved to the Panchayats. It is suggested that in order to conserve water resources, construction of check dams in the rivers should be entrusted to the Panchayats. If this function is given lock stock and barrel to the Panchayats, it being a basic requirement, will enthuse the people to participate in water management.

1 In inter-tier allocation of functions, the cardinal principle that what can be undertaken at a particular level should be entrusted to that level alone has been kept in mind. However, ample scope for improving the functional relationship between the three tiers is still there. Significantly, whatever functions have been allocated to the Panchayats in accordance with this principle have been taken away by Section 283, according to which the government may alter, amend or add to any of the entries made in the functions of the Panchayats. Hence this section should be repealed.

- To fully realize economic development and social justice, other functions like police powers and judicial powers should also be given to the Panchayats. Bihar, West Bengal, Punjab and Uttar Pradesh are the States which have given judicial functions to institutions at the grass roots level. Recently, the Madhya Pradesh State Assembly has also passed a legislation for constituting Gram Nyayalayas to administer justice in rural areas. The Karnataka government also proposes to introduce an amendment to the State's Panchayat Act in the coming session of the Assembly for setting up Nyaya Panchayats.

The Kerala Panchayat Raj Act does not make provision for constituting Nyayalaya at grass roots levels for dispensing justice to the people. It is, therefore, suggested that police and judicial functions should be given to the Panchayats for meaningful decentralization.

Functional autonomy has not been given to the Panchayats, because provisions such as the schemes being contingent on the availability of resources and placing of performance of vital functions under the supervision and guidance of the government have circumscribed the role of participatory planning through the institutions.

For ushering in an era of participatory planning for Panchayats, the State government should amend all the Acts pertaining to the subjects in the XIth Schedule of the Central Act, take out all relevant portions from the existing Subjects Acts and incorporate them in the Panchayat Act through an amendment by the State legislature.

For enabling the people to participate effectively in planning and development of their areas through

Panchayats, it is indispensable that these bodies should have their own officials. But this has not been provided for in the Kerala Panchayat Act.

- The secretaries of all the three tiers will be the government employees (Section 179) under the State Act. The power of transferring these employees is also vested in the government or in a prescribed authority if a resolution to that effect has been passed by the Panchayat by a simple majority. However, action on this resolution is not mandatory on the part of the government.

This provision is objectionable, because this does not entail autonomy of the people in their actions. What is the rationale behind insisting on a simple majority for a resolution for transferring an official? It is practised at the State and the Central levels? Hence this provision may have to be repealed.

- The Chairpersons of the Panchayats have been empowered to exercise supervision and control over the officials of the Panchayats and prepare their confidential reports (Section 156 (4) (b). It is a welcome feature of the Act. But provisions in the Kerala Munidipal Act [Section 14 (3) (b)] which say that Chairpersons prepare the confidential report of the Secretary as well as review the confidential reports prepared by the Secretaries in respect of their employees should also be made applicable to the Panchayats.
- An enabling provision for constituting a separate Service or Cadre [Section 179 (3)] has been made in the Act. Other States which have some such provisions are Karnataka [Section 196 (5) and Punjab (Section 26). But the provision in the Kerala Act is not substantial in nature as it has not been clearly specified as has been done in the Gujarat Panchayati Raj Act.

The provision under Section 179 (3) of the KPRA must be operationalized at once so that the Panchayats have their own officers and employees. Kerala may be benefited from Gujarat and Rajasthan Panchayati Raj Acts in which provisions for Panchayat cadre have already been incorporated. Under the Gujarat Panchayati Raj Act, there will be three cadres of Panchayat employees, namely the District cadre, the Taluk cadre and the Local cadre [Section 227 (3)]. For this purpose, a Gujarat Panchayat Service Selection Board shall be constituted. Besides this Board, a District Panchayat Service Selection Committee shall also be constituted at the district-level to recruit the primary education staff (Section 236).

In Rajasthan, a provision for establishing a District Establishment Committee under the chairpersonship of the President of the ZP has been made. This Committee shall make selections for the posts in different grades and categories for the Panchayats, prepare lists of the persons for promotion and deal with disciplinary matters affecting the officers and employee except officers of the State cadre.

Actually, a permanent solution of the cadre problem is to amend the Constitution, because the Panchayats after becoming local government must have their own employees as the State and the Centre have as per part XIV of the Constitution. But to begin with, the State government must invoke immediately the enabling provisions in the Panchayat Act.

The Gram Sabha (GS) is the comer-stone of participatory planning as it establishes direct democracy at the grass roots level, enabling the people to mobilize their collective wisdom for their development.

Thus, it is important to make this body strong and vibrant. But the Kerala Panchayat Raj Act, 1994 does not make it a strong body.

- As per Section 8 of the Act, the GS has been made a discussing and assisting body while it should have been made an approving and sanctioning authority for all programmes and schemes implemented by the VP, as it has been made in the Tamil Nadu and Punjab Acts.
- Meetings of the GS instead of being convened twice (Section 3) in a year, should be held quarterly as has been provided for in the Panchayat Acts of Madhya Pradesh and Bihar. The report of the Study Team on the position of the Gram Sabha in Panchayati Raj Movement (1963) had also recommended that its meetings be held more frequently, i.e. at least once in each quarter.

Moreover, to make sure that the meetings of the GS are held, provisions have been made in the Punjab and Haryana Panchayati Raj Acts that if a Chairperson, without genuine reasons, fails to hold two meetings he/she will automatically cease to function as Chairperson. A similar provision should also be included in the Kerala Act.

- The quorum for the GS (Section) is specified as not less than 50 members, while in most States it is one-tenth of the total number of the voters. However, in Tamil Nadu, the quroum for this body is specified as one-third of the total members. Keeping in view the educational and social development of Kerala where people are politically conscious, even fifty per cent of the total strength of the GS. An adequate representation of women in the quorum for the meeting should also be made mandatory for their effective participation.
- A provision for constituting a Vigilance Committee to oversee the functioning of the VP comprising members who are not members of the latter should

be made in the State Act on the pattern of the Panchayati Raj Acts of Bihar, Manipur, Rajasthan and Tripura. In these Committees, adequate representation of SCs/STs and women should also be ensured.

- The presence of the village-level officials in the meetings of the GS is also very important for participatory planning. Therefore, it should also be made mandatory that the Secretary of the VP and officials of the development departments at decentralized level should attend all the meetings of the GS and assist it as has been provided for in the Panchayati Raj Acts of Haryana, Punjab and Rajasthan.
- To further strengthen the GS, the three-decade old suggestions of the Study Team on Gram Sabha in Panchayati Raj movement (1963), like holding the meetings during the period when villagers are not busy in agricultural activities, and organization of entertainment programmes immediately after the meetings, are worthy of consideration to ensure adequate attendance.

The introduction of PRIs was a revolutionary step to wards rural uplift in this country. Almost all the States have constituted Panchayati Raj bodies, with the exception of Bihar, Orissa, Lakshadweep. Pondicherry and the hill districts of Uttar Pradesh. The PRIs will function as effective institutions of local self-government and they would prepare plans for economic development and social justice and implement them. The PRIs will be the umbrella for integration of sectoral programmes.

During the Ninth Plan, CAPART will continue to provide projectized financial assistance to voluntary organizations which will have to play a more dynamic role in empowering the poor through advocacy, awareness generation and formation of self-help groups. Decentralized planning will be made more effective through greater involvement of panchayats as also the voluntary organizations and people's self-managed institutions.

In the preceding pages we have discussed the objectives, strategies and various programmes which have been given priority in the approach to Ninth Five Year Plan.

We all know that Rs. 30,000 crore had been earmarked for rural development in the Eighth Five Year Plan, even then we have not been able to achieve the desired success and the plan period is nearing completion. It has been proposed to spend RS. 90,000 crore on rural development during the Ninth Plan. But even then we cannot be sure that the whole objective and approach to the proposed plan will be moving smoothly and we shall be able to achieve our goals.

In this connection, it may be added that our policies in the past had hardly been in question so far as development objectives are concerned. At the implementation level there existed many bottlenecks which came in the way of proper implementation of the programme and achieving the real targets.

The co-ordination problem had been so much chronic and the gap between plan formulation and its implementation so vast that we failed to achieve our goals. No doubt, the approach paper to the Ninth Five Year Plan makes a laudable attempt but the question still remains the same. Now we have effective Panchayati Raj system in our country and it is hoped that they will be capable of meeting the challenges at the implementation stage. But the question is whether the bureaucracy and State-level politicians will actually allow these institutions to take up the challenging task?

While concluding we may say that if there is real political will to achieve the objectives of approach to the Ninth Plan and the Panchayati Raj institutions are given real powers to implement, the objectives could really be achieved. However, keeping in view the hung nature of our Parliament and survival of the government on within and outside support by various political parties, it is still doubtful whether we will be able to achieve the objectives.

A very pessimistic view suggests that it would be beyond the comprehension of the government. But an optimist student of rural development, may take a brighter view of the picture and hope that if not 100 per cent, at least 50 per cent of the objectives will be achieved.

Performance: In order to have more national generalisation, the past performance can be reviewed separately for two categories, i.e., (i) those efforts related to income generation and self-employment and (ii) others related to self-employment-cum-entrepreneurship category.

The first category covers the programmes/schemes under KVIC, TRYSEM, SEEUY and some other institutions exclusively devoted for self-employment. During 1985-86, KVIC, provided employment opportunities to 39.8 lakh persons whose earning amounted to Rs. 349.53 crores. In the total employment under KVIC Programme the share of SC/ST was about 29% and women's participation about 46%. Under TRYSEM Scheme 200,650 youths were to be trained during 1985-86. Out of this, 56,500 youth were trained and 41.845 were reported taking up self-employment.

The second category by and large, refers to SSI entrepreneurs. Under Indian context the two strategies, i.e., developing entrepreneurship and small industries are interwoven. Between 1973-74 and 1986-87, the number SSIs increased by over three folds generation by about two and half times. It is difficult to assess as to how much oif it is the outcome of planned efforts.

But programme wise SIDO conducted more than 1638 EDPs and trained 50,130 potential entrepreneurs during 1978-88. During 1970-86 they conducted 287 programme specially for 6,757 engineer entrepreneurs. IDBI sponsored 550 EDPs benefiting 15,369 entrepreneurs. 6 Since its inception NSTEDB sponsored 147 EDPs benefitting 3,090 potential science & technology entrepreneurs. 7 SBI conducted 125 EDPs during 1978-87 and trained 2,939 persons with success rate of 33 percent. NIESBUD masseurs sponsored 42 EDPs benefitting 1125 potential entrepreneurs. Besides such national bodies large number of programmes were conducted locally by other governmental and non-governmental organisations which have not been recorded systematically. As per one estimate about 1,250 full EDPs of 6 weeks duration are conducted every year benefitting more than 40,000 potential entrepreneurs.

Success Rate: Since entrepreneurship development presently pursued by variety of organisations/agencies with different types of approaches/strategies and also with varying degrees of resources for varied target groups, their rate of success (in terms of the ration of number of entrepreneurs who actually set up their enterprises to the number of persons trained/promoted) naturally show a very wide range of variation (8% of 80%).

Recently nationwide study by NIESBUD, however, reported 27.8% success rate as national average since there are experiences of higher rates of success there seems to be enough scope for further improvement in all aspects of EDPs starting from Identification & Selection of Potential Entrepreneurs; and Quality & Content of Training; Support Services; and Availability/accessibility to infrastructural facility.

Cost of Employment Generation : There are very few, if any, published documents presenting quantitative and qualitative evaluation of EDPs. In the absence of uniform data for all reported programmes, it may be useful to consider cost of emploment generation from the typical programmes separately.

The cost of conducting full entrepreneurship development programmes include cost of initial campaign, identification & selection, 4-6 weeks training, and follow-up for about 4-6 months after the completion of training. These can be estimated from the existing pattern of expenditure. SISIs are conducting integrated EDP with an expenditure of Rs. 56,000/- for TCOs and other voluntary organisations who conduct EDPs sponsored by IDBI and other financial institutions; NSTEDB & NIESBUD, the cost comes in between Rs. 70-80 thousand. Under difficult areas and for special schemes such as women entrepreneurship the coast goes upto Rs. 100,000/-.

Considerig 30% as success rate and on an average 30 participants per programme the cost for promoting entrepreneurship comes in between Rs. 6000/- and Rs. 11,000/- (without establishment cost) per entrepreneurs who sets up an enterprise with an investment between few thousand to 35 lakhs. SBI Evaluation Study (1986) 10 further help us understand the pattern and size of investment and return by entrepreneurs promoted through such EDPs. The overall average investment by them was reported as Rs. 3.55 lakhs.

To be more precise maximum, i.e., 57.4% invested between 2-5 lakhs; and followed by those 27.9% who invested between 1-2 lakhs; and 8% invested upto Rs.

25,000/- and only 6% invested over Rs. 10 lakhs. In terms of benefits, out of such promoted entrepreneurs 83% sampled units reported making on an average a net profit of Rs. 48,200/- (about 4000/- per month) during 1985.

Another study that provided detailed information about cost/benefit refers to Assam Experiment-Self-Employment through entrepreneurship Motivation Training Centres during 1973-76. With the total expenditure of Rs. 17.96 lack that included the cost of training of officers, all recurring and non-recurring expenditrue of 6 EMTCs in Assam 534 units started functioning (another 593 received financial sanction but not considered for calculating benefits here) and accordingly the cost for promoting each succeessful entrepreneur was reported having net profit between Rs. 300/- to Rs. 1500/- per month (during mid seventies).

Further the total amount raised and invested by these entrepreneurs in the area amount raised and invested by these entrepreneurs in the area amounted to Rs. 1.2 crores to which Govt. contributed only 12.26 lakhs as seed money. The evauation study further revealed that more than 90% units thus established provided employment to 1-2 persons besides the self-employed owner.

Another valuable and more recent information related to cost-benefit of a typical entrepreneurship development programme for self-employment (in SBI sector) is available with Rural Development Self-emploment Training Institute (RUDSETI), Gurgaon which has been set up jointly by a Trust and two nationalised banks since 1984. RUDSETI trained 1,832 candidates and 1127 of them have already set up their enterprises, the total of cost on selection, two weeks training counselling and support activities comes to Rs. 795/- per successful self-employed entrepreneurs (this does not include the establishment cost).

In addition, the bank financing to these entrepreneurs on an average was reported as Rs. 18,214/- per self-employed person, enterprises set up by these entrepreneurs represented 'business' enterprises 28.7% followed by 'industries' 19.6% and 11.6% 'service units'. It was further revealed that 68% of thus promoted entrepreneurs have started earning net profit between Rs. 500/- to Rs. 1500/- per month.

Like in other spheres, Indian women have proved their great potential as successful entrepreneurs. Some of Indian women entrepreneurs today lead the biggest shipping companies, trading and export houses, brewing industry, plastic & electronics establishment. Garment and handicrafts exports are primarily in the hands of women entrepreneurs. However, such achievement by about 100,000 women entrepreneurs in India touches just the fringe of vast future potential promised to Indian women.

Out of the total 761 million people in India, female comprise 360.74 million representing 47.7% of the total population. There are 99.4 million women workforce (representing 28% of the female population), but as per 1981 census, there are only 150,000 self-employed women accounting for only 5.2% of the total self-employed persons in the country.

Majority of them are engaged in the unorganised sectors like agriculture, agrobased industries handicrafts, handlooms, and cottage based industries. Participation of women as industrial entrepreneurs, however, is comparatively a recent phenomena commencing from 70s onwards According to an estimate among 1.6 million SSI entrepreneurs in India during 1986-87, the total number of women entrepreneurs does not exceed 100,000.

Table Indian women's status in entrepreneurial terms

Item	Percentage
Women % to total population	47.7
Women % to total Workplace	36.4
Women % to total Unemployed	40.0
Women % to total Self-employed	5.2
Women % to total SSI Entrepreneurs	7.5

In late 70s, it became conspicuous that women offer great potential as entrepreneurs. Accordingly, besides encouraging more women to join regular EFP, a number of special programmes and strategies were thought out to ensure women to take up entrepreneurship as their career.

During 1978-87, Small Industry Development Organisation (SIDO) with its network of Small Industries Service Institutes (SISI) spread throughout the country conducted 248 Courses exclusively for women benefitting 8,904 potential women entrepreneurs.

During 1986, Industrial Development Bank of India (IDBI) launched a special Scheme for Women Entrepreneurs according to which the training support and counselling is offered in a package.

The scheme emphasized the need to set up modern small scale units in electronics engineering, plastic and chemicals, etc. consistent with the knowledge, skills and personal background of trainees further suggests to include women entrepreneurs so far as possible and provide long lead time and the post-training escort services by the conducting agency until the projects taken up by women entrepreneurs generally reach their break-even stage. The success rate under this scheme has crossed the 50% mark of the national averag. Further, a this helped several new voluntary organisations in acquiring and improving their competencies and infrastructural facilities for conducting effective EDPs for Women.

In September, 1986 the Government of India set up a National Level Standing Committee for Women Entrepreneurs under the Chairmanship of the Minister of State for Youth Affairs, Sports, Women & Child Development. The Standing Committee made suitable recommendations & suggestions to the Government regarding the problem of entrepreneurship amongst women.

In view of the growing importance of women entrepreneurship, several nationalised banks opened special Cells for women entrepreneurs. Many State Financial Corporation have also developed special schemes for assisting the women entrepreneurs. Several entrepreneurs associations are very active in promoting and supporting the cause of entrepreneurship development. Most of them are now having a separate Women's Wing.

Only about a few year ago, an women entrepreneur, in India was visualised as a maker of pickles, papads, masala (spices) and other such household goods. But the recent EDPs have helped them in organising enterprises of complex type, bigger in size, with sophisticated technology involving higher managerial abilities.

As such, the number of women entrepreneurs is increasing very fast. In order to further accelerate the process, it may be necessary to develop more man-power undertaking training and support to women entrepreneurs. Presently, two National Institutions, NIESBUD and EDII are organising half-a-dozen trainers training programme producing not more than 150 trainers in a year. To this even another 100 are added by other newly established institutions such as ICEW in Ahmedabad and IED in Lucknow hardly meeting the 50% of the total requirement.

Usually, it has been observed in the West that economic independence to women will increase the incidence of breaking of 'family tie'. Economic prosperity through entrepreneurial pursuits by Indian women has proved just the contrary. More often, women entrepreneurs have succeed in evolving other family members such as husband, father, mother etc. into her entrepreneurial folds.

This is supported by the fact that majority of successful women entrepreneurs were married (85.5%), mostly between the age 36-45 year (56.2%) and most of them (81.7%) had children of about the age of 10 years. These empirical evidences raises a great of early entrepreneurisation of the whole society by promoting entrepreneurisation of the whole society by promoting entrepreneurship amongst women. Through women participation, the movement is bound to add momentum.

Introduced in 1959, the Panchayati Raj is considered a political and administrative innovation of far-reaching importance. Initially, people envinced keen interest in the Panchayati Raj system and their representatives participated actively in local affairs.

With passage of time, the initial enthusiasm and public participation gradually diminished. Again, after the enactment of the Constitution (73rd Amendment) Act 1992, there is a resurgence of rural local bodies in India. The objects of this amendment are:

- To place more powers in the hands of rural people to determine their own destiny and to build a society;
- To enhance the capabilities of rural people to frame planning from below;

- To decentralize execution of all kinds of development activities with the effective participation of the people; and
- To alter the administrative methods in rural area.

The Panchayati Raj is the embodiment of rural local government with a three-tier system—village, intermediate and district levels—interconnected to provide for a community in experience as well as programme formulation and its implementation. To this system has been given powers and authority of governance as well as of plan formulation and execution.

It has three roles to play simultaneously: (a) as a unit of rural local government; (b) as an instrument of community development; and (c) as an agency of the State government.

XI Schedule: The Constitution Amendment Act 1992 has specified 29 items in the Eleventh Schedule which may be entrusted to the Panchayats in additon to any other schemes for economic development and social justice which may also be entrusted to them by the State governments.

The following items from the Eleventh Schedule are important from environment protection and improvement point of view:

- Agriculture;
- Land immprovement, implementation of land reforms, and soil conservation;
- Minor irrigation, Water management and watershed development;
- Social forestry and farm forestry;
- Minor forest produce;
- Rural housing;

- Drinking water;
- Fuel and fooder;
- Non-conventional energy sources;
- Health and sanitation.

If we compare the jurisdiction of Panchayati Raj with the aims of World Conservation Strategy, we find that Panchayati Raj is fully incorporating the aims in the following manner:

- To maintain essential ecological processes and life-support systems (such as soil regeneration and protection, the recycling of nutrients and cleaning of water) for human survival and development.
- To ensure the sustainable utilization of species and ecosystems (notably fish and other wildlife, forests and grazing lands) which support millions of rural communities as well as major industries.

Decentralized planning: The role of PRIs is crucial for environment protection and improvement. Each tier is involved in the process of local planning about their jurisdiction. The plans are made at village Panchayat and then examined and compiled by the Panchayat at intermediate level (known as Block or Panchayat Samiti). After this, at district level as Zilla Pairshad) all plans from intermediae levels are considered. At the district level, there is a District Plan Committee which consolidates the plan looking to rational utilization of natural utilization of natural resources and environment conservation and forward it to the State Government. Such planning process takes care of local conditions, needs of the people, natural resources and geography of local areas.

The Panchayati Raj institutions have an effective role in the implementation of various policies and programmes contributing to environment protection and improvement, formulated by State and Central governments. In the Rajasthan Panchayati Raj Act, it is specifically mentioned that the State Government by its direction assigns the task of management and maintenance of forests in Panchayat area to Panchayat.

The PRIs also provide necessary assistance to the other agencies engaged in environment protection such as land allotment for forest and establishment of research centres. Besides this, the following roles of PRIs are also important:

- To create will and determination among the rural people to protect and improve the environment;
- To understand the local situation and to share the information about environment;
- To achieve integrated approach by co-ordinating the activities of various agencies interested in environment protection in rural areas;
- To provide a an open forum for discussion on environment protection;
- To give guidance and training to rural people; and
- To restrain the people from those activites which are harmful to environment, if necessary by imposing penalty and fine.

Key to success

Development is the primary concern and responsibility of the people. They must prepare the plan and implement the same. This is much more true with the introduction of Panchayati Raj. The voluntary organizations may also be actively involved in this task. People are the primary concern. It is their confidence and credibility that needs to be obtained. It is mutual trust between government and the people that will repose faith in each other.

There are three basic principles of people-centred development. First, sovereignty resides with the people. Second, to exercise their sovereignty and assume responsibility for their own development and that of their communities, people must control their own resources, have access to relevant information, and have the means to hold the officials of government and voluntary organizations accountable. Third, those who would assist people with their development must recognize that it is they who are participating in support of the people's agenda, not vice-versa. The value of the outsider's contribution will be measured in terms of the enhanced capacity of the people to determine their own future.

The Gandhian model of development requires active involvement and participation of man building his own "destiny". This is possible if some of us belonging to the so-called rich and middle class voluntarily, instead of dfrifting toward consumerism, are willing to sacrifice and share our pleasures in the interests of the downtrodden of our society.

For rural India, time is running out and it must adopt strategies and methods to transform the socio-economic life of people to suit Indian ingenuity and culture. Integrated development sets forth a strategy of working with rural people—a strategy, in which participation by all is both the means and end itself.

In sum, the real wealth of a country lies in "human capital" and if you create conditions where human capital can flourish without being squashed by government controls, you can beat the rest of the countries of the Ninth Plan has to be very positive in building up "social capital" and infrastructure. Our social achievements are not outstanding despite our fifty years of Independence.

Our literacy rate is 52 per cent; infant mortality 74 per thousand; access to sanitation is available to only 16 per cent of the people. Though life expectancy has gone up to 62, the fertility rate is still 3.3 which would double India's population in the next century. Just as the proof of the pudding is in the eating, similarly the success of the Ninth Plan will depend on as to how far it has raised "human capotal" of India.

We have to shift the paradigm of development from a right centred-economy to a duty motivated economy, from self-centredness to the love of our fellowmen, if we want to succeed in our planned development of rural society.

Even though India is one of the few Third World countries which has constitutionalized protection and improvement of environment, the various enactment suffer from several lacunae including the non-recognition of the crucial role that PRIs can play in the endeavour. The involvement of PRIs as the watch-dog of environmental protection at the grass roots level needs to be duty recognized. The Constitution (73rd Amendment) Act 1992 now provides these institutions an opportunity to play their legitimate role. Environment protection represents one of the more recent and yet one of the more profound aspects new public affairs dimension in public administration. Environmental issues have aroused too much intellectual and academic interest both in developing and underdeveloped nations. They include envioronmental degradation, deforestation and desertification, atmospheric pollution and imbalances as well as disertifications in ecology resulting from the way natural resources—land, water, forests, minerals, etc are harnessed for fulfilment of human needs.

The UN Conference on Human Environment in 1972 proclaimed that the defence and improvement of human environment both natural and man-made had become an imperative good for mankind, to be pursued together with fundamental goals of peace and worldwide economic and social development. The achievement of these goals was the responsibility of citizens, communities, enterprises and institutions at every level. Later on, the World Conservation Strategy (1980) and the Brundthland Report also noted the irreversible destruction of ecosystems of the poor countries and the implicit threat to the world security and the consequent political instability and social problems. The problem of environmental crises of the developing countries is different from that of the developed countries.

The establishment of viable community-based institutions for environment protection was suggested with full legal, administrative and technical support. These institutions should be empowered to plan, to work out the modality and to implement the various measures for environment protection and conservation. The Panchayati Raj as an institution of local rural government is the excellent model for it in rural India.

Among the developing countries, india is also facing environmental problems and crises. The enormous increase in population is the most potent cause for acceleration of the overutilization of productive resources and downgrading the quality of environment.

India has a domesticated animal population of nearly 500 million. Considering that only 3.5 per cent of the land area are under grass, the population is supported by the forest and agriculture residues which are thereby diverted from agricultural land. Out of the total cultivable land, 175 million ha are degraded needing special treatment to restore productivity.

Of the 75 million ha designated as forest land, only

35 million ha are close forest. Despite all efforts, India has continued to lose forest cover. The deforestation causes loss in bivodiversity. Over 1,500 species of plants and animals are on the endangered list. Levels of air and water pollution are much beyond acceptable limits. These challenges disturb the environment equilibrium and the life of mankind.

The basic aim of our National Forest Policy must be to ensure environmental stability and maintenance of ecological balance including atmospheric which are vital for the sustenance of all forms of life—human, animal and plant. Rural India has different kinds of environmental crises compared to other countries. The rapid growth of rural population has placed inexorable burden on farm as well as on other land resources, on forests, on water resources and worsened the quality of life of the rural poor in respect of housing, health, ecological surroundings and other essentials.

Constitution & environmental protection: The Un Declaration on Human Environment in 1972 signalled India to initiate positive steps in the direction towards environment improvement.

The Constitution of India has conceptualized its thinking on environment in the form of the Directive Principles of State Policy in favour of protection and improvement of environment, and safeguarding of forests and wildlife (Article 48A), a fundamental duty to protect and improve the natural environment including forests, lakes, rivers and wildlife and to have compassion for living creatures [Article 51A(g)], and a subject in the Consurrent List in its Seventh Schedule (Item 17A and 17B). Both the Directive principles and Fundamental Duty are non-justiciable, but these provide the necessary constitutional sanction if the State intends to adopt a law in the matter.

Administrative control: The other component of the infrastructure for environment improvement and protection is provided by the existing legislation. There are 30 major enactments such as Water Cess Act, Forest Act, Forest Conservation Act, Wildlife Protection Act, Environment Protection Act, of Union and State Governments. Administrative actions—regulatory, negotiational and persuasive—under these enactments are mainly taken by the Central and State administrative organizations—the Central Ministry of Environment and Forests, the Central Pollution Control Board and the State Departments of Environment and State Pollution Control Boards.

Besides this, there also exist the other administrative mechanisms concerned with the implementation of policies on environment. The Panchayati Raj institutions have also become important instruments in rural India for environment protection and improvement.

5

Urban Poverty Alleviation Programme

Swarna Jayanti Shahari Rozgar Yojana

In a decision of far reaching consequences, the Union Cabinet on 5th August, 1997 approved the Swarna Jayanti Shahari Rozgar Yojana (SJSRY). The SJSRY has been launched as a replacement for Nehru Rozgar Yojana (NRY), Urban Basic Services for the Poor (UBSP), and Prime Ministers Integrated Urban Poverty Eradication Programme (PMI UPEP) on 1.12.97. The SJSRY seeks to provide gainful employment to the urban unemployed or underemployed poor through encouraging the setting up of self-employment ventures and provision of wage employment.

The Swarna Jayanti Shahari Rozgar Yojana will be funded on a 75:25 basis between the Centre and the States.

The Scheme consists of two special schemes, namely—

— The Urban Self Employment' Programme (USEP)

— The Urban Wage Employment Programme (UWEP)

Salient Features:

The Swarna Jayanti Shahari Rozgar Yojana rests on a foundation of community empowerment. This programme relies on establishing and promoting community organisations and structures to provide supporting and facilitating mechanism for local development. Towards this end nity organisations like Neighbourhood Groups (NGs), Neighbourhood Committees (NCs), and Community Development Societies (CDSs) be set up in the target areas based on the UBSP pattern. The CDSs shall be the focal point for purposes of identification of beneficiaries, preparation of application, monitoring of recovery, and generally providing whatever other support is necessary to the programme. The CDSs will also identify viable projects suitable for the particular area.

The CDSs, being a federation of different community based organisations, shall be the nodal agency for this programme. It is expected that they will lay emphasis on providing the entire gamut of social sector inputs to their areas including, but not limited to, health, welfare, education, etc. through establishing convergence between schemes being implemented by different line departments within their jurisdiction.

The Urban Self Employment Programme (USEP)

This programme has three distinct parts:

— Assistance to individual urban poor beneficiaries for setting up gainful self-employment ventures;

— Assistance to groups of urban poor women for setting up gainful self-employment ventures. This sub-scheme is called. The Scheme for Development of Women and Children in the Urban Areas (DWCUA)";

— Training of beneficiaries, potential beneficiaries and other persons associated with the urban employment programme for upgradation and acquisition of vocational and enterpreneurial skills.

Coverage

— The programme will be applicable to all urban towns in India;

— The programme will be implemented on a whole town basis with special emphasis on urban poor clusters.

Target Groups

— The programme shall target the urban poor, defined as those living below the urban poverty line, as defined from time to time;

— Special attention will be given to women, persons belonging to Scheduled Castes/ Tribes, disabled persons and other such categories as may be indicated by the government from time to time. The percentage of women beneficiaries under this programme shall not be less than 30%. SCs and STs must be benefited at least to the extent of the proportion of their strength in the local population. A provision of 3% shall be reserved for the disabled under this programme.

— There will be no minimum education qualification for beneficiaries under this programme. However, this scheme shall not apply to beneficiaries educated beyond the IX Standard.

— A house-to-house survey for identification of genuine beneficiaries will be done. Noneconomic parameters will also be applied to identify the urban poor in addition to the economic criteria of the urban poverty line.

— All other conditions being equal, women beneficiaries belonging to women-headed households, viz. widows, divorcees, single women of even households where women are the sole earners shall be ranked higher in priority.

Development of Women and Children in Urban Areas (DWCUA)

DWCUA aims at helping groups of urban poor women in taking up self-employment ventures. The group should consist of at least 10 women. The ceiling of subsidy under the scheme is Rs. 1.25 lakh or 50% of the cost of project whichever is less. Where the group sets itself up as Thrift and Credit Society, in addition to its self employment ventures, it will be eligible for an additional grant of Rs. 25,000 as Revolving Fund at the rate of Rs. 1000 maximum per member. The Fund is meant for purposes like purchase of raw materials and marketing, infrastructure support, one time expense on child care activity, expenses upto Rs. 500 on travel cost of group members to bank, payment of insurance premium for self/spouse/child by maintaining savings for different periods by a member and any other expense allowed by the State in Group's interest. The Revolving Fund can be availed by a Group only after one year of its formation.

Information, Education and Communication Component

States may utilise upto 2% of their allocation for activities under the IEC component. Once again, care shall be taken by the State to ensure that full use is made of the material made available by the Department of UEPA and the recognised national institution in this regard.

The Urban Wage Employment Programme (UWEP)

This programme shall seek to provide wage employment to beneficiaries living below the poverty line within the jurisdiction of urban local bodies by utilising their labour for construction of socially and economically useful public assets.

This programme shall apply to urban local bodies, the population of which was less than 5 lakhs as per the 1991 Census.

The material labour ratio for works under this programme shall be maintained at 60:40. The prevailing minimum wage rate, as notified from time to time for each area, shall be paid to beneficiaries under this programme.

Community Development Societies (CDSs) shall survey and draw up a list of available basic minimum services in their areas. Missing basic minimum services shall be listed thereafter. The term "basic services" above shall carry the same connotation as is carried under the scheme of EIUS.

The CDSs shall prioritise the above services into two lists "A" and "B". This prioritisation shall be final and not subject to change and modification by any other agency. List A will be the order of priority for the missing minimum services whereas List B shall be the order of priority for other required infrastructure. These lists alongwith the remarks of the CDS with respect to where such services should be located etc. shall be forwarded to the Town Poverty Eradication Cell at the beginning of the year. The DUDA or the ULB, whosoever is empowered in this behalf by the State Government, shall accord the final sanction.

Targets

No physical targets have been fixed and this matter has benefit to be decided by State Governments in conformity with the guidelines on the scheme and result of beneficiary survey. This has been done to ensure adequate flexibility of operation of the scheme.

Allocation of funds under Swarna Jayanti Shahari Rojgar Yojana (SJSRY):

The funds remaining unspent in respect of Nehru Rozgar Yojana (NRY), UBSP and PMIUPEP with various

States/UTs as on 30.11.97 was the opening balance for incurring expenditure under the now scheme. In addition, Central funds of Rs. 98.63 Crores had been released for 1997-98 (i.e. 1.12.97 to 31.3.98) and allocation of Rs. 183.20 Crores has been made for 1998-99 out of which till 31.12.98 a sum of Rs. 68.33 Crores has been released to the States/UTs.

Community Structure and IEC components

132.70 lakh beneficiaries have been covered under the community structure component till 31 December, 1998 and 19101 persons have be trained under the Programme as on 31.12.1998.

6

Water Supply and Sanitation

Water Supply and Sanitation are important basic needs affecting the quality of life and productive efficiency of the people. The State Governments/ Union Territories and urban local bodies are responsible for providing these services through proper planning, implementation, operation, maintenance and monitoring out of funds available under the State Plans, internal resource generation and/or by taking loans from financial institutions. The Ministry of Urban Affairs & Employment assists the State Governments/UTs by providing guidance for policy formulation, legislation, technical clearance of schemes, Central assistance, facilities for training, seminars/works hops and external assistance from 3426 bilateral/multilateral agencies. The programmes and activities undertaken by the Ministry during 1998-99 are as under:—

Low Cost Sanitation for Liberation of Scavengers

This Centrally sponsored scheme is under implementation through this Ministry since 1989-90. It provides for conversion of existing dry latrines into low cost water seal pour flush latrines and construction of new sanitary units where none exist to prevent open defecation. The basic objective is to liberate the scavengers from the obnoxious practice of carrying head loads of night soil and the scheme is being implemented on a "whole town" basis. The scheme is operated by providing subsidy from this Ministry and loans from the HUDCO in a synchronised manner so that the conversion/ construction of low cost sanitation units and liberation of scavengers is done on whole town basis. Financial & physical progress of the scheme as on 1. 1. 1999 is shown at Annexure-1 The Employment of Manual Scavengers & Construction of Dry Latrines (Prohibition) Act, 1993 was enacted by the Central Government on 5.6.93. It was a milestone achieved to bring an element of compulsion on the society for abolition of manual scavenging. A notification was issued by the Ministry on 24.1.97 which has brought it into force in all the Union Territories and States of Andhra Pradesh, Goa, Karnataka, Maharashtra, Tripura and West Bengal with effect from 26th January, 1997. The Act has already been adopted by the State Assemblies of Orissa, Punjab, Assam, Haryana and Bihar.

Accelerated Urban Water Supply Programme (AUWSP)

The Accelerated Urban Water Supply Programme (AUWSP) is a Centrally sponsored scheme initiated with the objective of solving the drinking Water problems in towns having population of less than 20,000 as per 1991 census. Considering the water scarcity and the narrow revenue base of these small towns, the scheme is funded by the Central and State Governments in the ratio of 50:50. The programme was launched during March, 1994. During the 8th Plan period an amount of Rs. 68.624 crores was released by the Ministry as Central share to various State Governments for implementation of 227 schemes with a total estimated cost of Rs. 218.50 crores approved during the said period. During the year 1997-98, detailed project reports for 35 schemes in 35 towns at a cost of Rs. 37.64 crores were approved by the Ministry and an amount of Rs. 27.95 crores was released to various State Governments. During the year 1998-99, detailed project reports for 47 schemes at a cost of Rs.

52.38 crores have been approved by the Ministry and an amount of Rs. 21.83 crores has been released to various Stale Governments (till 1. 1. 1999).

Solid Waste Management

The Urban Local Bodies and Municipalities are primarily responsible for the formulation and implementation of schemes for management of municipal solid waste. The Ministry's role is to act as a facilitator, wherever possible. The problem of waste management, around the vicinity of IAF airfields has been engaging the attention of the Government for quite sometime. Open dumping of waste and carcass disposal attract birds, which have caused a number of air accidents. An Inter-Ministerial Joint Sub-Committee constituted by the Ministry of Defence had, therefore, recommended that proper sanitation facilities, including solid waste management should be provided at the following 10 airfields to overcome the bird menace: (i) Gwalior (M.P.) (ii) Ambala (Haryana) (iii) Hindon (U.P.) (iv) Jodhpur (Rajasthan) (v) Tezpur (Assam) (vi) Dindigual (Andhra Pradesh) (vii) Sirsa (Haryana) (viii) Adampur (Punjab) (ix) Pune (Maharashtra) (x) Bareilly (U.P.) It was decided that 100% Central assistance may be provided through this Ministry for improvement of solid waste management and drainage in these towns. Improvement of slaughter houses and carcass disposal would be assisted through the Ministry of Agriculture. Feasibility reports for 10 towns have since been got prepared and forwarded to the concerned Urban Local Bodies/Air Force stations for their views/ comments. The concerned State Governments were also requested to convey their commitment for implementation of the scheme. Memorandum for Expenditure Finance Committee was circulated to the concerned Ministries and based on their comments, revised memorandum has been prepared. The matter will be taken up with the EFC after adequate allocation of funds and appraisal of projects by the Planning Commission.

A public interest litigation was filed in the Supreme Court (No. 888 of 1996) against the Union of India, all State Governments and some of the major Municipal Corporations regarding the deteriorating state of solid waste management in the country, *vis-a-vis* remedial measures needed to tackle the situation. As per the orders of the Hon'ble Supreme Court dated 16.1.98, a Committee was constituted under the Chairmanship of the Commissioner, Calcutta Municipal Corporation to look into various aspects connected with urban solid waste management in Class-1 cities (having population over one lakh). The Committee submitted its Interim Report on 30.6.98 to the Hon'ble Supreme Court. In order to obtain feedback on the recommendations contained in the report, with the approval of the Supreme Court, the Committee conducted 4 Regional Workshops at Calcutta, Chennai, Mumbai and New Delhi on 24.10.98, 21.11.98, 27.11.98 and 15.12.98 respectively., Representatives of the Central Ministries/ Organisations, State Govts., Urban Local Bodies, NGOs and experts in the field were invited to these workshops. The Committee is in the process of finalising its report.

The National Environmental Engineering Research Institute (NEERI), Nagpur was entrusted with the preparation of the Manual -on Solid Waste Management in October, 1995. The draft manual was completed in December, 1996 and the same was forwarded to 50 selected Urban Local Bodies for their comments/views. A Workshop for finalisation of the draft Manual was organized by the Ministry on 1-2nd September, 1997. The draft Manual was deliberated by the participants and 0 was unanimously decided that it needs to be redrafted by a group of experts. Accordingly, an Expert Committee comprising of 16 Members has been constituted under the, Chairmanship of Adviser (PHEE) for revision of the Manual. The Committee has held several meetings and is in the process of finalising the various chapters of the Manual.

Technical Clearance of Water Supply & Sanitation Schemes

The CPHEEO has approved IS schemes from 1.4.1998 to 31.12.1998 for implementation by different State Governments with loan assistance from LIC. A list of schemes approved and their estimated cost is at Annexure-III

Seminars/Workshops

The Economic and Social Commission for Asia and the Pacific (ESCAP) organised a Subregional Workshop on "Private Sector Involvement in the Water Supply and Sanitation Sector in collaboration with this Ministry from 28th to 30th April, 1998 at Kanishka Hotel, New Delhi. The Workshop was attended by senior level officials and sector professionals from the neighbouring countries, international organisations, State Governments/UTs and Central Ministries.

A National Conference of Chief Public Health Engineers and Heads of Implementing Agencies in charge of urban water supply and sanitation sector was organised by the Ministry/CPHEEO in collaboration with the Public Health Engineering Department, Government of Haryana at Chandigarh from 16-18 November, 1998 to discuss the important issues and programmes concerning the sector.

External Assistance

Considerable efforts have to be put in by the implementing agencies, viz. the State and Central Government to secure external assistance for urban water supply and sanitation projects.

Management Information System

The Ministry has since developed computer based Management Information System (MIS) softwares of urban water supply and sanitation. These softwares were provided to all the State/UT PHE Departments Water Boards and Metro Boards, etc., after demonstration workshops and meetings so that the, could use the MIS software for collection an(dissemination of information and for decision making

PHE Training

Development of trained manpower is one of the thrust areas of the Ministry. The CPHEEO organises various training courses for the in-service Engineers working in the State Public Health Engineering Departments/ Water Supply & Sanitation Boards through academic institutes and field departments. Grants are provided to the recognised Engineering Colleges and Training Institutes for conducting Post-Graduate, Short Term and Refresher Courses. During the year 1998-99 up to December, 1998, 885 in-service engineers and technical staff are expected to have been benefited from the programmes as detailed below:—

Post Graduate Course	Engineers 15
Short Term Courses	Engineers 15
Refresher Courses	800 Engineers & technical Staff

During January to March, 1999 more than 400 engineers and technical staff are expected to be trained. The Ministry had deputed more than 20 officials from the State Governments etc. for attending advanced training programmes abroad.

Research & Development Programme

During the year 1998-99, the R&D project entitled Hospital Waste Management sponsored by the Ministry has been completed by the All India Institute of Local Self Govt., Mumbai. Copy of the final report is being forwarded to concerned departments for perusal and possible implementation of the research findings. A research study to determine the status of water supply, sanitation and solid waste management in urban areas has been entrusted to the National Institute of Urban Affairs.

7

Urban Development

Urban Development is a State subject. The Ministry of Urban Affairs and Employment assists State Governments in their programmes of urban development by way of formulating broad policy framework; providing legislative support by way of constitutional amendment, legislation or issue of guidelines; implementing a number of centrally sponsored schemes; processing and monitóring assistance from multilateral/bilateral institutions for State Government projects; and, finally providing technical support and advice for promoting orderly urbanisation.

Policy and Legal Initiatives

National Urban Policy

The Ministry of Urban Affairs and Employment is in the process of formulating a National Urban Policy keeping in view the recommendations of the National Commission on Urbanisation, the economic reforms and the elements of National Urbanisation Strategy listed out in the regional Action Plan on Urbanisation adopted by the ESCAP countries vide the New Delhi Declaration. The National Urban Policy will take into account the suggestions of the State Governments, State Urbanisation Strategy papers prepared in the context of the IDSMT Scheme and the decentralisation reforms envisaged in the Constitution (74th) Amendment Act, 1992. Due cognizance would be given to overall development goals of States, their physical and financial resources, growth potential of towns in different regions and integration of spatial and economic planning. With the formulation of overall National Urbanisation Strategy, it would be possible to identify thrust areas and address the various urban problems such as infrastructural deficiencies, poverty and environmental deterioration in a systematic manner, keeping the goals of sustainable development in view.

The Planning Commission has constituted a National Task Force on Perspective and Policy in 1995. Three Technical Groups were also constituted on the subjects of Urban Perspective and Policy, Urban Infrastructure and Urban Planning System.

The Technical Group on Urban Planning System under the Chairmanship of Dr. Arcot Ramachandran has submitted its final report. The draft final reports of the Group on Urban Infrastructure under the Chairmanship of Shri Vaghul, the then Chairman of ICICI and the technical Group on Urban Perspective and Policy under the Chairmanship of Prof. Y.K. Alagh (the then Vice-Chancellor of JNU and former Minister of Power) have been received. The Groups have been requested to furnish their final reports. After the final reports of the two Technical Groups are received, the report of the Task Force will be finalised. The recommendations of the Task Force will be an input for the National Urbanisation Policy.

The Constitution (74th Amendment) Act, 1992 relating to Municipalities (known as the Nagarpalika Act) was passed by Parliament in the Winter Session of 1992 and it received the assent of the President on 20.4.1993. This Act seeks to provide a common framework for the structure and mandate of Urban Local Bodies to enable them to function as effective democratic units of Local Self-Government.

Government of India notified 1st June, 1993 as the date from which the 74th Amendment Act came into force. The Act provided for a period of one year from the date of its commencement, within which the Municipal Laws which were in force at that time in States/Union Territories, were required to be changed/ amended/ modified in order to bring them in conformity with the provisions of the Constitution (74th Amendment) Act, 1992.

The salient features of the Constitution (74th Amendment) Act cover the following:

- Constitution of Municipalities
- Composition of Municipalities
- Constitution of Wards Committees
- Reservation of Seats
- Fixed duration of Municipalities
- Power, Authority and Responsibilities of Municipalities
- Appointment of State Election Commission
- Appointment of State Finance Commission
- Constitution of Metropolitan and District Planning Committees.

Action has been taken by the State/UT Governments to set up State Finance Commissions/ State Election Commissions as follows:

State Finance Commissions (SFCs): All States have set up their Finance Commissions. Most of the State Finance Commissions have already submitted their

Report to the concerned State Government. The concerned States have accepted nearly all of the recommendations made by their respective Finance Commissions. They are in the process of enacting detailed rules for the purpose.

Election Commission: All State Governments/UTs have set up their Election Commissions for conducting elections to Urban Local Bodies. Election to municipal bodies have been completed in all States/ UTs except Bihar and Pondicherry where elections are held up due to court cases.

Model Legislations

A Model Rent Control Legislation has been formulated and tabled in the Parliament on 14.7.92. This has been circulated among the State Govt./UTs Administrations for amending the existing Acts or enacting new Rent Acts on the lines of the Model legislation. Governments of Gujarat, Karnataka, Tamil Nadu are considering amendments to respective Acts. Punjab has already passed a Rent Bill and is awaiting President's assent.

The Model Apartment Ownership Bill provides for heritable and transferable ownership rights to every apartment owner. It also provides for an association of apartment owners and effective management and maintenance of common areas and facilities in which every apartment owner has a percentage of undivided interest. The Model Apartment Ownership legislation provides for enforcement of obligations on promoters and apartment owners. The bill is under circulation to the State Governments.

A Model Apartment and Property Regulations Bill has also been drafted for circulation and guidance for the State Governments. Under the New Housing and Habitat Policy 1998, the role of the Government has become more as a facilitator rather than a builder. As such, housing activity would be increasingly undertaken by private builders. With an increased role of the private sector in land assembly and development, housing and infrastructure sectors, it has become necessary to regulate the activities of private builders and estate agents for healthy growth of the housing sector and also to ensure protection of the interests of prospective buyers. Model Apartment and Property Regulations Bill is under circulation.

Delhi Apartment Ownership Act 1986

This was found to be defective and suggestion for major amendments and revisions came from various quarters. The provisions regarding competent authorities and the penal provisions were being criticized. After taking into account various factors, it was decided to introduce a fresh bill in Parliament on the lines of the model bill. A revised Delhi Apartment Ownership Bill is under formulation.

Delhi Real Estate Developers Regulation Bill

This Ministry proposes to bring up a legislation with a view to regulate the construction and sale of apartments, development of colonies and activities of promoters, builders and estate agents in the NCT of Delhi. The Bill in this regard is under formulation.

Delhi Rent Act 1995

Delhi Rent Bill, which was introduced in Rajya Sabha on the 26th August, 1994 had been passed by both the Houses of Parliament and assented to by President on 23.8.95. However, the Act did not come into force as it was proposed to introduce some amendments. An Amendment Bill was introduced in the Rajya Sabha and it was referred to the Standing Committee.

Urban Land (Ceiling & Regulation) Act, 1976

The enactment of ULCR Act was made with the objective of preventing concentration of urban land in a few hands and facilitate equitable distribution of urban land to sub-serve the common good. The Act failed to achieve the objective on account of hurdles in implementation due to inherent defects in the Act and numerous litigations against the land acquired under the Act. A Bill to repeal the Act was introduced in Parliament last year and Speaker, Lok Sabha referred the Bill to the Standing Committee on Urban and Rural Affairs for examination. The Committee recommended repeal of the Act immediately and suggested some modifications in the Bill. An ordinance was issued on 11.1.99 to repeal the ULCR Act 1976 with modified provisions suggested by the Committee. The ordinance will be replaced by a repeal Bill during the current Budget Session.

Integrated Development of Small & Medium Towns (IDSMT):

The total population of the country has increased from 361 million in 1951 to 844 million by 1991, whereas, urban population increased from 62 million to 217 million, while in the same period, the number of urban agglomerations has increased to 3768 from 2843. This indicates that the increase in urban population was 250% whereas increase in urban agglomerations was only 32%. Thus, it is evident that there was a clear shift towards large towns, perhaps due to lack of employment opportunities and poor urban infrastructure bass of small and medium towns.

To improve the economic and physical infrastructure and also to provide essential facilities and services and also to slow down the growth of large cities by developing small and medium towns through increased investments in these towns, the centrally sponsored scheme of Integrated Development of Small and Medium Towns (IDSMT) was initiated in the year 1979-80 and is continuing with timely amendments and modifications. Investment in the development of small urban centres would also help in reducing migration to large cities and support the growth of surrounding rural areas as well.

The guidelines has since been revised and the new guidelines sent to the State Governments and UT Administrations. The State Governments have been requested to prepare revised State Urbanisation Strategy Paper alongwith a list of priority towns and submit the project reports for the current financial year 1998-99 conforming to the revised guidelines.

Objectives

— Improving infrastructural facilities and helping in the creation of durable public assets in small and medium towns;

— Decentralising economic growth and employment opportunities and promoting dispersed urbanisation;

— Increasing the availability of serviced sites for housing, commercial and industrial uses.

— Integrating spatial and socio-economic planning as envisaged in the Constitution (74th Amendment) Act, 1992.

For the current year 1998-99, central assistance of Rs. 35.00 crores (RE), has been earmarked under IDSMT Scheme. Central assistance of Rs. 9.71 crore has been released to 51 ongoing towns. Also Rs. 0.68 crore has been released under Central Urban Infrastructure Support Scheme for preparation of project reports. The balance amount shall be released on receipt of progress reports and utilisation certificates from State Governments and UT Administration.

During the year 1997-98, a sum of Rs. 26.02 crore (includes grant-in-aid released under CUISS) has been released to 16 new towns and 141 on-going towns covered during 7th Plan, two annual plans and 8th Plan. The overall achievement vis-a-vis target of this Ministry in the financial year 199798 was 104% in terms of coverage of new towns as per revised guidelines and in terms of release of central assistance. The tentative allocation of towns during the year 1997-98 was 51 whereas 16 towns have been covered besides evaluation of the on-going towns.

Infrastructure Development in Mega Cities

Keeping in view the recommendations of the National Commission on Urbanisation (NCU) and in response to persistent demands made by the State Governments for central assistance to undertake the development of infrastructure in Mega Cities, the Centrally Sponsored Scheme for Infrastructural Development in Mega Cities was initiated during 199394. The primary objective of the scheme is to enable the mega cities to build a Revolving Fund by the end of the Ninth Plan for sustained investment in urban infrastructure through adoption of direct and indirect cost recovery measures.

The main features of the scheme are as follows:

(a) The Scheme is applicable to Mumbai, Calcutta, Chennai, Bangalore and Hyderabad.

(b) The funds under the scheme are channelised through a specialised institution/nodal agency at the State level.

(c) The sharing between Central Govt. and State Govt. is at 25%: 25%; the balance 50% is to be met from institutional finance/capital market.

(d) The projects under the Scheme consist of a suitable mix/basket of (i) remunerative, (ii) user charge-based and (iii) basic services projects.

(e) The nodal agencies are required to provide project related finance for urban infrastructure including water supply sewerage, drainage, sanitation, city transport networks, land development, slum improvement, solid waste management, etc.

Funds flow from the Central and State Governments to the nodal agency as grant. However, the amounts flowing from the nodal agency to the implementing agencies for projects, are a mix of loans and grants in such a way that 75% of the Central and State shares are recovered back into a Revolving Fund at the level of the Mega City Scheme nodal agencies. The objective is to create and maintain a special fund for the development of infrastructural assets on a sustained basis.

The nodal agencies for the Mega City Scheme are:

Mumbai	Mumbai Metropolitan Region Development Authority (MMRDA)
Calcutta	Calcutta Metropolitan Development Authority (CMDA)
Chennai	Tamil Nadu Urban Finance and Infrastructure Development Corporation (TUFIDCO)
Hyderabad	Andhra Pradesh Urban Infrastructure and Finance Development Corporation (APUIFDC)
Bangalore	Karnataka Urban Infrastructure Development Finance Corporation (KUIDFC)

The projects under the Mega City Scheme are sanctioned by a Sanctioning Committee constituted at the state level with 3 members of the State Government and 1 member each from the Planning Commission and the Ministry of Urban Affairs and Employment.

The Planning Commission notionally indicated an outlay of Rs. 700 crores for 8th Plan Period for Mega City Scheme (Mumbai Rs. 200 crores, Calcutta-Rs. 200 crores, Chennai Rs. 100 crores, Hyderabad -Rs. 100 crores and Bangalore-Rs. 100 crores). Against this an amount of Rs. 290.50 crores was provided under Mega City Scheme in the 8th Five Year Plan period (Rs. 70.50 crores—1993-94; Rs. 75.00 crores—1994-95; Rs. 84.00 crores—1995-96 and Rs. 61.00 crores—1996-97). During 1997-98, an amount of Rs. 69.00 crores was allocated for the scheme. During 1998-99, an amount of Rs. 86.50 crores was originally allocated for the scheme which has been reduced to Rs. 75.00 crores. Out of this, an amount of Rs. 43.00 crores has already been released to the State Level Nodal Agencies. The details of funds released to the five mega cities as central share upto 30.9.98 are given at Annexure-1

The State Level Project Sanctioning Committee in all the Mega Cities have so far approved 238 projects amounting to Rs. 2339.89 crores for implementation. Upto September, 1998 an amount of Rs. 681.69 crores has been spent on approved projects. The Mega City Nodal Agencies are also making efforts for mobilising Institutional Finance and an amount of Rs. 530.64 crores has so far been mobilised from HUDCO/other sources. The details of financial and physical progress under the Mega City Scheme are at Annexure II.

Urban Mapping Scheme

The Constitution (74th Amendment) Act provides a

framework for physical and economic development of urban areas and envisages a three tier planning structure in States: (i) at local level, planning b, Panchayats and Municipalities; (ii) at regional level District Development Plan and Metropolitan Are Development Plans to be prepared by District Planning Committee and Metropolitan Planning Committee respectively; and (iii) at State level, State plans to be prepared by the State Governments. The planning exercises need continuous data collection analysis, interpretation and updating of data. A computer based data base and information system in GIS environment should be developed at various levels which would provide support to planners development planning, particularly for the present and future development of rapidly growing cities and metropolitan areas.

2. In this connection, the use of modern aerial photography and remote sensing techniques could be better utilised for preparation and updating of the existing base maps by adopting computer-based Geographic Information Systems. The National Commission on Urbanisation (1988) had also suggested the use of the techniques of remote sensing for urban planning and development particularly in monitoring the dynamic aspects of the urban environment. Urban maps need to the multipurpose so that they can be used by various agencies like Town Planning Departments, Local Bodies, Public works Departments, Services and utilities agencies, taxation departments, Directorate of Survey and Land Records etc. for planning and monitoring of development and management of towns.

To meet the requirement of base maps for towns and cities a scheme for preparing urban maps using aerial photography was started during the Eighth Five Year Plan. The original estimates were to the tune of 19.72

crore for preparing large scale base maps for about 150 towns with the help of aerial photography. The project envisaged development of technical capabilities of the town planning organisations at Central and State level so as to enable updating of the maps in a reservation cycle. In the first phase 25 towns from six states were selected on priority basis for coverage under this scheme in consultation with the State Governments by the Town & Country (NRSA) was assigned the task of alongwith line maps after rectification, ground control etc.

An amount of Rs.5.50 cror. was allocated in the 8th Five Year Plan for the Urban Mapping Scheme and Research & Training in Urban & Regional Planning. A sum of Rs. 8.08 crores has been released to TCPO under Urban Mapping Scheme upto 1997-98(Rs.1.12 crores—1992-93; Rs. 2.81 crores—1993-94; Rs. 2.15 crores—1994-95, Rs. 1.00 crore 1996-97 and Rs. 1.00 crore—1997-98) out of which an expenditure of Rs. 6.51 crores has been incurred so far, towards payment to NRSA for the work of aerial photography and base Mapping and for upgrading hardware /software facilities and training of personnel.

The Executive Agency for the project, the national Remote Sensing Agency (NRSA) has completed aerial photography and they have supplied photographs and aerial maps for all the towns. TCPO in collaboration with concerned State Town Planning Departments is undertaking interpretation of aerial photographs and collection of other secondary data/ information to generate thematic maps and graphic data base for the development of GIS and processing of information for use as multi purpose maps.

As envisaged in the 8th Five Year Plan document, the second phase of Urban Mapping Scheme involving 25 more towns was approved to be covered in the Ninth

Year Plan period. For the second phases of Urban Mapping Scheme 25 towns have been proposed and aerial survey work has been completed by NRSA for 10 towns. For rest of towns, State Governments have submitted/are in the process of submitting the technical specifications for taking up aerail work.

An amount of Rs. 2.80 crores was originally allocated for the yew 1998-99 for the Research and Training in Urban & Regional Planning and Urban Mapping out of which a sum of Rs. 1.00 crore was earmarked for release to TCPO for the second phase of Urban Mapping Scheme. However, at Revised Estimate stage the allocation for Research &Training in Urban & Regional Planning and Urban Mapping has been reduced to Rs. 1.40 crore and consequently a sum of Rs. 0.60 crore has finally been earmarked for Urban Mapping Scheme.

Promotion of Non-Handicapping Environment for the Disabled and Elderly Persons

The Ministry of Urban Affairs & Employment is the nodal Ministry for implementation of barrier-free built environment for the disabled and elderly persons as envisaged in the Economic and Social Commission for Asia and the Pacific (ESCAP) Resolution adopted in its 48th session held in Beijing in 1992. The New Delhi Pilot Project for promotion of Non-Handicapping Built Environment for the Disabled and Elderly Persons was launched in 1996 with the support of ESCAP.

One sq. km. area was selected in Indraprastha Estate Complex jointly by ESCAP and the Working Committee set up under the Chairmanship of Joint Secretary (DD) for implementation of the project. A number of buildings located in this area which are frequently being visited by the disabled persons were taken up for implementation of the project. Besides, Nirman Bhawan and Shastri Bhawan housing the Ministries of Urban Affairs &

Employment and Social Justice and Empowerment respectively have also been included in the list of buildings identified for implementing the project. The project was completed and a final workshop was held in June, 1998. A number of important recommendations were adopted during the workshop. A Working Committee was reconstituted under the Chairmanship of JS (DD) to oversee the implementation of the recommendations.

The Ministry of Urban Affairs & Employment has also prepared Model Building Bye-Laws which contain a number of provisions for providing accessibilities to disabled persons to various public buildings. These Building Bye-Laws have been sent to all the State Governments, Union Territories, DDA, MOD, NDMC etc. for adoption.

Besides, the Chief Ministers of the States and UTs have been addressed to implement the provisions relating to promotion of barrier-free built environment for the disabled in the buildings in their States/UTs, especially the buildings belonging to State Legislatures, High Courts etc. Similar request has been sent to Secretary Generals of Lok Sabha/ Rajya Sabha and Registrar, Supreme Court to carry out suitable additions/ alterations in their buildings to provide barrier-free built access to the disabled. The Railway Board and Ministry of Civil Aviation, Ministry of Communication, Ministry of Surface Transport, Department of Health and Department of Education have also been addressed in this regard.

A committee set up under the Chairmanship of Director General (Works) has prepared Guidelines and Space Standards for Barrier-Free Built Environment for the disabled. These guidelines have been circulated to State Governments for guidance and adoption.

Prime Minister's Award for Excellence in Urban Planning and Design

It has been decided with the approval of the Prime Minister to institute two National Awards for:—

(i) implemented Urban Planning and Design Projects signifying built environment of exceptional quality; and

(ii) innovative ideas / concepts and plans in Urban Planning and Design, where the projects are still the pipeline or at implementation stage.

These awards are open to all Indian architects, town planners and allied professionals, their firms and government, public and private sector institutions/ organisations who have planned/ implemented projects anywhere in India.

The first prize in each category will carry a cash award of Rs. 5 lakhs including a citation, and the second prize will carry a cash award of Rs. 2.50 lakhs including a citation. These prizes will be awarded on a biennial basis.

Applications were invited for the Award for 1996-97 biennium. The entries were evaluated by the Jury and the recommendations have been finally accepted by the Prime Minister. It is expected that the prizes would be distributed shortly.

Externally Aided Urban Development Projects

The World Bank assisted TNUDP with a project outlay of Rs. 988.5 crore was completed on 30.9.97. One of the components of the project was Municipal Urban Development Fund (MUDF). This was set up to provide debt finance to city Governments on a pilot basis.

The successful track record of MUDF encouraged Govt. of Tamil Nadu to broaden the scope of the Fund with a view to attract private capital into urban infrastructure and facilitate better performing Urban Local Bodies (ULBs) to access capital market. In 1996, Govt. of Tamil Nadu with the assistance of World Bank established the Tamil Nadu Urban Development Fund.

TNUDF is a Trust Fund managed by an Asset Management Company holding shares by Tamil Nadu Urban Infrastructure Financing Services Ltd. (TNUIFSL), ICICI, HDFC and IL&FS in the ratio of 49%, 21%,15% and 15% respectively.

Bombay Urban Infrastructure Development Project

Based on the concept of Financial Intermediaries for financing urban infrastructure projects, the Govt. of Maharashtra proposed setting up of an Intermediary for financing Mumbai Urban Infrastructure Project. The project proposal was recommended to the World Bank through Ministry of Finance (Deptt. of Economic Affairs). The Bank has advised to hold off the project preparation work until agreements on institutional arrangements are finalised.

West Bengal Municipal Development Project

Two separate agreements have been signed with the World Bank on 26.6.98 for grants amounting US $ 468,750 and US $ 927,050 respectively. The objectives of the project are to assist selected Municipality in developing strategy and comprehensive plans for environmental, economic and social management and to strengthen the capacity of municipality to deliver the objectives.

Karnataka Municipal Development and Urban Infrastructure Project

The Govt. of Karnataka had forwarded a proposal for development of urban infrastructure in the cities and towns of the State. The estimated cost of the project is US

$ 150 million. The project proposal was recommended to World Bank through Ministry of Finance (Deptt. of Economic Affairs). The Bank had held discussions with the State Govt. in September, 1998 on the proposal.

Preparation of Country Infrastructure Framework Report

The World Bank Group in its paper on "An Action Programme for Facilitating Private Involvement in Urban Infrastructure" had suggested to conduct studies to review/examine (i) existing initiatives for private sector involvement in India (ii) new initiatives required (iii) preparation of Country Assistance Strategy and (iv) preparation of status report on current trend in implementation of private sector infrastructure projects. Based on these suggestions, the Ministry prepared a Concept Paper for the Bank's intervention in urban sector. The paper is expected to be discussed by DEA with World Bank and a Project Concept Document prepared thereafter. This would be discussed with selected State Govts. to help them to prepare project for funding by the Bank.

WHO Project

Healthy City Programme

The Ministry of Urban Affairs & Employment formulated a proposal on "Healthy Cities Programme" in the country with financial assistance from WHO based on the concept of Healthy Cities Programme of WHO. The objectives of the programmes are (i) Capacity building for integrating environmental health programme into all major urban policies and programmes including Mega City Scheme and (ii) taking up pilot projects to demonstrate the application of Healthy Cities Programmes in the five mega cities. The estimated cost of the project is US $ 125.000. The agencies involved in implementing the programme are: HSMI, New Delhi: All India Institute of

Local Self Government, Mumbai; All India Institute of Hygiene and Public Health, Calcutta Regional Centre for Urban Environmental Studies Hyderabad; Administrative Staff College of India, Hyderabad; National Environmental Engineering Institute, Nagpur; Municipal Corporations of Greater Mumbai, Calcutta, Bangalore, Hyderabad and Chennai and Hyderabad. These proposals have been forwarded to WHO for funding

Asian Development Bank (ADB) Projects

The Karnataka Urban Infrastructure Development Project

The Karnataka urban Infrastructure Development Project costing US$132 million (ADB loan US $ 85 million) is under implementation. The main focus of the project is to promote decentralisation of economic growth from the rapidly expanding Bangalore city to four selected towns namely Mysore, Tumkur, Channapatnam and Ramanagram to be promoted as counter magnets. The Karnataka Urban Infrastructure Development Finance Corporation is the implementing agency of the project. As on 31.8.98, an expenditure of Rs. 37.34 crore has been incurred on the project.

Rajasthan Urban Infrastructure Development Project

On the basis of study conducted under the ADB assisted Technical Assistance for development of six towns in Rajasthan, the Bank has agreed to provides funding for an Urban Development Project namely the Rajasthan Urban, Infrastructure Development Project Loan negotiations were held in Manila in October 1998 for a loan of US $ 250 million. The objective of the project is for development of six cities in the state namely Ajmer, Bikaner, Kota, Jaipur, Jodhpur and Udaipur.

ADB Technical assistance

Karnataka Coastal Environmental Management and the Urban Development

The ADB has approved technical assistance for assessing needs and priorities for policy intervention as well as investment in environmental management and urban infrastructure and services in three coastal districts of Karnataka viz. South Canara, Udupi and North Canara at a total cost of US $ 8 lakh. The draft final report of the TA has already been submitted and final report is expected to be submitted shortly.

Based on the study under the TA the Bank is expected to approve the Karnataka Urban Development and Coastal environmental Management Project which would focus on improving the living conditions in urban centres located along the West Coast of Karnataka through the provision of essential urban infrastructure and municipal services to meet basic human needs and support sustainable development of the region. The estimated cost of the project is US $ 251.4 million of which the Bank is expected to finance through a loan amounting to US $ 175 million and the balance is to be funded by the State Government and Local Governments.

Projects Preparatory Technical Assistance for Calcutta Municipal Environmental Improvement Programme

A proposal for undertaking Technical Assistance study by ADB for undertaking a technically and financially viable programme for improvement of drainage, waste water management and solid waste management as well as other investments necessary for improving environmental quality over the next 20 years within the Calcutta Municipal Corporation is being considered by ADB. The estimated cost of the TA is US $ 1,310,000. The TA is included in the Bank's Country Assistance Programme 1998 and subsequent loan amount estimated at US $ 200 million is tentatively scheduled for processing in 1999 and approval in 2000.

TA for Urban Environmental Infrastructure Fund

ADB in association with Govt. of India has undertaken a Technical Assistance (TA) Project for the design of an Urban and Environmental Infrastructure Fund (UEIF). The Fund is expected to support the development of Urban and Environmental Infrastructure. The objective of the TA is to assist the Government in developing means to mobilise 'resources to meet the rapidly growing needs of urban development and environmental improvement through (i) the establishment of an Urban and Environmental Development Fund to leverage private sector and external resources for urban development and environmental improvement and (ii) the preparation of suitable projects involving public-private investment for financing under the Fund. Presently the Consultants are involved in the studies and the reports are expected shortly.

Matters Relating to Research Projects/ Studies

This Ministry considers various research proposals submitted by Government, Semi-Government, Academic and Research Institutions and Voluntary Organisations and releases grant-in-aid to them. These funds are mainly released for conducting research studies pertaining to subjects such as the evaluation of on-going plan schemes in the Urban Development and Housing sector, Urban Management, Upgradation of the Financial and Administrative Capability of the Urban Local Bodies, System of Devolution of State Resources to Municipalities, Operation of Urban Land Market, Measures for Promoting Privatisation/Public Private Partnership, etc. and also for relevant Training Programmes for Municipal/Town Planning functionaries. The grant-in-aid under this head are also released for conducting seminars and conferences which covers the above mentioned subjects.

8

Diversity of India

Over the fifty years, the interrelated set of characteristics have got exemplified in an institutional and political framework. Today if we are led to a retrospective insight that it has in fact turned out to be a story of fifty years consisting of both the playing out of these cultural and political contours and gravely failing to do so. It nonetheless does provide us with a holistic framework of perceiving the fifty years as one major, continuously unfolding, often times paradoxical, yet somehow integrated, episode. Perhaps the most remarkable aspect of India's fifty years story has been the almost continuous coexistence of democracy and poverty.

It is the story of a country so deeply mired in not only poverty but also high levels of illiteracy, unemployment, ill-health and depressed conditions, in which the dalits, diverse "minorities" and large numbers of women and children still continue to both have faith in and actually work through the democratic process. What is more, it is precisely the poor and these suffering classes of people that have kept the democratic process alive, far more than the elite and the affluent classes.

The clear reason for this is that for the poor and the deprived it is only through the democratic political process that their condition has any chance of improving. They are increasingly aware of this, there is a considerable rise in political consciousness among them and they have after a long period of waiting for the State and its institutions to deliver the goods, decided to themselves intervene politically and find ways to fend for themselves and bend the system as a whole for their own deliverance. As we look at the situation at the end of fifty years of independence it is becoming increasingly clear that what has saved the poor from total eclipse is not some poverty alleviation scheme launched by the bureaucracy or the Planning Commission and its economists but the poor people's own struggles against the system, their own strategies of survival and gradually, their own growth in confidence and sense of dignity and self-esteem. What is remarkable is that in doing so the poor in India are making full use of the caste basis of the peculiar hierarchical order found in India for changing the nature of the inherited social order, the multi-cultural structure of the "State" by growing resort to the politics of identity and self determination. The highly flexible ethical code that is allowing such a vast variety of contradictions, paradoxes and indeed so much hypocrisy in public life which is all getting slowly exposed and the system forced to accept norms of accountability, transparency and "right to information", under pressure not so much from the media and a handful of intellectuals but from the suffering masses themselves, even if this may still be part of the continuing hypocrisy. Elsewhere, in other parts of the world, the scourge of poverty and of growing inequity was removed by the rise of a class of intellectuals and politicians who were concerned about the "state of affairs" and began intervening in them–this in course of time lead to the rise of what came to be known as the "Left" consisting of parties, universities, journals, study circles, "clubs" and "societies" (like the Fabians) as well as new thinking on the role of the state in the economy, as represented by the Keynesian revolution, and of course the organisation of the working class and the economically deprived, all of this slowly producing a new idea and ideology of the state, often called the welfare state. In India, despite much rhetoric, some stirring resolutions (Avadi and the rest) and a whole lot of legislative measures, constitutional amendments and plan schemes, this has just not happened.

On the contrary, vested interests, the growing power of the rich who have lost all sense of social responsibility and have instead decided to abandon the poor who they increasingly hold responsible for holding back the country's "progress" and, now their adoption of the neo-liberal doctrine of globalisation and liberalisation, have all stopped such measures from being implemented. Hence, the new reality as faced by the poor which is producing new responses from them as we approach the ends of the first fifty years of our independence. It is by the poor gaining new insights, greater confidence in themselves and intervening for the purpose of realising the original vision that the 50-year dream will start unfolding. It is indeed the unfolding of one single integrated episode that the fifty years represent.

For example, on the eve of Independence only, a small section of the urban population of India had access to western medical facilities. The majority of the rural population relied on indigenous practitioners of the Ayurvedic, Unani and Homoeopathic systems of medicine and to a few far flung government dispensaries, private practitioners, missionary hospitals and some private philanthropic institutions. Though the government did provide some rudimentary services during epidemics of plague, cholera and smallpox these were far from adequate because of a lack of resources, trained health personnel and the problems of delivery.

In 1946, the Health Survey and Planning Committee of the Government of India under the chairmanship of Sir Joseph Bhore submitted a report which had a major on the improvement of the existing health services and establishing a rational and durable health infrastructure in this country. The Bhore Committee advocated a decentralized health structure with the distinct as the main unit for planning and coordination and the Primary Health Centre as the nucleus for an integrated service in rural areas. Health care in India has undergone a major transformation and there have been substantial achievements in disease control and a marked improvement in health indices. In 1983, a National Health Policy was formally adopted by the Indian Parliament. This laid special emphasis on the preventive, promotive and rehabilitative health services. It established a comprehensive network of Primary Health Centre services, creation of an army of health volunteers and effective community participation.

Thus the health care establishment has become more widespread and accessible. Together with this, training facilities for medical and paramedical personnel in both western and indigenous systems have been increased and a solid foundation laid for medical research especially into diseases effecting the Indian people.

The budget investment on health has increased from Rs. 65.2 crores during the first Five Year Plan (1951-56) to Rs. 3,393 crores during the Seventh Plan. This has increased the health facilities in terms of training, personnel and hospitals. The number of Primary Health Centres increased from 725 in 1955 to 16,735 in 1988. Hospitals increased from 2,717 in 1970 to more than 8,000 in 1988. There were only 59,000 doctors at the time of Independence; now this number has grown to over four lakhs.

Thus whilst the doctor-population ratio was only 17 doctors per 1 lakh in 1950, it is now 50 per lakh. The number of beds available has also increased from one to seven lakhs and there has also been an increase in other categories of health personnel such as dentists, nurses and other health workers. There has been a four to five-fold increase in the number of nurses, midwives, auxiliary midwives and lady health visitors.

The number of training establishments have also shown a marked increase–medical colleges rose from 42 in 1950 to 140 in 1991 and dental colleges from 4 in 1950 to 43 in 1989. On the recommendations of the Bhore Committee certain National Institutes for Medical Education and Training were started. The first of these was the All India Institute of Medical Sciences in New Delhi which was started in 1956.

The main purpose for establishing such institutes for undergraduate and postgraduate models for undergraduate and postgraduate medical education, for rendering specialised medical care and to undertake investigation into indigenous medical problems.

During the First Five Year Plan many programmes were launched to control communicable diseases such as malaria, smallpox, tuberculosis, leprosy and cholera. The number of cases of smallpox was 1.6 lakhs in 1950 and out of these 41,000 were fetal. By 1975 the disease had been completely eradicated. Plague has also nearly disappeared.

The number of case of cholera was 1.8 lakhs in 1950 out of which 19,000 were fatal. Improvements have also been made in the control of leprosy, tuberculosis, goiter, blindness, and diarrhoeal and sexually transmitted diseases. A major effort is being made to control the spread of the Acquired Immunodeficiency Syndrome

(AIDS) which has over the year acquired fearful dimensions.

The major achievement in this area has been the establishment and spread of the Integrated Child Development and Services, popularly known as the ICDS. This project was started in 1976 on an experimental basis to provide a package of services for pre-school children and expectant mothers. These services included immunization, regular medical check-ups, supplementary nutrition, non-formal education for the children and nutrition and health education for the children and nutrition and health education to women in the reproductive age group.

The services are now provided on a national scale including the tribal areas. The basic unit of the ICDS is the Anganwadi which is staffed by an Anganwadi worker who covers a population of 1000. There are now about 1,00,000 anganwadis who cover a population of 130 lakhs (in 1971 the population covered was 6.6 lakhs).

Infant mortality, which probably is the best index of the quality of a country's health care, has fallen from 134 per 1,000 live births in 1950 to 95 in 1987. In certain states like Kerala which have a higher female literacy rate and more widespread health facilities this figure is 60.

Birth rate declined from 39.9 in 1950 to 32 in 1987 and is expected to be less than 25 by the turn of the century. The death rate was 27.4 per thousand population per year in 1950 and 10.8 per thousand population per year in 1987. It is expected to be 8 per thousand per year by the year 2000. Life expectancy at birth was 32 years in 1950 and 58 years in 1991. By the year 2000 it may reach 65 years.

India has developed a strong medical research base and has been called a third world giant in this area.

Indian Medical Scientists rank eighth in the world in research output and account for over half of the third world's publications.

The Indian Council of Medical research (ICMR) is the apex body controlling research activity in medicine and is one of the oldest medical research bodies in the world. It started as the Indian Research Fund Association in 1911-81 years ago. It has 20 permanent research institutes which are carrying out specific research into tuberculosis cholera, malaria, nutrition, reproduction and cancer. It also funds ad hocresearch projects in medical colleges and other institutions and there have been major contributions from this country in the areas of protein energy malnutrition, Vitamin A' deficiency, female contraception, the domicililary treatment of tuberculosis, oral rehydration therapy, the control of habitual abortion, high attitude pulmonary edema, operations for leprosy, the treatment of Kala azar, epidemic hepatitis and the discovery of J-receptors in the lungs. The budget of the ICMR which was Rs. 13 crores in the Sixth Five Year Plan has been increased to Rs. 40 crores during the Seventh Plan.

There are other government organisations which also carry out and fund medical research such as the Department of Science and Technology, the Council for Scientific and Industrial Research and the Indian National Science Academy.

Although this litany of achievement suggests all round success this is by no means true. The infrastructure of the Indian Health Services has been erected on a very sound and broad base but the heights have by no means been reached. Compared with many other developing countries, including China, our health indices such as infant morality, maternal mortality and life expectancy are much worse. Our population continues to grow at an alarming rate 50 that by the year 2025 it may exceed the population of China. Many of our 140 medical colleges, of whom some are basically private business ventures, are not producing doctors whose quality is comparable to those produced in western countries. This has led to the de-recognition of certain Indian medical degrees by some countries and this devaluation by others i.e. a doctor with an Indian degree is paid considerably less in their countries than one with a western degree.

Gone are the days when a medical graduate from Calcutta, Madras and Lucknow was respected as one from London, Edinburgh or Boston. Our research, although large in quantity, when it is assessed critically, is generally of poor quality. In terms of citation rates, the number of times that a paper is referred to by another, Indian publications rank low even in a third world league table.

The time has probably come to have a fresh look at Indian medicine. The first step would be to establish a nationwide health database to find out the facts as they are. At the same time it is important to pay much more attention to quality to the quality of patient care, the quality of medical education and the quality of research.

The advance in health care since Independence has been to establish a health system which is acessible to all our countrymen. The effort now should be to make this system function at a high level of excellence.

India is a land of physical, ecological, social, cultural and linguistic diversity. Bounded by the Himalayan mountain ranges in the north and the Indian Ocean in the south, it has a multitude of climates, soil types and geographical areas—and consequently of habitats and wildlife. But it is not only the physical and biological diversity that is enormous. The census reports 1,652 languages as mother tongues. Of these, 33 are spoken by over a 100,000 people each. India is also home to many religious communities and its ancient tradition of secularism is manifested in its Constitution.

Each of these languages and religions contributes to the vibrancy and variety of Indian life, and to the mosaic of India's social, cultural and economic life. 'Unity in Diversity' has been the maxim of cultural pluralism in India. But at times of resource shortages and allocation, it is not always easy to keep regional or sectorial aspirations subservient to national ones. To maintain the unity of India with all its diversity remains a challenge—but the binding forces evolved over centuries help meet this challenge.

India's population of 844 million is today growing at 2.11 per cent every year. This is expected to stabilize only in the second half of the next century, when India will be the most populous country in the world. Adding over 17 million people each year puts considerable pressure on the country's natural resources and reduces the gains of development.

The challenge underlying limiting population growth was brought out by Prime Minister P.V. Narasimha Rao who stressed recently the need for the country to "take upon itself the challenge to deal with population-related issues whish are inextricably linked to the total development of our nation." The `link' is usually misunderstood. It is not that population control will lead to development, but that development leads to a decrease in population growth rates.

High population growth rate is usually an indicator of poverty, and not the cause of it. This is perhaps best seen in the case of women's development. Taking just one indicator—female literacy—some trends become clear. States such as Kerala and Tamil Nadu which have among the highest female literacy rates in India (86.93 per cent and 52.29 per cent, respectively) are also among the states with the lowest decennial population growth rates (13.98 per cent and 14.94 per cent). This is just one development factor out of the many which act together to affect population.

Based on ideals long cherished by its people, the Constitution of India defines India as a 'Sovereign, Socialist, Secular, Democratic Republic'. the system of government is parliamentary with a federal structure, power and responsibility being shared between the Central and State Governments, and in turn with many local and district level authorities. The cooperation between various levels of government is crucial to development.

A challenge before a large country like India is to find the right blend between centralized and decentralized decision-making and between micro-level planning and macro-level planning. Decision-making that involves people at various levels brings in different perceptions and enriches the process.

The importance of involving local people in decision-making, to bring in a better perspective of their requirements and in finding implementable solutions, is also being recognized. Starting from colonial times, several policies, laws and procedures have tended to alienate people from their natural resources. Evolving methods for the participation of local people in the management of common property resources is a major challenge for natural resource management.

The floodplains of the great rivers are India's food bowls. So far, food production has kept abreast of population increase. But the Green Revolution, which was largely responsible for this, has raised some questions of environmental costs. High-yielding varieties, making crops more vulnerable to disease. Soil health problems such as deficiency of micro-nutrients and organic matter, incidence of soil salinity, and damage to the physical structure of soil have arisen in the intensively cultivated areas.

The need for higher inputs has resulted in chemical inputs going up from about 1.9 kg per ha of gross cropped area in 1960 to over 72 kg per ha by 1990-91. The challenge is not only to sustain and increase agricultural growth, but to do so without damaging the environment.

Of the total 329 million hectares (mha) of land, it is estimated that only 266 mha possess any potential for production. Of this, 143 mha is agricultural land and it is estimated that 85 mha suffers from varying degrees of soil degradation. Of the remaining 123 mha, 40 are completely unproductive. The balance 83 mha are classified as forest lands, of which over half are denuded to various degrees.

India has the world's largest cattle population. The 406 million head of livestock have to be supported on 13 mha, or less than 4 per cent of the land which is classified as pasture lands, most of which is overgrazed. Thus, out of 266 mha, about 175 mha or 66 per cent is degraded to varying degrees. Water and wind erosion account for the degradation of almost 150 mha of this.

The challenge of prevention of erosion, and indeed of restoration of India's land resources, is intricately related to strategies for the management of land, water and vegetative cover. Forests in India have been shrinking for several centuries owing to pressures of agriculture, commercial and industrial use, urbanization and other uses. The process continued after Independence. Vast areas that were once green are today wastelands. Bringing these back under vegetative cover is a major challenge.

Like indigenous people all over the world, the tribal communities that live in forests respect the trees, and the birds and animals that give them sustenance. Strategies are being developed for a greater degree of people's participation in forest management.

The role of forest-dwelling communities in restoring and conserving forests is now being increasingly recognized. The challenge is to attempt to integrate the modern knowledge and skills of the Forest Department with the traditional knowledge and experience of the local communities, and to evolve strategies for the joint management of forests.

As in most places in the world, the forests and the agricultural plains have an intimate relationship. Forests usually act as catchments for rivers. With the increasing demand for water, plans were made to harness the mighty rivers through large irrigation projects.

Typically, these would submerge forests, displace local communities and benefit agriculture in the plains. Today some of these, like the dam on the river Narmada and the Tehri dam, have become areas of debate. This is an issue which poses very difficult questions regarding the relationship between environment and development, and resolving these is a challenge the country faces.

If the world's rainfall were averaged over its landmass, it is seen that India receives more than one-and-a-half times the rain that other parts of the world get. But this rainfall has a large spatial and temporal variation and is highly seasonal. Eighty per cent of the country gets 80 per cent or more of the annual rainfall during the four months of the monsoon.

Managing water so that it is available when and where it is required is a major issue. Of the total 400 million hectare metres (mham) annual precipitation that

India receives, approximately 150 mham percolates into the soil, 180 mham joins the surface flow and 70 mham evaporates. Of the 150 mham which enters the soil, about 110 mham constitutes soil moisture while 40 mham percolates into groundwater aquifers. Of the 180 mham run-off, major and minor irrigation projects have so far succeeded in trapping 17 mham in their reservoirs. Another 4 or 5 mham are stored in tanks and small reservoirs. Thus only about 16 per cent of the annual rainfall is available for irrigation.

Large dams which replaced traditional water-harvesting techniques in modern India were initially seen as the solution. But today the problems of displacement, submergence and drainage are subjects of serious debate.

Increasing demands and new technologies are leading to the over-exploitation of groundwater, leading to an alarming drop in water tables in certain areas. This has even led to the problem of extreme salinity in some parts of the country. Rationalizing the use of groundwater is another important issue.

Community wastes, industrial effluents and excessive use of chemical fertilizers and pesticides are polluting surface water and affecting the quality of groundwater. The implications of this on human health and aquatic life are obvious. Finding optimal strategies for the conservation of water, provision of safe drinking water and keeping warer bodies clean are difficult challenges.

India is very rich in biodiversity. Preserving this heritage is a major challenge, as also utilizing this for development. With the considerably large financial resources and research capabilities available with the North, the benefits emanating from this biodiversity are being exploited more rapidly by the North than by the countries of its origin.

Although India is largely rural and agricultural, the 27 per cent Indians who live in urban areas constitute a large number in absolute terms.

A very large number of these are the urban poor who live in highly degraded slums. Urbanization and industrialization pose a host of environmental problems that need urgent attention. Over 30 per cent of urban Indians live in slums. Out of India's 3,245 towns and cities, only 21 have partial or full sewerage and sewage treatment facilities. Coping with rapid urbanization is a major challenge facing the country today.

Several of India's cities started out as trading towns centred in agricultural area. As these grew, urban land requirements ate into some of the best agricultural lands. Location policies for urban and industrial growth from this point of view are other challenges to planning in India.

While on the one hand India has some of the most sophisticated industrial plants, there are many more using outdated, polluting technologies and makeshift facilities, with negligible provision for treating their wastes. As a result, there are many cities and industrial ares that would perhaps be classified among the worst in terms of their air and water pollution.

Major initiatives are however being taken. The Environment Protection Act (1986), the Water (Prevention and Control of Pollution) Act, 1974, and the Air (Prevention and Control of Pollution) Act, 1981, have set standards that certain industries must fulfill. Much pollution control equipment is now available in the country. The Central Pollution Control Board and State Pollution Control Boards have their own machinery to monitor emission and pollution levels.

The choices, however, are difficult. Substantial

resources, technical expertise, political and social will, awareness among the people and their support are required to implement these rules. Industries may need to be relocated, and new equipment added to treat the wastes.

New, clean technologies need to replace older ones. In some cases plants may even need to be scrapped. These measures may involve loss of jobs in the short run and have an immediate consequence on the cost of products. These are difficult choices, especially in a developing country.

The Challenges of meeting India's growing energy requirements are many. presently, commercial and non-commercial sources contribute almost equally to fulfilling these needs. The current use of bio-resources for meeting energy requirements is far in excess of their regenerative capacities. Each source of commercial energy-hydel, thermal or nuclear—has major environmental consequences and the challenge is to utilize these resources with the least environmental damage. This involves determining the optimal technology, scale and location of such projects.

There is considerable scope for energy saving. For instance, the inefficiencies of the system can be seen from the fact that 100 tonnes of coal mined for the purpose of power generation provide only the energy equivalent of 5 tonnes of coal in the form of actual irrigation when we use electric pumping in the agricultural sector. A full 95 tonnes of coal is lost in energy euqivalent terms in the process of power generation, transmission and distribution, inefficiencies in the pump set itself and the irrigation system which finally reaches water to the farmer's field.

Major investment would be required in the area of technology upgradation for increasing efficiency of generation, transmission and utilization of commercial energy. There are also technology constraints in using existing sources. Huge quantities of natural gas estimated to be worth about Rs. 50 million a day are today flared, rather than utilized for power generation, domestic fuel or feedstock for the production of fertilizer.

Another challenge is that of reorienting to today's conditions and needs, institutions, attitudes and infrastructures essentially built up during the colonial times. This change must take into account India's traditions of resource use, management, education etc. The change needs to come about in education, in attitudes, in administrative procedures and in institutions, for it affects the way people view technology, resources, and indeed development itself.

Poverty, however, remains the central issue and the biggest challenge. While the annual per capita income has been slowly rising over time, about 40 per cent of the people are below what is considered the poverty line. The challenge is therefore not only to find development paths and models which are environmentally sustainable but that are also socially just and culturally acceptable.

For a very large number of the poor who depend on the resources of their immediate environment, poverty has been compounded by environmental degradation. Not only does the natural resource base of the immediate environment provide their basic requirements, it is also the basis of their livelihood and security. The challenge of poverty and the challenge of environment are therefore not two different challenges but two facets of the same challenge.

The problems are complex and the choices difficult. Each issue needs its own resolution, not a borrowed solution. A large number of areas need research and constant monitoring. Citizens and decision-makers need to become more aware of their environment and the intricate relationship it bears to development. Today in India we see the seeds of this effort. A national Ministry of Environment and Forest was set up in 1985. Most states have set up Departments of Environment and associated agencies.

Several hundred institutions and several thousand NGOs are today, in one way or another, working towards coping with the challenges of environment and development. But the most hopeful sing perhaps is an increasing number of people who, individually and through their communities, are taking action—action that leads to a better environment and a better life. It is these efforts that need to be shared widely. The efforts of the people, NGOs and the Government.

Gandhiji was not a professional economist, but he held strong views on the problems that are certainly the domain of economics.

He did not deny the impact of one's surroundings and material resources upon one's character, but he did not subscribe to the Marxian view that the final causes of all social changes and political revolutions were to be sought, not in man's sould, not in man's insight ito eternal truth and justice, but in changes in the modes of production. "I believe" Gandhiji said "and I have noticed too that thought transforms man's features as well as character".

He rejected outright the sordid figure of the economic man, who was always motivated by the tinkle of gold. He did not believe that man lives by bread alone. He saw faith as the mainspring of social well–being.

Like Hawtrey and Bohson, he believed that economics could not be dissociated from ethics. In him we find a powerful denunciation of the neutrality of economics as between ends preached by Senior, Cairness and Say, and rehabilitated recently by Robbins. "True economics", he said, "never militates against the highest ethical standard just as all true ethics to be worth its name must at the same time be also good economics".

His simple way of living earned for his economic views the nickname of loin—cloth economics. It was mistakenly though that he stood for a state of wantlessness or pleaded for a low, depressed standard of living. His approach was pragmatic and realistic. How could he lead a life of ease and luxury, when the millions of India were submerged in abysmal poverty? He gave up all possessions because being in the service of the poor he though he had no claims on those "I came definitely to the conclusion" hesaid, "that if I had to serve the people in whose midst my life was cast and to whose difficulties I was witness from day to day, I must discard all wealth, all possessions....and a time came when it became a positive joy to give up those things". He further remarked, The golden rule...is resolutely to refuse to have what millions cannot". If the need of his fellow beings for something that he possessed was greater than his, he looked upon that thing as stolen property.

The theory of trusteeship of property is a logical projection of his theory of non—possession of what others cannot afford to get. He wanted the industrialists, the landlords and the other fortunate sections of the community t act as trustees of the wealth, which they were to use for the betterment of their poorer brethren.

He was against the blind application of economic theory as developed in the West to Indian conditions. Like Justice Ranade he was for the evolution of an Indian economy suited to the peculir conditions of Indians. "Each country has its ownb economies. German textbooks are different from the English. Free trade may be England's salvation. It spells our ruin." His denunciation of free trade and solicitude for Swadeshi is a re—echo of List's plea for protection.

He was no enemy of machine, but he stood against it when it evslaved man or elbowed him out of the factory. Lack of capital ckoupled with a surfeit on man—power in India and theevils of the factory system led him to advocate a decentralised economic system with its accent on small–scale and cottage industries. "The salvation of India lies in cottages," was his slogan.

In his advocacy of cooperative farming he anticipated the presentday emphasis on it in the context of our backward agriculture and food deficit. "Ifirmly believe," he wrote in the 'Harijan', "that we shall not derive the full benefits of agriculture until we take to cooperative farming. Does it not stand to reason that it is far better for hundred families in a village to cultivate their lands collectively and divide the income therefrom than to divide the land anyhow into a hundred portions."

He was not blown off his feet by the material achievements of socialism in the West. He believed in the evolution of and indigenous variety of socialism. "Let us study our eastern institutions in that spirit of enquiry and we shall evolve a truer sokcialism and a truer communism that the world has yet dreamt of". His socialism can be classed with that of the Utopian socialists, who received the undisguised contempt of Marx.

He was not against communism as such. He claimed for himself the title of "a foremost communist." His communism was, however, based on non–violence and pure means to achieve it. "If communism comes without violence", he said, "would be welcome." These words ring in sharp contrast to the Communist Manifesto of 1843.

Gandhian economics, in sum, is rooted in non–violence, truth, love and self—sacrifice. It rejects coercion, regimentation, self–interest, centralisation of means of production and wealth, and above all a mad pursuit of the material goods of life.

The Indian Constitution is a remarkable document as it strikes a balance between tradition and modernity, between a federal structure and a strong centre and between the demands of social justice and the rights of the individual. However, as we enter the 50th year of our Independence, perhaps it would be desirable to take a close second look at the Constitution with a view to removing possible distortions and streamlining its functioning, feel the author.

Democracy is often described as government of the people, by the people and for the people. The Constitution, written as in the United States and other countries or unwritten but dependent on tradition as in the United Kingdom, lays down the framework for this form of government. But written or unwritten, there is a remarkable similarity between the two. In the United Kingdom the centre of power shifted first from the Crown to the nobles and then to the House of Commons. In the United States, judicial pronouncements have changed the complexion of the government. The federal Government has far more powers than was envisaged at first. All this was achieved by a process of evolution either by consensus as in the U.K. or by judicial pronouncements as it came up and a solution was found.

India became independent on August 15, 1947 and the Founding Fathers worked post haste to give the nation a new Constitution. The constitution was adopted by the Constitutent Assembly on November 26, 1949 and came into force on January 26, 1950. It was a remarkable achievement because many countries which became independent along with India were still floundering and trying to find their way in framing the Constitution. Countries, which became independent later, were looking at India's efforts. The Indian Constitution is a remarkable document as it strikes a balance between tradition and modernity, between a federal structure and strong centre between the demands of social justice and the rights of the individual and between conflicting demands in other areas.

Though the Founding Fathers were proud of the Constitution they had framed, they were also aware of their own limitations. As people move into a new house, they notice defects which had escaped the architect. Also conditions change and needs grow. Similarly, defects come to light as a Constitution comes into operation. Changes therefore become necessary and have to be made quickly and easily.

As Dr. B.R. Ambedkar, the Law Minister, said on the day the Constitution was adopted, "The Assembly has not only refrained from putting a seal of finality and infallibility upon the Constitution by denying the people the right to amend the Constitution or making the amendment of the Constitution subject to the fulfilment of extraordinary terms and conditions, as in America or in Australia but has provided a more facile procedure foramending the Constitution". The President of the Constituent Assembly Dr. Rajendra Prasad observed "another important feature of the Constitution is that it enables amendments to be made without much difficulty".

Prime Minister Jawaharlal Nehru was even more forthright. Speaking on the first amendment made in 1951 he said, "People must realise that this great

Constitution of ours, which we laboured for so long, is not a final or rigid thing which must either be accepted or broken. A Constitution which is responsive to their ideas, in that it can be revised here and there, they will respect it all the more and they will not fight against it. Otherwise if you make them feel that it is unchangeable and cannot be touched the only thing that can be done by people who wish to change it, is to try and break it.

That is a dangerous thing and a bad thing. Therefore it is a desirable and a good thing for people to realise that this very fine Constitution which we have fashioned is good in so far as it goes but as society changes, as conditions change, we mend it in the proper way".

The members of the Constituent Assembly were conscious that they had been elected by members ofthe Provincial Assemblies who had themselves been elected on a limited franchise. How could they put restrictions on the House of the People which was to be set up on the principle of universal adult franchise ?

The leaders were also aware that in the years to come, conditions would change, new demands would be made and met and it would be the duty of the new rulers to meet the challenges as they came up. It was therefore that they left the way open for easy amendments without going through the arduous process of forming a new Constituent Assembly.

Events proved that the Founding Fathers of the Constitution showed robust common sense when they decided that the process of amending the Constitution should be easy. The first amendment was made in 1951 to make it possible among other things to carry out land reforms and abolish the zamindaris. Also, it was decided that reasonable restrictions could be placed on the exercise of Fundamental Rights in the interests of society.

Since then, the Constitution has been amended more than 75 times. Most of these amendments were made to remove difficulties in the working of the Constitution, but others like the one about Panchayati Raj and Municipalities gave an entirely new dimension to administration by devolution of powers to local self-government bodies. The amendment about reservation for women in legislative bodies will add one more dimension to the Constitution.

The result is that the Constitution today resembles an ancient edifice to which additions and modifications have been made from time to time to suit the needs but in the process, the character of the original structure has been changed beyond recognition. Some of the provisions of the Constitution like introducing prohibition or banning cow slaughter have been found to be impossible to implement. Others like drafting a Common Civil Code have met with stiff opposition form sections of society. Similarly many of the Directive Principles of State Policy have been reduced to mere expression of pious intentions.

The Constituent Assembly utilised the period between August 15, 1947 and November 26, 1949 to draft the Constitution which came into force on January 26, 1950. On August 15 1997 India completes fifty years of Independence. It will be in the fitness of things if the task of taking a second look at the Constitution is attempted so as to remove the cobwebs and to streamline the working. A Committee of Parliament can undertake the job with inputs from politicians, experts in constitutional law, academics and journalists. The changes can be made by the time the nation celebrates the 50th anniversary of the enforcement of the Constitution and the establishment of the Indian Republic.

One in every seven persons on this planet lives in

India. With 16 per cent of the world's population and only 2.4 per cent of its land area, there is obviously a great demand on the natural resources including land. This is so in spite of the fact that an average Indian consumes a much lower quantum of resources than a person in the developed world. If an average person in the South were to consume as much as an average person in a developed country, the environmental crisis would be unimaginable.

While, to a large extent, the lower per capita consumption is due to poverty, an important reason is also that a majority of the population in India follows a sustainable lifestyle which is based on environmentally sound practices evolved over thousands of years.

The environmental problem today is being precipitated partly because practices which were appropriate earlier, like shifting cultivation and unrestricted cattle grazing, are not so anymore. For instance, as a result of increasing population and decreasing availability of land, crop-fallow cycles in shifting cultivation have been reduced to a mere five years from a more sustainable 20-40 years in the past.

But just as there were learnings and difficulties with regard to traditional practices, so was the case with newly introduced technologies. Many measures, at one time seen as solutions, are today extracting an unanticipated price.

The Green Revolution of the 1960s met India's growing demand for food. While it helped India to dramatically increase foodgrain production, what was not fully appreciated then was that the Green Revolution would on the one hand affect the country's natural resource capital, and on the other, create dependencies on inputs such as chemical fertilizers and pesticides. There are indications of soil health problems such as deficiency of micronutrients and organic matter, incidence of soil salinity and damage to the physical structure of the soil, apart from increasing dependence on chemical inputs, many of which are imported.

Today there is widespread realization that there can be no readymade solutions, that technology alone cannot solve problems, that we have to use all our ingenuity to find solutions which combine the best of the old practices with the benefits that modern science and technology can offer.

The challenges are staggering in number, scale and complexity. We need to develop and to modernize in less wasteful ways than is the current paradigm, but not lose our sound traditional values and practices. India will have to leap-frog over wasteful and polluting technologies and go for technologies which are the most environmentally sound, and are based on maximizing recycling and efficient use of resources practices which are inherent in India's traditions. It is when such development comes about that the population pressures will ease, as development brings down demographic growth rates.

The task is stupendous. For while the challenge of development might seem to be 'how to get there' the real challenges is 'how not to get there'. Urbanization, industrial growth, transportation systems, agriculture, housing... all have to stop imitating practices that are already being phased out in the developed world. With the North becoming more conscious about the condition of their own environment, 'dirty' factories are moving South.

To cite only one example, the production of harmful and toxic dyestuff intermediates such as H-acid, K-acid, gamma acid and metanilic acid taken up in the 60s stands at over 41,000 tonnes in the country today, with an estimated Rs. 6 billion worth for export to the developed countries.

The forces which are taking India, and much of the developing world, on the conventional and largely imitative and unimaginative development path are many. But this path is not sustainable—for India or for the world. As Mahatma Gandhi remarked over 60 years ago. "God forbid that India should ever take to industrialism after the manner of the West.

The economic imperialism of a single, tiny... kingdom is today keeping the world in chains. If an entire nation of 300 million took to similar economic exploitation, it would strip the world bare like locusts.

When the West developed, it did so perhaps in ignorance of the environmental impact of its activities. Today we know that such a path is neither practicable nor desirable for countries which are raising their standards of living. We, along with other developing countries, have to find alternative paths to an alternative goal. A goal which ultimately is the true goal of development—an environmentaly sound and sustainable quality of life, which is socially just and equitable.

A goal that must be common to all citizens of the planet. A goal that is perhaps as distant from the developing world as it is from the over-consuming, wasteful societies of what is currently referred to as the 'developed' world.

It is this goal of development that we seek together as people, as organizations and as governments at the United Nations Conference on Environment and Development. It is this intermeshing of environmental and developmental concerns that must form the goal of humankind.

The world is rapidly realizing that environmental issues such as global warming and ozone depletion, acid rain, marine pollution and the threat to biodiversity are global and not merely national issues. But in a world where per capita GNP varies from US $ 80 in Mozambique to US $ 29,880 in Switzerland; where life expectancy at birth varies from 42 years in Sierra Leone to 79 years in Japan; and where literacy rates vary from about 12 per cent in Somalia to over 95 per cent in the United States, what is not as explicitly understood is that development too is a global issue.

And perhaps even less understood is the fact that a sustainable and viable planet requires that development be global. As Mrs. Indira Gandhi, then Prime Minister of India and the only visiting head of government to attend the UN Conference on the Human Environment in Stockholm in 1972, said, the removal of poverty is an integral part of the goal of an environmental strategy for the world.

It is towards this goal that several efforts are under way in India. These are environmental initiatives—not merely of government at various levels, but of people and organizations outside the government. They are efforts which may not all succeed, but they represent initiatives that are continuously under review and change.

They represent the broad base of concern and the vibrancy of environmental efforts in India. These initiatives need to be shared in an effort to find the alternative paths that will lead all nations towards the true goal of development without environmental and social damage.

The total Scheduled Tribe population in India, as per 1991 census, is about eight per cent of the entire population in the country. Of this, aboupt 55 per cent

Scheduled Tribe population are concentrated in central region; roughly 28.14 per cent in western religion, 12.02 per cent in north eastern region; 4.22 per cent in southern region; and the remaining in other regions. Since Independence, the Government of India continued to emphasize the programmes and schemes for raising the socio-economic levels of the tribal people.

One of the main tasks of planning was to identify and remove the large disparities that existed in the country across regions and social groups. A number of Departments and Ministries in the Union and State governments had been entrusted with the task of implementing the constitutional provisions to ensure speedy development of the Scheduled Tribes. The financial allocation for their development had also been increased. Yet, why is there no perceptible improvement in their condition? Is there something wrong with the policy and planning as also the implementation?

As for the general policy approach to tribal development, it is pertinent to go back to the statements made by Dr. Rajendra Prasad and Jawaharlal Nehru, and the proposals of the Planning Commission for the Second Five Year Plan. They constitute, as a matter of fact, the policy statements towards tribal development.

Dr. Rajendra Prasad, the first President of India, indicated that "there should be no idea of forcing anything on the tribals either by way of religion, language, or, even mode of living and customs. Facilities for education and for general improvement in their economic life should be provided for them, and it should be left to them to choose whether they would like to be assimilated with, and absorbed by the surrounding society, or would like to maintain their own separate tribal existence."

"They are our own people and our work does not end with the opening of so many schools, and so many dispensaries and hospitals. Of course, we want schools, hospitals, and roads and all that, but to stop there is rather a dead way of looking at things, what we ought to do is to develop a sense of oneness with these people, a sense of unity and understanding. We must approach the tribal people with affection and friendliness and come to them as a liberating force. If they feel you have come to impose yourselves upon them, or, that we go to them in order to try and change their methods of living, to take away their land to encourage our businessmen to exploit them, then the fault is ours, for is ours, for it only means that our approach to the tribal people is wholly wrong."

One of the most urgent and crucial tasks was the identification of the primitive tribal groups. The VI Plan emphasized the identification of these groups and then taking up unique programmes for each group relevant to its ecosystem. The Working Group on tribal development for the Sixth Plan admitted that in planning for tribal development, the basic handicap was the lack of basic statistical data relating to the Scheduled Tribes.

The Dhebar Commission also mentioned that many tribals in order to circumvent the provisions of the Act related to land, changed their names and adopted non-tribal names. Mundas changed to Mahadeo Pal because Mahadeo Pal is not a Scheduled Tribe. This change of name resulted in the parting of lands by the tribals.

In Darjeeling areas, the Bhutias took advantage of the Alienation Act and got lands from poorer sections of the tribals, i.e. Lepchas, at very nominal prices.

Article 350A of the Constitution lays down that adequate facilities for instruction in the mother tongue at the primary stage of education shall be endeavoured to be provided. To protect and promote tribal language and culture and to search out talent, tribal language must be promoted as medium of instruction at the primary level. The Central Institute of Indian Language, Mysore, NCERT, and State Tribal Research Institutes have been making their contributions in the preparation of textbooks and teaching aid and materials.

The Dhebar Commission also mentioned that the tribals and their leaders emphasized that the instruction in primary schools be imparted to them through their mother tongue. Teachers from amongst them, or tribal dialect-knowing teachers may be appointed. Boys and girls may be taught in their mother tongue up to the primary stage. In Sikkim, Lepcha language is being taught up to the primary stage.

A recent report of the Planning Commission also mentions that 'a policy decision had to be taken in regard to adoption of tribal language as medium of instruction at the primary stage', and suggested that the efforts of various agencies in this direction might be coordinated.

Another important aspect involving the improvement of life of the weaker tribe is education. While the overall situation in the field of tribal education improved as the literacy percentage went up from 11.3 in 1971 to 16.35 in 1981, and 23.03 in 1991, yet the general awareness of the tribal community to protect itself from economic and exploitative onslaught from outside has not improved much.

Formal and non-formal education, forest education, and vocational courses need to get due emphasis. Teacher should be recruited from amongst the tribals so as to engender confidence among the children and make the school functional, and minimize absenteeism among teachers. As the Christian missionaries have done for the spread of education in the north-eastern States, so should the voluntary organisations be encouraged to do among the tribal people. A few years ago, the Ministry of Education at the Centre set up a committee consisting of social scientists, educationists and administrators et al to examine the relevance of educational curricula and contents to the tribal context and make appropriate recommendations. What happened to the Committee is not known. The committee should be revived to take up its work urgently.

The VII Plan emphasized that education in tribal areas be given highest priority; and scheduled Tribe boys in large number be placed on vocational courses; non-enrolment and drop-outs be reduced; low literacy areas and low literacy groups among Scheduled Tribes be identified; and residential schools be opened in such areas.

Surprisingly, an element of exploitation entered into the tribal areas through educational institutions permitted to be run by non-government outside agencies. Permission to such new schools to be opened may not be granted, no foreign funds be allowed to flow to educational institutions in these areas whether through foreign agencies or voluntary organizations within the country, unless a specific clearance had been obtained.

Hostel facilities at primary, middle and secondary levels both for boys and girls, sports facilities and encouragement to various aspects of tribal culture in the sphere of art, music, painting and dance be provided. Institutions like Lalit Kala Akademi, Sahitya Akademi, Sangeet Natak Akademi, besides, Tribal Research Institutes should undertake to encourage these.

According to jawaharlal Nehru, avenues of tribal development should be pursued within the broad framework of the following five fundamental principles:

1. People should develop along the lines of their own genius and we should avoid imposing anything on them. We should try to encourage in every way their own traditional arts and cultures.
2. Tribal rights in land and forest should be respected.
3. We should try to train and build up a team of their own people to do the work of development and administration. Some technical personnel from outside will be needed in the beginning. But we should avoid introducing too many outsiders into tribal territory.
4. We should not over-administer those areas or overwhelm them with a multiplicity of schemes. We should rather work through, and not in rivalry to their own cultural and social institutions.
5. We should judge results, not by statistics, or the amount of money spent, but by the quality of human character that is involved.

The proposals of the Planning Commission for the Second Five Year Plan also emphasized that the tribals themselves must play their part in schemes of their own development:

"Welfare programmes for the tribal people have to be based on respect and understanding of their culture and traditions, and an appreciation of the social psychological and economic problems with which they are faced. In their implementation, the confidence of the people, and in particular, the understanding and goodwill of the elders of the tribal communities are of the highest importance. It is necessary that the welfare extension workers should be found as far as possible from amongst the educated youths in tribal communities. In the adoption of new techniques, tribal leadership has a major role. Tribal people have to be assisted largely through their own institutions. Details of development programmes should be formulated in consultation with members of Advisory councils, leaders of tribal opinion, and institutions engaged in the study of tribal problems. The tribal people feel that these programmes area response to their own urge for better standards of living and the development of their own culture. If the programmes are implemented with popular support, they will give the tribal people a sense of partnership and integration with the nation as a whole."

These statement of the national leaders and the Planning Commission briefly set out the schemes of tribal development.

The overall policy approach towards the tribals had been (i) isolationist, (ii) assimilative, and (iii) integrationist. The first approach is: 'let them choose their own way, let them remain isolated, touch them not.'

The second approach is 'to absorb them and assimilate them.' The third approach is 'to integrate them into the national mainstream, let them develop a sense of oneness with other people, a sense of unity and understanding.'

The story of the tribals is much worse. They are living in the resource rich areas of this county. Most of the minerals and forest products come from this area. But thanks to the way our industrialisation is going on, they do not get any employment. They lose their territory because of industrialization. At the same time, their source of income from the forests has declined. They are raising the question of equity in modern development activities. These are the hunger prone areas. To make these areas free from hunger is not an easy task. Providing food at reduced price through the public distribution system (PDS) is a step in the right direction. The PD system must take their culture into account. They eat millet and mahua which should be provided by the

PDS in the tribal belt. Area planning is necessary with the help of foresters, agriculturists and social workers who can plan such a manner as to liberate these areas from hunger. They are questioning the concept of modern education and health services. New educational and health technology has to be developed to suit their needs. That is why planning at micro level linking with national objective has to be worked out.

The Ninth Plan document reflects the social, cultural and economic needs of these communities. In developing a proper economic, educational strategy one has to see that the benefits are going to reach them. The present government is backed by popular support from these communities. The government has to satisfy their material needs which can sustain the democratic system. That will prove a point that planning is an instrument of social integration by allocating resources in agriculture, primary and vocational education, primary health services, and help in developing intermediate technology which will help these communities. The approach paper to the Ninth Plan has brought a lot of fresh thinking. It has brought back the role of planning to the centre of activities once more. It has provided space for the State in the era of market economy, that the State has constitutional obligation to the vast masses who are pauperized in the process of liberalization. In providing both economic and social security, the State has to strengthen the public distribution system,, education and health services by providing more resources to agriculture, rural development, primary education and primary health services. Let us hope that the spirit of the approach paper becomes a reality.

There is no end to the debate on environment and development. However, instances of the preservationist approach is to be found in the local indigenous communities living in and around forests. In real life, such communities have been seriously affected as a result of both degradation of forest land and their reduced accessibility to forest resources on account of strict forest laws. Degradation of surrounding environment and rigid forestlaws have adversely affected food accessibility, livelihood options and quality of life of local indigenous communities. Such degradation has often caused periodic phases of hunger and malnutrition in the absence of supportive means of livelihood for acquiring basic essentials of life.

Forest plantations of eucalyptus and other species no longer provide the rich biodiversity available earlier in natural forests. Common property resources, in which groups of local people have co-equal use rights, such as community pastures, community forests, wastelands, village ponds, rivers, etc have declined at a rapid pace. Such phenomenon has led to a diminished role of local natural resources which have traditionally constituted invaluable asset-base for meeting basic needs and livelihood requirements of indigenous communities.

Such relatively undisturbed lands include forests, grasslands, wetlands, water bodies, etc which constitue habitat for indigenous communities, plants and animal species and thus contribute to maintenance of human and biological diversity. Such lands perform important environmental functions and also constitute essential means of livelihood. As far as fragility of such ecosystems is concerned, the indigenous communities have traditionally presented little threat to sensitive ecological zones, because their production systems have been sustainable, scattered over a large area, and they have traditionally kept encroachers, poachers and others out of the area.

The benefits provided by forests, trees and common

property resources are basic to such communities and amongst direct benefits, the following are included:

- food such as nuts, wild fruits, vegetables, leaves, flowers, roots, stems honey, wild animals insects, etc;
- habitat and shelter;
- raw materials like bamboo, canes, fibres, oils, bhabbar grass, waxes, resins, gums, dyes and wood for furniture and capital equipment for agriculture, artisanship, etc;
- wood for building, fencing, tool making, etc;
- firewood;
- medicines and drugs;
- fodder such as grass, branches, twigs and leaves, grazing sites;
- means of livelihood, both seasonal and annual;
- shade;
- ornaments, religious items and cultural symbols; and
- drought relief.

Apart from direct benefits, forests, trees and common property resources also provide indirect benefits, such as preventing erosion, conserving moisture, conserving water, recycling nutrient, preventing drought or reducing its impact, providing leaf manure, fixing nitrogen by leguminous trees, regulating climate and rainfall, providing greenery and beauty and reducing pollution.

Forests as safety net: In short, forests, trees and common property resources provide safety nets to the local indigenous communities. In the presence of spiraling prices, reduced wages in real terms, unemployment, sickness, reduced productivity from land, and recurring shortages, forests, trees and common property resources act as a kind of safety net for local communities, protecting them from the harshness of market forces.

They come to the rescue by providing a safety net against food and livelihood insecurity, drought attacks, pest attacks, illness, pollution, high prices, high rents, etc. They play a dominant role in providing alternative sources of livelihood and in offering coping strategies to local communities.

The strategy for development of the Scheduled Tribes is based on the TSP (tribal sub-plan) approach which came into operation since 1974-75 (V Plan) in 16 States (now 18 States) and two Union territories. The main objective of the tribal sub-plan is to (i) raise the socio-economic condition of the tribal population and strengthen infrastructure in the tribal areas, and (ii) to protect and promote tribal interests through legal and administrative support.

The programmes are now being implemented through (i) 194 Integrated Tribal Development Projects (ITDPs) comprising generally blocks/tehsils with 50 per cent or more Scheduled Tribe population; (ii) 277 pockets of tribal concentration (Modified Area Development Approach Projects) having a total population of 10,000 or more, and Scheduled Tribe population of 50 per cent or more; and (iii) 90 primitive tribe projects or micro-projects.

The tribal sub-plan has a two-fold thrust, viz (i) socio-economic development of the tribal areas, and (ii) socio-economic development of the tribal families.

It was expected that during the Seventh Plan period, there would be cent per cent coverage of Scheduled Tribe population under the tribal sub-plan. Benefits were also proposed to be extended to the scattered Scheduled Tribe population which was not covered by any specific project through family-oriented programmes. It may be mentioned that the tribal population coverage during the Sixth Plan period was only 75 per cent. During the Seventh Plan, the following were the objectives under tribal sub-plan approach: (i) taking up family beneficiary programme through raising productivity-level of the beneficiary families in the field of agriculture, horticulture, animal husbandry, small industry, etc. (ii) elimination of exploration of the tribals in the sphere of alienation of land, money-lending, debt bondage, forest, etc. (iii) human resource development through education and training programmes, (vi) infrastructure development, (v) development of vulnerable tribal areas and groups like, forest villagers, displaced tribes and tribal women; and (vi) upgradation of environment of tribal areas.

For the year 1985-86, the target of tribal families to be economically assisted was fixed at 8.35 lakh, and the achievement reported was 8.3 lakh families. For 1986-87, the target fixed was 8.35 lakh tribal families and for 1987-88, a tentative target of assisting 8.50 lakh tribal families had been kept.

Special Central Assistance: Under tribal development, Special Central Assistance (SCA) is an additive to the State Plan efforts for Scheduled Tribes. The Eighth Plan had a target to cover 46.50 lakh families. Against this, 28.69 lakh families were covered during the first three years of the Plan (8.88 lakh in 1992-93; 10.42 lakh in 1993-94; and 9.39 lakh in 1994-95). This constituted 61.7 per cent of the target. To improve the literacy rate among tribal women, a new scheme was introduced since 1992-93, and is being implemented through non-governmental organizations in 48 districts with tribal concentration where female population is less than two per cent.

Financing tribal sub-plan: There are four sources for financing tribal sub-plan programmes: (i) Special Central Assistance (SCA) administered by Ministry of Welfare, (ii) State Plan funds, (iii) centrally-sponsored schemes, and (vi) institutional finance.

Since the V Plan period, with the launching of the tribal sub-plan approach, special programmes for extremely backward tribe groups had been taken up. These were micro-projects or projects for primitive tribal groups. These primitive tribal groups had three criteria for their identification: (i) almost stagnant population, or extremely low growth rate facing the danger of extinction, (ii) having are pre-agricultural level of technology, and (iii) extremely low level of literacy.

Another important factor was the ecosystem in which they lived. There were also other factors which entered into the situation of each of these tribal groups calling for a sensitive and in-depth study of each, precedent to enforcement of any action plan.

The Planning Commission also mentioned that particular care need to be taken of the small primitive tribal groups, some of which were on the verge of extinction.

The Dhebar Commission (1961) alluded to them as the 'lowest layer}, and listed 50 tribes in various States which were in an extremely underdeveloped state. During the V Plan period, the Ministry of Home Affairs identified 52 tribal communities as primitive, their estimated population being 10 lakhs. During the VI Plan period, an additional 20 tribal groups were identified raising their total number to 72 with an estimated population of 14 lakhs. Now the clusters of tribal concentration have gone up to 90.

There had been emphasis since the V Plan period on

preparation of a project report for each of these groups relative to its situation. Nevertheless, there had been considerable neglect in this regard. Apart form the continued misery of conditions in which they lived, the risk of extinction of some of these tribes was also great.

Special Development Programmes for Scheduled Tribes living outside the ITDP should also be taken up. Not merely economic support but also social support is required to be given to the weaker tribes. Voluntary agencies should be encourage to take up work to improve and change their socio-cultural conditions and to stop conversion among them.

Need-based and appropriate type of village industries, such as basket making for packaging oranges and other fruit like guava, plum, peach, etc. and for packaging tea which grow in the north-east, and Darjeeling areas need to be developed.

Tribal technology and craft in Darjeeling region such as devices for irrigation and drinking water on bamboo pillars and tree trunk by connecting split up bamboo pieces from the hilly source of water to their villages and orchards need to be improved and properly exploited for the optimum use of water resources. The scheme of orange production should be taken up as intensively and extensively as the apple production in Kashmir Valley and Himachal Pradesh to boost the tribal economy.

Institutional finance, and the co-operative sector should be encouraged; voluntary organizations and other such agencies should also be encouraged and taken into confidence in all programmes and schemes of socio-cultural and economic development of the tribal communities.

Programmes of socio-economic and cultural improvement should go together. In this direction, the cluster approach, mutual competitive approach and family-oriented beneficiary approach need to be vigorously pursued. The smaller and weaker tribes should be encouraged to develop mutual support and competitive growth approach among the tribal groups of the same economic level.

Programmes of tribal development for the betterment of weaker and primitive tribes are laudable in premise. What is required is vigorous implementation through determined administrative action for which constant monitoring and evaluation would be necessary. This should be the responsibility of the State governments. The role of voluntary organizations, and Tribal Council would also be crucial, and must receive due emphasis and importance. At the same time, the realization must grow among the tribal groups that self-support is crucial to all socio-economic and cultural developments, all outside supports were meant only to strengthen it.

The VII Plan proposed to have cent per cent coverage of tribal population under tribal sub-plan. Its benefits were also expected to be extend to the scattered tribal population not covered by any specific project through family-oriented programmes.

The plan proposal suggested that while allocating Special Central Assistance (SCA), care need to be taken to earmark beneficiaries and amounts to utilized for Scheduled Tribes within the identified tribal units like ITDP, MADA pockets, primitive tribe projects and clusters on the one hand and the rest of the scattered tribal population on the other. But, for want of adequate and reliable data about the primitive tribes, scattered tribal groups, rationalization of allocation of special Central assistance seemed to difficult.

However, since there are four sources of financing tribal sub-plan programmes, viz—(i) SCA (Special Central Assistance), (ii) State Plan Funds, (iii) Centrally-Sponsored Schemes, (iv) Institutional finance; over-all rationalization in the allocation of resources for tribal development could be possible provided adequate data about the tribal population at various levels of development were available, and determined administrative action was initiated by:

- taking up family beneficiary programme through raising the productivity level of the beneficiary families in the field of agriculture, horticulture, animal husbandry; small-scale industries, etc.;
- elimination of exploitation of the tribals in the sphere of alienation of land, money-lending, debt bondage, forest, etc.
- human resource development through education and training programme;
- infrastructure development;
- development of vulnerable tribal areas and groups like forest villagers, displaced and migrant tribals including women; and
- upgradation of environment of tribal areas.

The Employment-orientation Programme was proposed to diversify the occupation of Scheduled Tribes who were primarily agricultural labour, through different types of income generating schemes. The main thrust was on the development of skills of tribals in their traditional and other trades and crafts.

West Bengal example: The West Bengal Scheduled Castes and Scheduled Tribes Development and Finance Corporation had been set up to give margin money loan linked with bank loan and government subsidy to provide various packages of schemes to Scheduled Caste and Scheduled Tribe target group families to assist to cross the poverty line.

The Tribal Development Co-operative Corporation (TCCC) and (LAMPS) (Large Agricultural Multipurpose Societies) are mainly involved in providing crop loans from co-operative banks.

The Training-cum-Production Centres (TCPC) were run departmentally to provide training in traditional traces and some new trades like textile, leather, carpentry, sericulture, tailoring, knitting and other handicrafts, and miscellaneous trades to the Scheduled Caste and Scheduled Tribe population. Ex-trainees were provided with one-time grant linked with bank loan to establish in trade.

The Working Group on development of Scheduled Castes and Scheduled Tribes during the VII Plan laid down that every State should prepare project report on every weaker tribe formulated by inter-disciplinary teams having social scientists and representatives of voluntary organisations in addition to administrators.

Any scheme of economic development among primitive tribes, should be undertaken after careful consideration and screening with a view to selecting only those which have relevance and suitability from the point of view of their acceptability, traditions, skills and environment.

After listing out these economic schemes, the initial approach should be to saturate each tribal group with them. The saturation approach might help these groups a great deal. The genetic approach to go into the causes of the declining population trend of some of the tribal groups might also be useful.

As far as the official machinery was concerned, the State government should make sure that it consisted of the component, empathetic and dedicated persons who should be well-rewarded as they had to serve in difficult terrains, and inhospitable areas. It was suggested that in addition to paying them handsome special allowances, they should also be allowed to retain official residence for their families at the previous place of posting. The construction of staff quarters in these areas should receive top priority. It had also been suggested that the project administrator of Integrated Tribal Development Project should be placed in over-all charge of the micro-projects for primative tribal groups.

It is a matter of concern that the detailed project reports which were required to be prepared in respect of 77 primitive tribal groups have not been done. The Government of India had been making available to the State governments financial assistance on cent per cent basis for development of primitive tribal groups since 1975-76. The State were required to gear their machinery appropriately and adequately to take up relevant programmes for these groups.

Primitive tribes—special measures: The Working Group recommended the following special measures for the development of primitive tribes:

- The saturation approach towards the economic development of the entire group with individual family as the base should be adopted. Familywise economic development plans and programmes should be formulated while adopting a holistic approach to their development;
- Special measures should be taken for improving education, health, nutrition, drinking water supply, transport and communication;
- The nearest ITDP project administrator should be declared as the direct supervisory officer of the project for primitive groups. The Project

Implementation Committee of ITDP may also function as the Project Implementation Committee of the Primitive Tribes Projects with induction of one or more heads of the traditional institutions of these groups as member in the Project Implementation Committee;

- The block having primitive tribes should be included under the Integrated Child Development Services on a priority basis;
- A complete ban on purchase and settlement of land and other with outsiders in the area should be imposed. Special attention should be paid to protective and non-exploitative measures, and a special watch be kept on flow of foreign funds into the area.

In all programmes for these groups, the leaders and functionaries of the traditional tribal institutions must be actively involved at formulation, implementation, field visits and review states.

Degradation of forest land and denial of forest resources due to rigid local forest laws have seriously affected the local indigenous communities. Limited substitution possibilities or alternative sources of livelihood have added to their improverishment. Better management of forest resources by redefining their access to forest resources and clarifying their roles and responsibilities is the need of the hour. Their deprived status can be improved, if not fully restored, by involving them in decision-making regarding regeneration of forest wealth. The subject of environment and development has become a critical topic especially in the context of the modern race towards industrialization. As more and more of industrialization is taking place leading to sizeable increase in national income, the costs in terms of permanent loss of limited environmental resources is also being realized in most quarters. Experts across the world are searching for models which would yield 'industrialized development' which at the same time is 'environment-friendly'. The search is still on but the 'trade offs' in terms of destruction of environment has become continuous phenomena.

In the current development literature, there are at least four schools of thought on environment and development. The conventional or old school of thought is the 'exploitative school' which is preoccupied with maximum gain in terms of the present generation and takes a narrow view of 'development' as that of creating material assets.

It propounds the view that natural resources like any other resources exist for the purpose of development and maximum effort should be made to maximize use of such resources for obtaining higher returns. In recent decades, this school has fallen from grace and three other schools have emerged which are propounding the theory of sustainable development, where the development needs to be sustained much beyond that of the present generation. Such schools emphasize on the fragility of environmental resources, the critical life-support system which environment provides and the permanent damages inflicted to environment as a result of development activity.

One such school is conservationist school which argues that any development activity needs to consider the 'trade off' in terms of environment and any such damage done to environment needs to be adequately compensated.

Another school is the preservationist school which believes in having standards set and areas and zones of nature preserved from development activities. The environment is not meant for development and there has to be rules, regulations and standards for preserving nature. Still another school is the extreme school of sustainable development which believes in maximum ecological preservation where human beings are to live in harmony with nature. Hence, sustainable development has different dimensions contours depending on the school propunding it.

Culture of India which is composite in nature is essentially an expression of inner urges and cumulative beliefs of people gathered through centuries of experience. It is the perennial flow of this culturtal stream which determines the nation's strength, character and capacity to survive as an integrated living reality despite heavy odds and its continuous march forward on the path of progress.

Keeping this in view, preservation of cultural heritage, inculcation of art consciousness among people and promotion of high standards of creative and performing arts and dissemination of culture have been made part of the objectives of State policy.

The Central and state governments strive for promotion and dissemination of art and culture through national and regional academies of art, dance, drama, music and letters. Zonal cultural centres have been set up for projecting, preserving and sustaining cultural kinship that transcends territorial limits. In addition, Indira Gandhi National Centre for Arts has been set up at New Delhi as a resource centre and data base. All these institutions and Departments of Art and Culture are helped in their objective by media and voluntary agencies. Apart from this, some eminent persons in the field of fine arts are nominated by the President to the Rajya Sabha.

To promote and propagate understanding of Indian art, both within and outside the country, the Government established Lalit Kala Akademi (National Akademi of Fine Arts) at new Delhi in 1954.

To decentralise its activities, the Akademi has set up regional centres called Rashtriya Lalit Kala Kendra at Lucknow, Calcutta, Madras and Bhubneswar as well as a small office at Bombay. The Akademi has also set up Community Artists Studio Complex with workshop facilities in painting, sculpture, printmaking and ceramics in Garhi village in New Delhi. The workshops and all regional centres are headed by experts to give technical guidance in these disciplines.

Since its inception, the Akademi organises national exhibition of contemporary Indian art with 10 national awards, each of Rs. 25,000. Three to four special exhibitions every year are organised with some concept involving known and eminent artists of India.

Every three years, the Akademi also organises Triennale-India, a most significant exhibition of contemporary art in this part of the world. The last, Seventh Triennale was held in 1991 while the next one was inaugurated on 16 February 1994. The Akademi also organises a Rashtriya Kala Mela (National Art Fair) where artists from all over India present their work. The Eighth Rashtriya Kala Mela was held in Bangalore in 1995, while sixth was held in Bombay in January 1993 and the seventh Mela was held in New Delhi in February 1994.

The Akademi honours eminent artists and art historians every year by electing them as fellows of the Akademi. So far 45 persons have been conferred with this fellowship. To propagate Indian art outside, the Akademi regularly participates in International Biennales and Triennales abroad and also organises exhibitions of works of art from other countries. To foster contacts with artists ouside, it sponsors exchange of artists with other countries under the various Cultural Exchange Programmes and Agreements of the Government of India.

The Lalit Kala Akademi accords recognition to art institutions/associations and extends financial assistance to these bodies as well as state Akademis every year. It also gives scholarship to deserving young artists of its regional centres.

Under its publication programme, the Akademi brings out monographs on the works of Indian contemporary artists in Hindi and English and books on contemporary, traditional, folk and tribal arts authored by eminent writers and art critics. The Akademi also brings out bi-annual art journals, Lalit Kala Contemporary (English), Lalit Kala Ancient (English) and Samkaleen Kala (Hindi). Apart from these, it brings out large size multicolour reproductions of contemporary paintings and graphics from time to time. The Akademi has started a regular programme on research and documentation. Scholars are given financial assistance to undertake projects in contemporary folk, tribal and traditional arts. It has set up an Artists-Aid Fund to give financial assistance to ailing artists and other artists who may be in penury. The first National Exhibition of Photography was held in 1995. The Akademi has decided to give five awards of Rs. 10,000 each and five Hon'ble Mentions for the Exhibition.

Centre for Cultural Resources and Training (CCRT) was set up in May 1979 as an autonomous organisation by the Government of India. The CCRT took over the scheme 'Propagation of Culture' among college and school students which was being implemented by Delhi University, since 1970. The Centre is under the administrative control of Department of Culture, Ministry of Human Resource Development.

The broad objectives of the CCRT have been to revitalise the education system by creating an understanding and awareness among students about the plurality of regional cultures of India and integrating this knowledge with the education.

The main thrust is on linking education with culture and making students aware of the importance of culture in all development programmes. The training being imparted stresses on the role of culture in science and technology, housing, agriculture, sports, etc. An important component of training is creating an awareness amongst students and teachers of their role in solving environmental pollution problems and conservation and preservation of the natural and cultural heritage. To fulfil these objectives, the Centre organises a variety of training programmes for teachers, educators, administrators and students throughout the country. It has also been organising academic programmes on Indian art and culture for foreign teachers and students. Workshops are conducted in various art activities lilke drama, music, narrative art forms, etc., to provide practical training and knowledge in the arts and crafts. In these workshops, teachers are encouraged to develop programmes inwhich the art form can be profitably utilised to educational curriculum.

The CCRT organises various educational activities for school students, teachers and children belonging to governmental and non-government organisations under its extension and community feedback programmes, which includes, educational tours to monuments, museums, art galleries, craft centres, zoological parks and gardens, camps on conservation of natural and cultural heritage, camps on learning crafts using low cost localilty available resources, lectures and demonstrations by artists and experts on various art forms, demonstrations by artists and crafts persons in schools.

The CCRT collects materials on the arts and crafts of the country in the form of audio recordings, slides, photographs, films and written texts in order to disseminate the information on culture and provide participants and other research institutions with material on the arts of India.

The Centre also aims to disseminate information and foster an understanding of Indian culturre amongst teachers, administrators, educators and students. Publications for institutions and members of the community are prepared on topics related to aspects of Indian culture and ecology and the natural environment.

The CCRT implements the Cultural Talent Search Scholarship Scheme, which was taken over from the Department of Culture in 1982. The scheme provides scholarships to outstanding children in the age-group of 10 to 14 years studying, either in recognised schools okr belonging to families practising traditional, performing or other arts to develop their talent in various cultural fields particularly in rare art forms. The scholarship continues till the age of 20 years or first year of university degree. The Centre has also instituted CCRT Teacher's Award which is given every year to selected teachers in recognition of the outstanding work done by them in the field of education and culture.

Zonal cultural centres have been conceptualised with the aim of projecting cultural kinships transcending territorial bounds. The idea is to arouse and deepen awarreness of the local cultures and how these merge into zonal identities and eventually into the rich diversity of India's composite culture. Besides, these are also intended to document, preserve and to sustain the vanishing art forms and oral traditons. The involvement of artists and creative people has been in built in the set-up through a system of autonomous governance.

The seven zonal cultural centres established under the new scheme are: (i) North-Zone Cultural Centre, Patiala; (ii) East Zone Cultural Centre, Santiniketan; (iii) South Zone Cultural Centre, Thanjavur; (iv) west Zone Cultural Centre, Udaipur; (v) North-Central Zone Cultural Centre, Allahabad; (vi) North East Zone Cultural Centre, Dimapur and (vii) South-Central Zone Cultural Centre, Nagpur. The participation of states in more than one zonal cultural centre according to their cultural linkage is a special feature of the composition of the zonal centres.

The Ramakrishna Mission Institute of Culture, Calcutta is engaged in the promotion of thought, knowledge and education. Apart from being engaged in cultural activities at national and international level, the Institute also maitains several schools of instructions.

Indira Gandhi National Centre for the Arts (IGNCA) was established to commemorate the memory of the late Prime Minister, Mrs Indira Gandhi.

This Centre launched on 19 November 1985 as a fully funded autonomous trust, is visualized as a centre encompassing the study and experience of all the arts-each for its own integrity, yet within a dimension of mutual interdependence, inter-relatedness with nature, social structure and cosmology. Through diverse programmes of research, publication, training, creative activities and performance, the IGNCA seeks to place the arts within the context of the natural and human environment. the fundamental approach of the Centre in all its work is multi-disciplinary and inter-disciplinary.

The Indira Gandhi National Centre for the Arts, comprises five main divisions viz. (i) Kala Nidhi; (ii) kala Kosa; (iii) janapada Sampada; (iv) Kala Darshana and (v) Sutradhara. During 1994-95, the reference library of Kala

NIdhi Division added 2,204 selected works of eminent authors to its collection, 478 rolls of microfilms of rare Indian manuscripts from abroad and 1,532 microfiches from SMPK, Berlin University of Vienna were also added to its collections.

The Kala Kosa Division under its programme of Kalathttvakosa, a lexicon of fundamental concepts of Indian arts, is engaged in the preparation of its volume engaged in the preparation of its volume III and IV. The institution organised a 17 day workshop on 'Manuscriptology and Palaeography' in collaboration with Shri Lal Bahadur Shastri Rashtriya Sanskrit Vidyapeetha as part of training programme for younger generation of researchers from within IGNCA and outside. During the year, the janapada Sampada Division under its Loka Parmapara programmes, recieved interim reports on various projects including Santhal Perception of Sound", "Seed and Eaarth in Oral Tradition of Vraja", etc. Under its publication programme, a number of manuscripts were assigned to the co-publishers.

The first and second issues of IGNCA Newsletter, Vihangama, have been brought out during the year and the third issue is under publication. The Kala Darshana Division organised a number of exhibitions abroad in collaboration with Mr. Jacques Pimpaneau of Musee Kwok On, France, photographic exhibition of photographs by David Ulrich titled Hawalii Landscape of Transformation; and Raja Deen Dayal Exhibition at Bombay and Bhopal. The IGNCA also co—sponsored a session on "Cave art of India and China" at Dunhuang (China), and deputed three delegates to participate in the International Seminar held there as a part of the Dunhaung Academy Golden Jubilee celebrations.

One of the important activities undertaken by the Government of India has been the commemoration of the centenaries ofdistinguished Indians who have left an indelible impression on the history and life of our country. National committees are set up for centenaries which are considered to be of such importance. Year long programmes are drawn up by the committees for implementation during the centenary year.

These programmes normally include organisation of national seminars, installation of statutes, other functions, stamp release, publications and exhibitions. The Department of Culture also provides financial assistance to registered voluntary organisations for celebrating the centenaries of outstanding personalities which are not taken up for celebration by the Government of India. Another mode of organising centenaries is where one or more state governments are requested to set up the centenary committee and the Government of India on its part organises a few programmes like release of commemorative postage stamps, seminars/lectures, publication, etc.

Gandhi Smriti and Darshan Samiti (GSDS) was set up by the Department of Culture in 1948 primarily to maintain and look after the national memorial where gandhiji was assisinated and now called 'Gandhi Smriti', and a permanent photo exhibition at Rajghat called' Gandhi Darshan', which was created at the time of Gandhiji's birth centenary in the year 1969. The institution has brought out a number of books on Gandhi, communal harmony and national integration. It also publishes a quarterly newsletter to create awareness about the GSDS and also organises annual Gandhij Memorial Lecture by an eminent scholar both in India and abroad.

The year 1994-95 happens to be the 125th birth anniversary year of Gandhiji and, therefore a series of programmes commenced with an inaugural function at

Vigyan Bhawan on 2 October 1994 chaired by the President. The Samiti has since organised a programme of painting by the children, a photo exhibition put up at Paris on the eve of the 1st UNESCO Gandhi Memorial Lecture delivered by the Prime Minister; a massive programme of creating awareness for the youth in all the districts of Kerala; another programme involving several thousand youths and others for creating awareness about the literature on Gandhi. Programmes have also been organised for women, especially for those elected for Panchayats. Orientation programmes comprising discussions, film shows, visit to an exhibition and cultural programmes in several rural settings were the other highlights. The GSDS also participated and collaborated in the regional Conference organised by UNESCO on tolerance in April 1995 at New Delhi.

Maulana Abul Kalam Azad Institute of Asian Studies, under the administrative control of the Department of Culture is the centre for research and training of the life and works of Maulana Abul Kalam Azad and with the study on social, cultural, political and economic movement in Asia from the middle of the 19th century. The Institute also maintains library of books, newspapers, still photographs and materials on the secular traditions of modern India and events of the 19th century which is suitable for the public to collect papers and library sources for study and research from India and abroad. It also maintains personal museum at the former residence of Maulana Abul Kalam Azad. The Museum highlights the life and works of Maulana Abdul Kalam Azad as a distinguished national leader and thinker.

The other arts

All festivals have a common purpose of creating a greater awareness amongst the people of the receiving country of

India's rich cultural heritage and contemporary development in vrious spheres of modern India. This helps to generate an appropriate climate of goodwill and understanding for mutual exchanges in different spheres including technology, commerce and tourism on a more permanent footing. The main thrust of the Festival of India has been to project its multifaceted cultural life, while also highlighting scientific and technical progress and advancement through a series of exhibitions, programmes of performing arts as well as through seminars, readings, workshops, youth meetings, sports festivals etc.

The Festival of India in China was inaugurated on 9 May 1994 at Ply Plaza at Beijing by the Human Resource Development Minister and his Chinese counterpart. The inaugural ceremony consisted mainly of performing art event with the underlying theme 'Harmony'. Eight Indian films were screened at different venues in China during the Festival of India. The National Institute of Fashion technology mounted fashion shows during the festival.

The Performing Arts programme for the Festival of India in China was the single largest component among the festival events. About 75 performers visited China during the period of festival. Indian handicrafts combine varied styles and colours, fine workmanship, profound traditions and have a distinctive national flavour, Karigari provided a glimpse of these patterns of handicraft traditions that have survived in India for many thousand years. It was inaugurated on 10 May 1994. In this exhibition, an effort was made to give the viewers an impression of Indian science as a whole, in all its rich diversity through Indian experience in science and technology in its long history of 4500 years.

Around 1500 titles, mostly recent and some old titles

of perennial value, brought out by almost 150 publishers were displayed at the exhibitions in China. The books selected for the exhibitions in China covered a wide range of subjects such as arts, history, biography, literature, philosophy, religion, social sciences, technology and books of general reference.

Rediscovery of ancient and medieval Indian literature and development of modern literature in major Indian languages and English mark literary activities of present-day India. A large number of literary periodicals and magazines, literary institutions and All India Radio have given impetus to the growth of modern Indian literature.

Sahitya Akademi was set up by the Government on March 1954. Being an apex national body for the promotion of literature, the Akademi has all through devoted itself to recognise men of achievement in letters, to educate public taste and to improve standards of literature and literary criticism. With this Akademi has a big publication programme and some of the major publication projects which are continuing are publication of series of Markers of Indian Literature, series of Histories of Indian Literature, publication of a bi-monthly journal entitled Indian Literature in English, a quarterly journal entitled Samkaleen Bharatiya Sahitya in Hindi and a periodical journal entitled Sanskrit Pratibha in Sanskrit. The six volume project of Encyclopaedia of Indian Literature is now complete. During 1994, 22 Akademi awards to writers and 19 translation awards to translators were given by the Sahitya Akademi and it published 143 books and organised 46 book exhibtions and workshops.

The national Bibliography of Indian Literature published by Sahitya Akademi in four volumes hitherto covered Assamese, Bengali, English, Gujarati, Hindi,

Kanada, Kashmiri, Malayalam, Marathi, Oriya, Punjabi, Sanskrit, Sindhi, Tamil, Telugu and Urdu for the period from 1901-1953. Its fifth volume covering Dogeri, Konkani, Maithili, Manipuri, Rajasthani and Mepali for the period 1901 to 1980 has been brought out in 1990-91. It is now proposed to publish a second series of the National Bbliography of Indian Literature form 1954 to 1980/90 for all the languages covered in the first series.

To provide financial support to outstanding artistes for creative work in various fields of performing, plastic and literary arts the following schemes are being implemented by Government.

The scheme of Emeritus Fellowships has been formulated to extend financial support to artists who have achieved a high degree of excellence in their respective fields but have since retired from the profession to enable them to continue experimentation in the spirit of financial freedom. Nine fellowships are awarded every year for a period of two years. The rate of fellowships is Rs. 5,000 per month. In addition to this fellowships amount, Rs. 10,000 as annual incidental grant for fellowship is also granted.

A fellowship in memory of Pt Kumar Gandharv has been instituted from 1992-93. The fellowship is conferred to distinguished senior artistes in various fields every year.

The scheme gives financial assistance to young artistes of outstanding promise for advanced training in the fields of music, dance, painting, sculpture, book illustration, design, etc. The duration of scholarship is two years and the value is Rs. 1000 per month, while the number of scholarship is 200 per year.

The scheme provides for financial assistance to persons distinguished in letters, arts, etc., who may be in indigent circumstances and are above 58 years of age and in certain cases, to their dependents who are left unprovided for. Under the scheme, expenditure is shared by the Central and the respective state governments. The maximum assistance that could be given to an individual is Rs. 1,500 per month.

The scheme provides for the award of Senior Fellowships of the value of Rs. 3,000 per month and Junior Fellowships of the value of Rs. 1,500 per month each. Fifty Senior Fellowships and 150 Junior Fellowships are awarded every year. The duration of fellowship is two years and in exceptional cases, this can be extended a year more.

Financial assistance is being given to institutions of all India character, engaged in the development of cultural activities, to meet part of their expenditure on maintenance and development activities. The institutions assisted include the Institute of Historical Studies, Calcutta; Numismatic Society of Inda, Varansi; Institute of Traditional Culture, Madras; Bharatiya Vidya Bhawan; Bombay and the Institute of Numismatic Studies, Nasik.

Two main schools of classical music Hindustani and Carnatic continue to survive through oral tradition being passed on by teachers to disciples. This has led to the existence of family traditions called gharanas and sampradayas.

Dance in India has an unbroken tradition of over 2,000 years. Its themes are derived from mythology, legends and classical literature, two main divisions being calssical and folk. Classical dance forms are based on ancient dance discipline and have rigid rules of presentation. Important among them are Bharata Natyam, Kathakali, Kathak, Manipuri, Kuchipudi and Odissi. Bharata Natyam though derives its roots from Tamil Nadu has developed into an all India form, Kathakali is a dance form of Kerala and Kathak is a classical dance form revitalised as result of the fusion of Mughal influence with Indian culture. Manipur has contributed a delicate, lyrical style of dance, Manipuri, while Kuchipudi is a dance form owing its origin to Andhra Pradesh, and Odissi from Orissa, once practised as a temple dance, is today widely interpreted by artists. Folk and tribal dances are of numerous patterns.

Both classical and folk dance owe their popularity to institutions like sangeet Natak Akademi and training institutes and cultural organisations. The Akademi gives financial assistance to cultural institutions and awards fellowships to scholars, performers and teachers to promote advanced study and training i different forms of dance music especially those which are rare.

Theatre in Indian is as old as her music and dance. Classical theatre survives only in some places. Folk theatre can be seen in its regional variants practically in every region. There are also professional theatres, which are mainly city-oriented. Besides, India has a rich tradition of puppet theatre, prevalent form being puppets, rod puppets, glove puppets and leather puppets (shadow theatre). There are several semi-professional and amateur theatre groups involved in staging plays in Indian languages and English.

Sangeet Natak Akademi, the national academy of music, dance and drama, was set up in 1953 to promote performing arts in collaboration with states and voluntary organisation.

It seeks increased public appreciation of these art forms through sponsorship, research and dissemination. It holds seminars and festivals, presents awards to outstanding performing artites, gives financial assistance for theatre productions, extends financial help to traditional teachers and grants scholarships to students. It operates a scheme of inter-state exchange of troupes to promote national and cultural integration through regional festivals and bringing rare art forms of the regions to the fore.

The Akademi has set up a special unit for surveying and docmenting various theatrical, musical and dance forms in the country. Its disc and tape unit has the largest collection of Indian classical, folk and tribal music, dance and theatre items.

The Sangeet Natak Akademi runs two zonal institutions for training in dance, Kathak Kendra, New Delhi and Jawaharlal Nehru Manipuri Dance Academi, Imphal. It took over the Rabindra Rangshala as the third unit with effect from 2 April 1993. It gives subsidy for publication of books in various Indian languages and English on music, dance and drama and confers awards and fellowships to distinguished artistes and scholars. The fellowship carry a purse of Rs. 40,000 and the awards Rs. 25,0000 and a Tamrapatra.

The National School of Drama (NSD) - one of the foremost theatre training institutions in the world and the only of its kind in India was set up by Sangeet Natak Akademi in 1959. Later in 1975, it became an autonomous organisation, financed entirely by Department of Culture, ministry of Human Resource Development, Government of India.

NSD gas produced a galaxy of talents - actors, directors, script writers, designers, technicians, educationists who work not only in theatre but in film and television also - winning several awards, national and international. The training in the School is based on a thorough, comprehensive, carefully planned syllabus. The systematic study and practical performing experience of Sanskrit drama, modern Indian drama, traditional Indian theatre forms, Asian drama and western drama give the students a solid grounding and a wide perspective in the art of theatre. In order to establish links between traditional theatre forms of India and modern expressions, the School brings experts to train the students in these forms and also sends students to regional centres for training in traditional theatre.

The School has also attracted to its training faculty some of the finest creative talents from within the country and abroad. The school has a Repertory Company and Theatre-In-Education Company in Delhi and Regrional Resource-cum-Research Centre at Bangalore. NSS's extension programme seeks to extend and diffuse its activities in all regions of the country. A programme for research, documentation and publication is recently added to the School's record of academic activities.

The primary objective of the Indian Council for Cultural Relations (ICCR) is to establish and strengthen cultural relations and mutual understanding between India and other countries.

One of the major activities of the Council is administering scholarship schemes for international students. There are at present 1,792 international students from around 70 countries pusruing a variety of courses on scholarships. Two new scholarship were instituted in the memory of the late Appa Saheb Pant, the first Commissioner of India in Kenya, and the Okita Memorial Scholarship at the request of the family of the former Japanese Foreign Minister, the late Dr. S. Okita.

The ICCR celebrated the birth anniversary of its founder, Maulana Abul Kalam Azad on 11 November as 'International Students Day'. Special get-togethers and cultural programmes were arranged on this occasion for international students and Indian students.

Festival of India in China held in May 1994 has been one of the major highlights of ICCR in 1994.

Some o fth other major events include 'India Today 1994' in Australia, which was inaugurated by the Vice-President of India; the India Trade Fair at St Petersburg; 'India in Dubai'; the 125th Death Anniversary Celebrations of Miraz Ghalib in Mauritius; and the 'India Night' at Alter Opera, Frankfurt. During April-december 1994, the ICCR sponsored visits of 17 cultural troupes abroad. The ICCR also organised performances by a number of incoming delegations and several Indian cultural programmes in honour of visiting delegations and several Indian cultural programmes in honour of visiting delegations/VVIP functions.

On the occasion of 125th Birth Anniversary of Mahatma Gandhi, the ICCR organised a major exhibition titled 'Ashoka-Gandhi-Nehru-The Healing Touch' at the Tokyo Fuji Art Museum in October 1994. Other exhibitions organised by ICCR during 1994 are the exhibition of Indian Children's Paintings (Republic of Korea) and the Children's Paintings (Cairo). The ICCR also presented busts of Gandhiji to the USA (for installation at International Peace Garden, Salt Lake City, San Francisco) and Cuba (for installation at Central Park, Havana) and that of Gurudev Rabindranath Tagore to Japan (for installation at Soka University Campus).

The Council sponsored and assisted 45 Indian scholars, intellectuals, academics and artists to participate in seminars, symposia, study tours, etc., abroad in 21 countries and received 78 visitors from 11 countries. The ICCR organised the International Symposium of India Studies (ISIS) during November-December 1994 at Kovalam, Kerala in which 31 scholars from vrious parts of the world participated.

In keeping with India's foreign policy that has a cultural dimension for promoting greater people-to-people contact, the Council has set up cultural centres in Geogetown, Jakarta, Moscow, Port Louis, Paramaribo, Cairo, Berlin, London, Tashkent and Almaty. These centres, except in Berlin and London, impart lessions in Indian music, dance, yoga and languages and organise lectures,l symposia, exhibitions, essay competitions, performances of dance and music, staging of plays, screening kof films and publication of news bulletins.

ICCR presently has 18 professors teaching Indian languages, Indology and allied subjects in Belgium, Bulgaria, China. Finland, France, Hungary, Indonesia, Republic of Korea, Mauritius, Poland, Thailand, Turkey, Trinidad and Tobago.

In August 1994, Ted Tanen from American Secretariat of the Indo-US Sub-Commission on Education and Culture visited India and had meetings with the Indian Co-Chairman of the Sub-Commission, Shri Salman Khurshid and several other leading persons, in various cultural and academic fields.

The Press Information Bureau in collaboration with the ICCR sponsored the visit of four women delegates from the media to participate in the 'Women & Media' programme in the USA in October 1994. The ICCR hosted the visit of four Indian film directors from USA to India to participate in the film festival'From India to America; New Directions in Indian American Films and Video' in New Delhi and Bombay in December 1994 organised by the Smita Patil Foundation in collaboration with the Indo-US Commission and Whitney Museum of American Art, USA.

The 28th Maulana Abul Kalam Azad Memorial Lecture was delivered on 9 September 1994 by Secretary General of the United Nations on 'Current World

Challenges as Reflected in the United Nations Today' and the 29th Lecture was delivered on 12 January 1995 by Tan Sri Ghazali Shafie, former Malaysian Minister for Foreign Affaisrs, Home and Education. Renowned Canadian environmentalist Mr. Naurice FS Kong was nominated for the Jawaharlal Nehru Award for International Understanding, 1992.

The Council brings out six quarterly journals in different languages: English (India Horizons and Africa), Hindi (Gangananchal), French (Recontre Avec L'Inde), Spanish (Papeles de la India) and Arabic (Thaqafatul Hind). A special issue of Indian Horizons on India-China Relations was brought out on the occasion of Festival of India in China and is considered to be one of the finest and most comprehensive books available on the age-old contacts between the two countries. The ICCR co-published India and Egyypt: Influences and Interactons and 'The Divine Peacock: Understanding Contemporary India'.

The ICCR also participated in the 11th New Helhi World Book Fair, the Exhibition of Indian Books in China, the Australian Book Fair in Sydney, the 46th Frankfurt Book Fair, the Exhibition of Indian Books in Male, the Special Book Exhibition in New Delhi and the Book Exhibition of ICCR publications at New Delhi.

The ICCR gifted 1,050 books to institutions, distinguished persons, academicians and opinion makers in 35 countries and 200 musical instruments, audio/video tapes and art objects to institutions in 18 countries.

Education about India's common cultural heritage has been identified in National Policy on Education as one of the core areas under the national system of education.

While spelling out the cultural perspective in

education, the policy has stressed on the need to bridge the schism between the formal system of education and India's rich and varied cultural traditions. It has called for enriching the curricula and processes of education in as many manifestations as possible and laid considerable emphasis on value education by highlighting the need to make education a forceful tool for cultivation of social and moral values.

Within these overall objectives, a Centrally-sponsored scheme of Assistance for Strengthening Culture and Values in Education has been designed for providing assistance to Government agencies, educational institutions, Panchayat Raj institutions, registered societies, public trusts and non-profit making companies.

The scheme has two broad components (i) strengthening cultural and value education inputs in the school and non-formal education system and (ii) strengthening the in-service training of art, craft, music and dance teachers. A total grant of Rs. 98 lakh has been approved for sanction to 33 organisations during 1994-95.

National Open School (NOS) was established in November 1989 as an autonomous organisation with the objective to provide quality education through distance education mode upto secondary stage for the school dropouts and children who cannot attend formal schools.

This school is vested with the authority to examine and certify students registered with it upto pre-degree level courses. The certificates issued by this school are recognised for admissions for pursuing higher education and also for employment. The students have the freedom to choose the set of subjects according to their needs, interests and abilities and are also encouraged to choose vocational subjects in combination with academic subjects. The marginalised groups, viz., rural youth, girls and women, SC and ST, handicapped, ex-servicemen are given priority by NOS.

The NOS provides student support services through a network of study centres known as accredited institutions (AIs) for academic courses and accredited vocational institutions (AVIs) for*. As on 31 March 1994, 306 AIs were functioning under NOS.

The number of students enrolled by the National Open School during the years 1992-93, 1993-94 and 1994-95 for its secondary and senior secondary courses was:

Year	Secondary	Senior secondary
1992-93	31,375	20,932
1993-94	35,098	25,777
1994-95	36,766	29,054

It is proposed to extend the open learning facilities in a phased manner at the secondary level in all parts of the country. In order to facilitate setting up of state open schools, the NOS provides consultancy services to the state goverments and serves as an agency for effective dissemination of information related to distance education and open learning.

The National Council of Educational Research and Training (NCERT) was established in September 1961 in New Delhi as an autonomous body. Qualitative improvement and excellence in school education and teacher education are some of its major objectives. They maintain effective liason with state education authorities for providing academic inputs to school education system.

The NCERT develops curricula, syllabi and prepares textbooks for classes I-XII which form the basis for prescription of schemes of studies by Central Boaard of

Secondary Education (CBSE) for the schools affiliated to the Board. It also develops instructional material for childhood education and training packages for teacher educators and supervisory personnel.

It provides technical assistance for national population education programmes designed to introduce population education in the formal education system. NCERT also provides its expertise to states/UTs. It also designs courses and material, generates software systems and sets up resource centres for computer literacy and studies in school project. NCERT organises Jawaharlal Nehru National Science Exhibition every year in which a large number of school students from all over the country participate.

The Council produces science kits for the use of school students. It prepares comprehensive guidelines for curriculum evaluation and school industry linkages as well as for pre-service education of teachers on vocationalisation of education. Training courses for the officials involved in the Integrated Education Programme for Disabled Children are also conducted.

The NCERT is providing very useful assistance to the Department of Education in implementing the District Primary Education Projects (DPEPs) in several states towards fulfilment of the recommendations made in Education For All (EFA) Summit of nine high population countries held in New Delhiin December1993.Oneof the major projects entrusted to the NCERT is the Sixth All India Educational Survey which the Council is implementing in collaboration with the National Informatics Centre (NIC).

The objective of inculcating the message of small family norms and other population related issues in the minds of school and college students and the clientele of adult and non-formal education is being achieved through National Population Education Project.This project is now being implemented through school and non-formal education, higher education and adult education.

Since its inception in 1980, NPEP has done much towards achieving its main objective of institutionalising population education through the school education system.

During the second cycle (1986-1990) the main focus was on consolidation of the project's multidimensional activities and further expansion of its network. During the third cycle, special attention was paid to girls and SCs/STs through various curricular activities with an emphasis on community participation. The process of interweaving population education elements into the syllabi, textbooks and of instructional and training materials will continue.

One of the main factors responsible for slow pace of growth of enrolment of adolescent girls of rural, tribal and other remote areas is the traditional social inhibitions against their movement outside the family precincts. Moreover the high/higher secondary schools in schools in such places are sparsely located. In order to actualise the recommendation in POA 1992 for formulating a special enabling plan to ensure increased enrolment of girls in secondary education and the NPE directive for encouraging NGO participation in education, the scheme for strengthening of boarding and hostel facilities for girl students of secondary/higher secondary schools was launched in 1993-94 with the objective of providing the following types of assistance to the existing hostels run by the NGOs: (i) Non-recurring assistance as non-time grant for provision of essential furniture, utensils and meeting basic recreational needs at the rate of Rs. 1,500 per boarder: and (ii) recurring assistance for food, emoluments of cook and bearer at the rate of Rs. 5,000 per annum per boarder.

During the early phase of the Independence Movement, leaders like Gokhale, Ranade, Naoroji and others tried to bring home to the Indian elite the illiberality of the so-called liberal education offered to the elite in the country. They, however, did not reach the masses, the downtrodden and the opressed in rural areas who did not have any infrastructure to receive any kind of education. This resulted in mass illiteracy, ignorance, cultural backwardness and all the miseries associated with the lack of literacy and education.

In fact, nobody except Mahatma Gandhi advocated the education of the masses in a manner conducive to national development. Perhaps Gandhiji was the first in modern India to think of the enormity of the problem in a holistic manner and offer national solutions for the removal of ignorance, illiteracy and the lack of education. One reason for the massive illiteracy, ignorance and cultural backwardness prevalent even today is this indifference (forced by education) among the educated elite of pre-and post-independence India.

Gandhiji's vision of modern India was related to his ideas about education. Whatever Gandhiji said or did was relevant to the building of an India of his dreams because he had an integrated vision. like Ivan Illich or Paulo Freire whom he anticipated by several decades, Gandhiji questioned the relevance of the colonial type of education for a free and independent India. "I would revolutionize college education and relate it to national necessities".

Even about industry-university interaction, job-degree delinking, privatization of education and such other vital topics that agitate the minds of modern educationists, Gandhiji had clear ideas. For example, he advocated self-supporting schools and industry-institution-supported colleges.

The revolutionary aspects of the Gandhian vision of education for New India were summarized by himself as follows:

- For primary education extending for seven years, taken as a whole, a vocation or vocations are the best medium for all-round development of a boy a girl, and therefore all syllabus should be woven round vocational training.
- Higher education was to be left to private enterprise and it ought to meet national requirements 'whether in the various industries, technical arts, belles-letters or fine arts'.
- University charters should be given liberally to any body of persons of proved worth and integrity, it being always understood that the universities will not cost the State anything except that it will bear the cost of running a Central Education Department.
- Education should lead to the highest development of the mind but this development can take place only through a scientific cultivation of the faculties of the mind and body at various levels.
- Education should make the educated aware of what is going on in their surroundings, and enable them to analyze and why's and the wherefore's of every thing in their immediate environment.

Gandhiji was not opposed to literacy training, physical exercises or religious instruction.

He opposed literary training without vocational training physical exercises for body beautification purposes, and relligious instruction of a narrow kind. His thrust was on vocationalization of education at school and college levels because he believed that true learning could be imparted only through DOING. Education for self-aggrandisement was, according to him, anti-social education. Only that which served society, especially the poorest of the poor, could be termed true education.

But while advocating vocationalization, Gandhiji opposed the evils of mechanization and repetitive and mononotonous work.

"By working with the machines we have ourselves become machines and have lost all sense of art and handwork", Gandhiji said. He, however, said that in order "to develop the whole personality of the students, education through manual work is essential. The true development of the mind and the heart could be achieved only through manual labour. Thus Gandhiji questioned the usefulness of liberal arts education in a country where a very large number of young people remained unemployed after obtaining higher education.